It is a pleasure to commend this se̶r̶ and piety. The theological, historic̶ and the range of the contributors, fr̶ and Chad Van Dixhoorn, to older sc̶h̶o̶l̶a̶r̶s̶ ̶o̶ffi̶c̶i̶a̶l̶ ̶P̶e̶r̶g̶ Godfrey, give this *Festschrift* a compelling attractiveness. Each of the essays focus on areas of Reformed doctrine and practice dear to Joel Beeke's heart and dear to Christians who prize experiential divinity. It is to be hoped that this collection of essays will be read widely and digested deeply.

IAN HAMILTON
Associate Minister, Smithton Culloden Free Church of Scotland,
Inverness, Scotland

This book marks the milestone of the publication of Dr Joel Beeke's 100th book—and it is so like the man and those 100 books that he has authored and edited. It is full of biblical wisdom, robust theological reflection, and warm and inviting piety. Dr Beeke is a gift to the twenty-first century church precisely because he has spent so much time traveling the ancient paths, paths which can be traced right back to the riches of Holy Writ. Dr Beeke is industrious and devoted, astoundingly prolific and joyfully dutiful. May this book, like Dr Beeke's 100 books, nourish the church and cause us to look past our cloud of witnesses and to the Author of our faith.

STEPHEN J. NICHOLS
President of Reformation Bible College and
Chief Academic Officer of Ligonier Ministries,
Sanford, Florida

Who more deserves a festschrift than Dr Joel Beeke for his industry, piety, family life, soundness, Catholic spirit, evangelism and warm outgoing personality? To distant Aberystwyth he has come on four occasions and preached most helpfully to us Welshmen. To the English he has given volumes of Puritan treasure which they had never heard of but then have marvelled at and eagerly read. He has promoted the translation of the second Reformation divines of the Netherlands, and so is loved by the Dutch. We all hail you our dear brother thanking God for you. You were not disobedient to the vision of the grandeur of the Reformed faith that you saw as a teenager. May your last years be your very best!

GEOFF THOMAS
Conference Speaker and author, Aberystwyth, Wales

It was my privilege to meet Dr Beeke first in the 1980s while in Grand Rapids for preaching. I have had the pleasure of meeting him often since and of preaching at his kind request. I am very pleased that he has written a hundred God-honouring books. I endorse this Festschrift with the prayer that many may read them and be blessed.

MAURICE ROBERTS
Conference speaker and author, Inverness, Scotland

This enriching volume is a truly appropriate honouring of Joel Beeke, for each of the writers in general deals with a particular theological doctrine as taught by certain Puritan writers. The teaching here has a balance central in Joel's mind and heart, for not only is it instructive in enriching our thinking, but these chapters are also warm enough to inflame our hearts and motivate our actions, moving us to live out what we have understood. Just why and how Joel Beeke has done so much in opening again for today many Puritans and in himself adding abundantly to their writing.

EDWARD DONNELLY
New Testament Professor Emeritus, Reformed Theological College, Belfast.

As well as being a fitting tribute to the contribution which Dr Joel Beeke has made to our understanding of Puritan history, theology and culture, this varied collection of high quality essays will itself add to the corpus of material which will inform, educate and stimulate further interest in Puritan study.

IVER MARTIN
President of Edinburgh Theological Seminary, Scotland

Writings in Honor
of
Joel R. Beeke

PURITAN
PIETY

Edited by
Michael A.G. Haykin
& Paul M. Smalley

CHRISTIAN
FOCUS

Copyright © Michael A. G. Haykin 2018
Each contributor retains the copyright for their individual chapter

paperback ISBN 978-1-5271-0158-6
epub ISBN 978-1-5271-0228-6
mobi ISBN 978-1-5271-0229-3

10 9 8 7 6 5 4 3 2 1

Published in 2018
in the
Mentor imprint
by
Christian Focus Publications Ltd,
Geanies House, Fearn, Ross-shire,
IV20 1TW, Great Britain.

www.christianfocus.com

Cover design by
Daniel Van Straaten

Printed and bound by
Bell & Bain

Contents

Contents continued

On Piety and Puritans—
Past and Contemporary

MICHAEL A. G. HAYKIN

*A*N historian must ever be wary of confusing historical eras. Thus, depending upon one's understanding of what lies at the heart of Puritanism, this movement as an historical entity ended, either in the expulsion of the Puritan leadership from the Church of England in 1662 with the Act of Uniformity, or it came to an end after the passing of the Act of Toleration in 1689 that officially enshrined Dissent as a part of the religious landscape of England and Wales. So, to speak, as some have done, of the Victorian preacher C. H. Spurgeon or the twentieth-century preacher D. Martyn Lloyd-Jones as the 'last of the Puritans' is really a faux-pas from the point of view of historical scholarship. And yet, surely these two men—as well as our brother whom this Festschrift honors—embodied so much of the ethos of the Puritans that it is not inappropriate to speak of them as 'Puritan-like' (I would have used the adjective 'Puritanical,' but that word sadly seems to have no positive associations in contemporary English).

I first met Dr Joel Beeke close to twenty years ago now, and I count his friendship as one of the extraordinary blessings of my life (as I am sure, all of the contributors to this Festschrift would attest to in their own ways). He has been extremely kind to me, especially since our ecclesial convictions differ somewhat. But this is very Puritan-like, for the best of these men and women recognized that what bound them together was a shared spirituality, a common Reformed heritage, and a like-minded devotion to the Scriptures and the Lord of whom the Scriptures pre-eminently spoke.

However, Dr Beeke not only shares the theological and spiritual emphases of the Puritans, but he has also played an absolutely key role, through writing and publishing, in the *ressourcement* of Puritan literature. He is rightly convinced that the Puritan era was one of the most remarkable eras of piety in Church History, and contemporary Evangelicalism has been much the poorer for not immersing itself in the theological riches of this period of time. By pen and voice he has sought to rectify this problem and give modern-day Evangelicals a more biblically-robust foundation to their thinking and doing. The bibliography of his works at the close of this volume attests to some of the energy he has poured into this endeavor.

The bulk of the essays in this Festschrift deal with individual Puritan authors and theological themes dear to our brother's heart—two of them, mine and Dr Oliver's, examine two key figures deeply indebted to Puritan thought and piety. All of them are written with deep thanksgiving to the Triune God who has given Dr Beeke a passion for mining the rich deposits of Puritan spirituality and gifts to translate this passion into written text. We would also like to thank Esther Engelsma (Beeke) for providing the bibliography of Dr Beeke's writings. May this God, the true and living God, give our brother many more years in theological reflection, writing, and speaking—and may the God of the Puritans ever be his and all of those who have contributed to this Festschrift.

CHAPTER ONE

Introduction: The Puritan Piety of Joel Beeke

PAUL M. SMALLEY

TEN years ago in 2007 I was looking for a book about the doctrine of God at the book tables of a pastors' conference. There I met a man named Joel Beeke, and after he was done talking to me I had bought four large books, or more precisely, the four-volume set of Wilhelmus à Brakel, *The Christian's Reasonable Service*. I found in Brakel the most amazing combination of biblical, doctrinal, experiential, and practical theology I had ever encountered. I had been introduced to the Dutch Further Reformation—the Puritans of the Netherlands, so to speak.

What I did not realize then was that I also had been introduced to a living Dutch 'Puritan' who would become my boss and dear friend. In 2010, God brought me to Grand Rapids, Michigan, where I work as Dr Beeke's teaching assistant at Puritan Reformed Theological Seminary. Seven years of laboring alongside this brother and regularly praying with him have left me with a deep impression of the power of God's grace in the life of fallen humanity.

As we prepare this volume (of which Dr Beeke is blissfully ignorant at the moment!), we do so with a burden for the glory of God. The German word *festschrift* means 'celebration-writing'. The occasion is Dr Beeke's ministry, but the festival we intend is unto the Lord. One way in which we honor the Lord is by remembering His servants, as God commanded us: 'Remember them which have the rule over you, who have spoken unto you the word of God: whose faith follow, considering the end of their conversation' (Heb. 13:7). The next verse tells us why, for when we remember God's faithful servants, what we see is not them so much as 'Jesus Christ the same yesterday, and to day, and for ever.'

Personal Background

Joel Robert Beeke was born on 9 December 1952 in Kalamazoo, Michigan, to John Beeke and Johanna (VanStrien) Beeke. John Beeke had been born in Krabbendijke, Zeeland, the Netherlands, and emigrated to the United States of America when he was seven years old. He was a man of heartfelt piety who read John Bunyan's *The Pilgrim's Progress* to his family with tears in his eyes and urged them to follow the Lord. He often said to his children, 'Oh, that I could write these great truths of eternity upon your hearts with an iron pen!' John found much help in his understanding of sin and the gospel in *Human Nature in Its Fourfold State* by Thomas Boston (1676–1732). John served as an elder in the church, but did not enjoy consistent assurance of salvation until the last decade of his life. He died in 1993 from a heart-attack while he read a sermon from the pulpit.

Joel's mother, Johanna, was a woman noted for her remarkable life of prayer. Her children often found her on her knees. She was known to pray two hours a day, yet when asked at age eighty-five what she would do differently if she could do life over, she said: 'I would pray more.' She was also an amazingly patient woman, who rarely if ever spoke an angry or critical word about anyone— sometimes to the frustration of her children. Johanna died in 2012 at age ninety-two. A month previously, Joel read to her from Revelation 21, and asked her what it meant that Christ is the Alpha and Omega. She replied, 'Jesus is both first and last in our lives.' At the time of her death she had five children, thirty-five grandchildren, ninety-two great-grandchildren, and one great-great-grandchild.

John and Johanna Beeke raised Joel and their other four children in the Netherlands Reformed Congregations, a small, conservative Dutch denomination. The NRC is the American counterpart to the Gereformeerde Gemeenten (Reformed Congregations) across the Atlantic in the Netherlands, founded in 1907 by Gerrit H. Kersten (1882–1948).

When Joel was a teenager, he passed through a season of deep, heart-breaking conviction of sin by which the Lord brought him to trust in Christ alone for his salvation. In addition to the Holy Scriptures, a major influence upon Joel's budding spiritual life was the writings of the British Puritans. The Christ-centered writings of Thomas Goodwin (1600–1679) were especially precious to him in those early years. Not long after coming to assurance of salvation, Joel received a powerful sense of calling from God to preach the gospel to all nations.

Joel studied at Western Michigan University in Kalamazoo from 1971 to 1973, and then transferred to Thomas Edison College from which he graduated BA with a specialization in religion. He proceeded to the Netherlands Reformed Theological School in St Catharines, Ontario, studying there from 1974 to 1978 for the equivalent of a Master of Divinity degree.

Ministry in Church and School

Joel then entered the ministry of the Netherlands Reformed Congregations. His labors demonstrated unusual energy and diligence from the beginning. From 1978 to 1981 he was the minister of the NRC church in Sioux Center, Iowa, serving as the sole pastor of a congregation of seven hundred people. While there, he helped to start the Netherlands Reformed Christian School in Rock Valley, Iowa. He also served as the clerk of the Netherlands Reformed Synod (1980–1992) and president of the Netherlands Reformed Book and Publishing Committee (1980–1993).

In 1981, Revd Beeke moved to Ebenezer Netherlands Reformed Church in Franklin Lakes, New Jersey, again acting as the sole pastor of a large congregation and active supporter of the local NRC school. His involvement in writing and publication grew as

11

he took on the roles of being the editor of *Paul*, the NRC mission journal (1984–1993), and *The Banner of Truth*, the denominational periodical (1985–1993).

In 1982, Revd Beeke published his first books, *Jehovah Shepherding His Sheep*, a series of profound theological meditations upon the twenty-third psalm, and *Backsliding: Disease and Cure*, about spiritual decline and renewal. He also co-authored with his brother, James W. Beeke, the *Bible Doctrine Student Workbook*. During this period of time, he edited two volumes of *Religious Stories for Young and Old*. The scope of Revd Beeke's initial books demonstrates his heart for doctrinal and practical Christianity that reaches the youngest children.

God took Revd Beeke in a new direction in 1982 that would dramatically expand his horizons. He enrolled in the doctoral program of Westminster Theological Seminary, Philadelphia. There he became a student of and partner with members of the broader Reformed and Presbyterian tradition. Initially he directed his studies towards the doctrine of predestination, a matter of keen interest to him. However, reflection upon the needs of his denomination moved him to change his focus to the doctrine of assurance, for he longed for people to know more peace, joy, and liberty in the Lord. In 1988, he graduated with a PhD in Reformation and Post-Reformation Theology. Even before graduation, he taught at WTS's Center for Urban Theological Studies (1984–1986) and lectured at WTS (1985–1986).

In 1986, Revd Beeke returned to Michigan to become the pastor of the First Netherlands Reformed Congregation in Grand Rapids. He also provided theological instruction for the NRC theological school and became president of Inheritance Publishers, a worldwide distributor of booklets containing classic sermons.

At Grand Rapids, God brought to Dr Beeke the love of his life, his 'queen' as he likes to call her. In 1989, he married Mary Kamp. God has since blessed them with three children, and a growing number of grandchildren. Mary is also an author and speaker at women's conferences. Life as husband and father profoundly shapes Dr Beeke's view of piety.

The Netherlands Reformed Congregations divided in 1993 over matters of theology and church order, and Dr Beeke continued his ministry under the auspices of a newly formed denomination, the Heritage Reformed Churches. He remains at the same church in Grand Rapids, now called the Heritage Reformed Congregation. He has served as the editor of the HRC denominational magazine, *The Banner of Sovereign Grace Truth*. Since 1994, Dr Beeke has been the editorial director of Reformation Heritage Books, a publisher of books both old and new in the Reformed and Puritan tradition. That same year, he became vice-chairman of the Dutch Reformed Translation Society in order to help make the writings of Herman Bavinck and the Dutch Further Reformation available to English-speakers.

Dr Beeke has also continued to write numerous books of his own. He co-authored with Mark Jones *A Puritan Theology*, a landmark study of Puritan teachings across the loci of systematic theology. He served as the general editor of *The Reformation Heritage KJV Study Bible*. He published his hundredth book in 2017, *Knowing and Growing in Assurance of Faith*. An extensive bibliography of his books and articles is provided as an appendix of this book.

The HRC commissioned Puritan Reformed Theological Seminary in 1995 as its training institution. PRTS began with Dr Beeke as professor and four students meeting in the garage of a private home. Three years later, the Free Reformed Churches of North America chose to train its ministerial students at PRTS. In 2004, PRTS built a new building to accommodate its expanding student body and library. The building houses the Puritan Research Center, a long-term dream of Dr Beeke to gather and preserve primary and secondary sources on Puritan theology and piety. As of 2017, PRTS has more than a hundred students from many denominational backgrounds, using facilities double the size of its 2004 structure. Its ten faculty members and many staff and volunteers train students in three Master degree programs and a PhD program to train future seminary leaders. Those who work at the seminary would testify that the growth of the school cannot be attributed to any one person or factor, but only the unmerited mercy of God who hears the prayers of His people.

Presently Dr Beeke has much to do at Heritage Reformed Congregation, Puritan Reformed Theological Seminary, and Reformation Heritage Books. God has also given to Dr Beeke an extensive ministry of speaking at Christian conferences around the world. In recent years, he preached in Canada, England, Wales, Scotland, Ireland, the Netherlands, Portugal, Aruba, the Dominican Republic, Mexico, Colombia, Brazil, Korea, Thailand, Israel, the United Arab Emirates, Ethiopia, Mozambique, Zambia, and South Africa—as well as many conferences across the United States of America. Dr Beeke preaches with a sense of urgency, knowing that his life is but a vapor, but the needs of the world are vast, and the glory of God is worthy of our every breath.

The remarkable breadth of Dr Beeke's ministry should not be misunderstood, however, as a life of ease and success. Dr Beeke has known much sorrow through the years, and this too has played an important part in his service to Christ. For decades Dr Beeke has found comfort in the writings of others who have suffered in Christ, such as the *Letters* of Samuel Rutherford (1600–1661), who found sweet communion with Christ while under the cross.

Themes in Joel Beeke's Piety

Like Calvin before him, Joel Beeke prioritizes piety as the aim of all Christian doctrine and effort. Piety (Latin *pietas*) is an old word for godliness, and Dr Beeke's approach is profoundly shaped by the study of the old paths of the Reformers and Puritans. A detailed exploration of Dr Beeke's piety is beyond the scope of this chapter, but I would offer the following points as a summary. A fuller statement of these themes may be found in his book, *Living for God's Glory: An Introduction to Calvinism.* Dr Beeke is fond of lists, and therefore I present the following list of ten characteristics of biblical piety emphasized in Dr Beeke's ministry.

1. Biblical piety *is born of the word of God* (1 Pet. 1:23). Godliness without the Holy Scriptures is delusion and idolatry. Only God's word can create piety that pleases God. God's primary instrument to give piety is preaching that draws true doctrine

out of the Scriptures and applies it to Christian experience for practical obedience (Reformed experiential preaching).

Dr Beeke challenges us to make the Word of God the soul of all our practice and the substance of all our piety:

> Do we search, love, live, and pray over the Holy Scriptures? Is the Bible the compass that leads us through the storms and over the waves that we encounter in life? Is Scripture the mirror by which we dress ourselves (James 1:22-27), the rule by which we work (Gal. 6:16), the water with which we wash (Ps. 119:9), fire that warms us (Luke 24:32), and food that nourishes us (Job. 23:12), and sword with which we fight (Eph. 6:17), the counselor who resolves our doubts and fears (Ps. 119:24), and the heritage that enriches us (Ps. 119:111-112)?[1]

2. Biblical piety *arises from the knowledge of God's glory* (John 17:3). Godliness is human, but is not man-centered. Genuine piety is God-centered, a fearful and loving response to the beauty and majesty of the Lord. This is the essence of Reformed Christianity: the all-transforming knowledge of the sovereign God who reveals Himself in the Bible.

Dr Beeke says that this is 'the true marrow' of so-called 'Calvinism', namely, 'that God is the Lord of life and Sovereign of the universe, whose will is the key to history.' Yet, 'this sovereignty is not arbitrary but is the sovereignty of the God and Father of our Lord Jesus Christ.' Piety does not arise from isolating God's sovereignty from His love, but exalting His 'fatherly sovereignty,' which, 'is in perfect harmony with all of God's attributes.'[2]

3. Biblical piety *breaks the heart over our sins against God* (Ps. 51:4, 17). To see the glory of God is be pierced with the magnitude of our sins against His law, His authority, and His goodness. Contrition and repentance are not unhealthy, nor are they merely a gateway into salvation, but are of the essence of godliness

---

1. Joel R. Beeke, *Living for God's Glory: An Introduction to Calvinism* (Orlando: Reformation Trust, 2008), p. 134.

2. Beeke, *Living for God's Glory*, pp. 39–40.

throughout life. As the Heidelberg Catechism teaches, our eternal comfort depends upon knowing our misery.

Piety breaks the heart over sin because the power of sin is in the heart. Dr Beeke says: 'The very heart of man is unbelieving, selfish, covetous, sensuous, and always desiring to displace God Himself. Hence, the very desire to sin is sin.'[3] Repentance, then, is not the intrusion of legalism into Christianity, but the opening of the soul to its absolute need for grace.

Therefore, sinners cannot increase in piety without suffering and humiliation. Dr Beeke confesses that the greatest influence in his life toward practical Reformed Christianity 'has been the afflictions that my sovereign God has sent my way .... If God had not broken me deeply many times in His sovereign wisdom, I would be more prideful than I am.'[4] However, the necessity of the Christian's suffering arises not only because of his sin, but also because of his Savior—'because of the believer's union with Christ' whose 'life was a perpetual cross'.[5]

4. Biblical piety *lives by communion with Christ* (John 15:4-5). No misery is truly Christian if it is not joined to deliverance by Jesus Christ. Godliness is God's gift through the only Mediator. He is the Prophet to reveal God's ways to us, the Priest to reconcile us to God, and the King to reign over us. Christ is everything to the believer.

Dr Beeke says: 'If you a true son or daughter of the Reformation, Christ in His threefold office as Prophet-Priest-King will mean everything to you.' He presses us to consider whether the doctrine of Christ has entered our hearts and lives: 'Have you learned to know Christ personally and experientially as your Savior and Lord?'[6] He loves to quote William Perkins (1558–1602), 'Preach one Christ, by Christ, to the praise of Christ.'[7]

---

3. Beeke, *Living for God's Glory*, p. 53.

4. Beeke, *Living for God's Glory*, p. xiv.

5. Beeke, *Living for God's Glory*, p. 182.

6. Beeke, *Living for God's Glory*, p. 144.

7. William Perkins, concluding summary to *The Arte of Prophecying*, as quoted in Beeke, *Living for God's Glory*, p. 258.

5. Biblical piety *mingles doctrine and experience by Spirit-wrought faith* (1 Thess. 1:3-5). Faith in Christ is the life-blood of godliness. This faith is not mere emotion, nor is it bare ideas in the mind. Rather, it is the Holy Spirit's creation when He plants the living truth in a living heart. Faith is an experiential reality, though at times it may be concealed from a believer's own perception. Consequently, the ministry of the word is doctrine for life.

Like Perkins, Dr Beeke compares faith to a 'hand' to receive Christ—a hand that 'does not create; it only receives.' He writes, 'It flees in poverty to Christ's riches, in guilt to Christ's reconciliation, and in bondage to Christ's liberation.' He quotes Luther: 'Faith lays hold of Christ and grasps Him as a present possession, just as the ring holds the jewel.'[8]

6. Biblical piety *develops in the nurture of the Christian family* (Deut. 6:6-7). Christian parents, and fathers in particular, bear a covenantal responsibility to raise their children in the Lord. In addition to regular participation in the life of the church, this entails weaving the Scriptures and prayer into family life through daily times of family devotion and worship.

Covenantal piety is fostered in relationships with an eye on future generations.[9] In our individualistic and anti-authoritarian age, we can learn from the Puritans that 'the Christian's relationship with his family is inseparable from personal sanctification,' as Dr Beeke says. He explains: 'The Bible tells us to glorify God by raising children for Him for the well-being of society, the church, and the family itself.'[10]

7. Biblical piety *flourishes under the church's means of grace* (Col. 3:16). Godliness is not merely private and personal, but also corporate and mutual. The quest for piety shows us how much we need each other. Preaching the word, singing psalms, prayer meetings, fellowship, and the Lord's Supper are crucial to spiritual growth.

---

8. Beeke, *Living for God's Glory*, p. 139.

9. See Joel R. Beeke, *Parenting by God's Promises: How to Raise Children in the Covenant of Grace* (Orlando: Reformation Trust, 2011).

10. Beeke, *Living for God's Glory*, p. 333.

Dr Beeke calls the public means of grace 'corporate disciplines', and warns: 'A Christian life lived in isolation from other believers will be defective and spiritually immature.'[11] We must not expect to keep our hearts in the way of Christ without disciplined effort, but, as John Flavel (1628–1691) said, make 'a diligent and constant use and improvement of all holy means and duties, to preserve the soul from sin, and maintain its sweet and free communion with God.'[12]

8. Biblical piety *unites Christians despite our differences.* Since piety focuses us upon God, joins us to Christ, and breaks our pride, it draws Christians together. This is not merely a theoretical unity, but practical and affectionate cooperation between people of different genders, ethnicities, and cultures. However, as piety is doctrinal, so unity is built upon the truth.

By God's grace, Dr Beeke models in his ministry 'the unity of the faith, and of the knowledge of the Son of God' (Eph. 4:13). He is a team-builder. He has a remarkable gift for recognizing the gifts of others and entering into partnerships with them so that together they can do more than possible apart. At the same time, he is deeply committed to confessional Reformed Christianity. Such unity under the truth is the history of PRTS, and the backdrop of the many books that Dr Beeke has co-authored with others. For example, the book *Living for God's Glory* includes contributions from eight authors in addition to Dr Beeke. In it, Dr Beeke's friend Michael Haykin notes: 'The New Testament knows nothing of solitary Christianity. One of the great sources of spiritual strength is Christian friendship and fellowship.'[13]

9. Biblical piety *energizes Christians to do good works.* Godliness is not quietism, a passive waiting for new experiences, but activism, the energetic doing of God's will. Piety is spiritual life. This entails Christian activism in every sphere, for all are under

---

11. Beeke, *Living for God's Glory*, p. 210.

12. John Flavel, *A Saint Indeed* (sermon on Prov. 4:23), as quoted in Beeke, *Living for God's Glory*, p. 204.

13. Michael A. G. Haykin, 'Cultivating the Spirit', in *Living for God's Glory*, p. 168.

God's sovereignty. It especially calls for activism in proclaiming and publishing biblical truth, the ground of piety.

As Dr Beeke points out, sanctification is both 'mortification', or killing of our sins, and 'vivification', that is, 'being quickened from the heart to do the will of God.'[14] This motivates not only devotional disciplines, but also the 'neighborly disciplines' of evangelizing and serving other people.[15] Stephen Charnock (1628–1680) said: 'We do not glorify God by elevated admirations, or eloquent expressions, or pompous services for him, as when we aspire to a conversing with him with unstained spirits, and live to him in living like him.'[16]

10. Biblical piety *demands a battle for holiness that is idealistic, realistic, and optimistic*. The Christian life is war, hand-to-hand combat against sin and Satan. This warfare must be idealistic in its lofty aims to love God and keep His commandments with all our hearts. It must be realistic in its assessment of the remaining sin that indwells all believers and their experiential struggles and seasons of darkness. Yet it must remain optimistic by looking to the end, when Christ shall return to bring His kingdom, for He will not lose any whom God has given to Him.

To foster such piety, Dr Beeke says, we need 'experiential preaching ... that seeks to explain in terms of biblical, Calvinistic truth how matters ought to go, how they do go, and the end goal of the Christian life.'[17] As he explains: 'Telling how matters go without indicating how they should go lulls the believer to cease from pressing forward to grow in the grace and knowledge of Christ (2 Pet. 3:18). Only telling how matter should be rather than how they really are discourages the believer from being assured that the Lord has worked in his heart.' Dr Beeke reminds us, 'Every Christian is a soldier,' and experiential preaching not only directs

---

14. Beeke, *Living for God's Glory*, p. 204.

15. Beeke, *Living for God's Glory*, p. 210.

16. Stephen Charnock, *The Existence and Attributes of God*, as quoted in Beeke, *Living for God's Glory*, p. 202.

17. Beeke, *Living for God's Glory*, p. 256.

him in the daily battle, but also 'reminds him of the victory that awaits him, for which God receives the glory.'[18]

This biblical view of piety has energized Joel Beeke to preach Christ and live unto Christ for five decades. It is no self-generated religiosity. Rather it is what Paul described when he said: 'But by the grace of God I am what I am: and his grace which was bestowed upon me was not in vain; but I laboured more abundantly than they all: yet not I, but the grace of God which was with me' (1 Cor. 15:10).

---

18. Beeke, *Living for God's Glory*, pp. 265–66.

Part 1: Reformed Theology and Puritan Piety

What is Theology? A Puritan and Reformed Vision of Living to God, through Christ, by the Spirit

RYAN M. MCGRAW

DEFINITIONS are important. Soccer is, by definition, different than basketball or baseball. How we define and describe a sport helps ensure that we play it correctly. In a similar way, how we define theology helps determine how we study and pursue theology. If theology is to us merely a scientific and intellectual system, then our pursuit of theology can devolve into head knowledge to the exclusion of heart knowledge. On the other hand, if theology is treated as a matter of the heart only, then it can become devoid of truth. A large part of the great legacy of the Puritans and other Reformed orthodox authors is that they defined theology in a way that aimed to avoid both of these extremes.

Joel Beeke has contributed much to wedding doctrine and piety in the pulpit and in the seminary. The Lord has used him to help revive the spirit of Puritan piety for the benefit of the church generally and to strengthen my family and I in the Lord particularly. How Puritan and other Reformed orthodox authors defined theology highlighted its experimental quality in relation both to doctrine and to life. They defined theology largely as the doctrine of living to God,[1] adding, by implication at least, that this was possible through Christ and by the Spirit only.[2]

This essay seeks to illustrate the importance of Puritan and Reformed definitions of theology to Christian faith and practice. I will do so by explaining generally how and why Puritan and Reformed authors defined theology, by showing the biblical justification for these definitions, and by illustrating why such definitions of theology are useful for making saving fellowship with the triune God the goal of all theological knowledge. This is important because it provides us an example of why Joel's emphasis on Puritan theology can be so potentially helpful for today's church. Though I plan to introduce this material historically, I will primarily evaluate it biblically and appropriate it practically. In other words, while this chapter borrows from some historical theology it is weighted towards practical theology.

The Development of Puritan and Reformed Definitions of Theology

Puritan and Reformed definitions of theology were calculated to wed doctrine and practice. We see this in relation to medieval debates over the nature of theology, the Reformed development of defining theology as a term, and the implicitly trinitarian cast that definitions of theology began to take. In this section, I intend only to bring readers up to speed on this matter without fully treating this question in its historical context. As such, this treatment aims to shed enough

---

1. William Ames, *Medulla S.S. Theologiæ, in Fine Adjuncta Est Disputatio De Fidei Divinæ Veritate. Editio Tertia Priori Longe Correctior* (Apud Robertum Allottum: Londini, 1629), p. 1; Richard A. Muller, *Post-Reformation Reformed Dogmatics: The Rise and Development of Reformed Orthodoxy, Ca. 1520 to Ca. 1725*, 2nd ed. (Grand Rapids, MI: Baker Academic, 2003), 1:154–58. Henceforth cited as *PRRD*.

2. Peter van Mastricht, *Theoretico-Practica Theologia. Qua, Per Singula Capita Theologica, Pars Exegetica, Dogmatica, Elenchtica & Practica, Perpetua Successione Conjugantur* (Trajecti ad Rhenum, & Amstelodami: Sumptibus Societatis, 1715), p. 2. 'Doctrinam videndi Dei, per Christum.' The Spirit is implied in his treatment of *per Christum*.

light on the subject to avoid stumbling while we walk through it, yet not enough to make clear all of the objects in the room.

In the medieval period, theologians debated whether theology was theoretical, practical, or some combination of the two.[3] This grew out of a long-standing discussion in the church about the nature of theology. Reformed authors generally concluded that theology as a discipline had both theoretical and practical components.[4] This point was important because it set the stage for defining theology in a way that incorporated its theoretical and practical components.

In spite of the widespread attention that the church has given historically to defining theology, it may surprise some to learn that the term, 'theology', does not appear in Scripture. However, other terms, such as 'Trinity' and 'incarnation', do not appear in Scripture either, yet they are useful in describing biblical ideas.[5] Puritan and Reformed authors believed rightly that if they used the term 'theology', then they had to define it in a way that honored Scripture. Following Peter Ramus (1515–1572) as mediated via William Perkins (1558–1602) and William Ames (1576-1633),[6]

---

3. Muller, *PRRD*, 1:340–42.

4. Walaeus et al., *Synopsis Purioris Theologiae = Synopsis of a Purer Theology*, ed. Roelf T. te Velde, trans. Reimer A. Faber, vol. 1 (Leiden: Brill, 2015), p. 43: 'Therefore in Theology theory and practice are not placed in opposition to one another, but they are conditions associated with each other for the purpose of obtaining everlasting life, and placed in their proper order.' [Non ergo theoria et praxis sunt in Theologia differentiae oppositae: sed conditiones inter se ad vitam aeternam consequendam consociatae, suoque ordine collocatae.].

5. Francis Cheynell, *The Divine Trinunity of the Father, Son, and Holy Spirit, Or, the Blessed Doctrine of the Three Coessentiall Subsistents in the Eternall Godhead Without Any Confusion or Division of the Distinct Subsistences or Multiplication of the Most Single and Entire Godhead Acknowledged, Beleeved, Adored by Christians, in Opposition to Pagans, Jewes, Mahumetans, Blasphemous and Antichristian Hereticks, Who Say They Are Christians, but Are Not* (London: Printed by T.R. and E.M. for Samuel Gellibrand …, 1650), p. 94.

6. Donald Sinnema, 'The Attempt to Establish a Chair in Practical Theology at Leiden University (1618–1626)', in *A Companion to Reformed Orthodoxy*, ed. H. J. Selderhuis, vol. 40, Brill's Companions to the Christian Tradition (Leiden: Brill, 2013), pp. 416–17.

25

most Reformed authors defined theology as, 'the doctrine of living to God'.[7] This carried the advantage of recognizing that the term theology as it relates to Scripture addressed questions relating to the knowledge of God. The Bible is concerned not simply with knowing about God, but knowing God personally. The Reformed definition had the advantage of recognizing that theology must involve sound doctrine, but it must be more than mere doctrine. It is the truth that accords with godliness. Those who profess to know God must not deny Him in their works. The consensus was that the church must define theology in a way that honors the biblical teaching that the knowledge of God is experimental. As Edward Reynolds (1599–1676) wrote: 'Christ is not truly apprehended either by the fancy or the understanding. He is at once known and possessed. It is an experimental, and not a speculative knowledge that conceives him; he understands him that feels him. We see him in his grace and truth, not in any carnal or gross pretense.'[8]

Puritan and Reformed definitions of theology were trinitarian as well. While many believers today struggle with whether there are any practical implications to the doctrine of the Trinity, older authors believed that the Trinity was the primary locus in which doctrine and practice converged in experimental piety.[9] Since theology involved knowing God, it also involved knowing God as triune. Johannes Cloppenburg (1592–1652) argued that without the doctrine of the Trinity, we can never know who God is (*quis*

---

7. Petrus Ramus, *Commentariorum De Religiona Christiana, Libri, Quatuor, Eivsdem Vita a Theophilo Banosio Descripta* (Francofvrti, 1576), p. 6. Ramus defined theology as the doctrine of living well ('Theologia est doctrina bene vivendi'), which, he argued, we could do only if we looked to God as the source of our blessedness, through faith in Christ, as the Spirit teaches us through Scripture alone.

8. Edward Reynolds, *Meditations on the Fall and Rising of St. Peter* (London, 1677), p. 58.

9. Gijsbert Voetius, *Selectarum Disputationum Theologicarum Pars Prima (Quinta. Accedunt Dissertatio Epistolica De Termino Vitæ. Exercitatio De Prognosticis Cometarum. Antehac Seorsim Editæ).* (Ultrajecti, 1648), 1:473; Johannes Hoornbeeck, *Theologia Practica Pars 1* (Francofurti & Lipsiae: Bailliar, 1698), 1:136.

sit), even if we know that He is (*an sit*) and what He is (*quid sit*).[10] The trinitarian knowledge of God was embedded in most basic Reformed definitions of theology. For example, though Ramus defined theology simply as the doctrine of living well, he explained that we can live well only if we look to God as the fountain of all good.[11] This true knowledge of God comes only through Christ, whom both the Old and New Testaments reveal in relation to piety and to the remission of our sins.[12] Yet the Spirit reveals Christ to believers by teaching us true heavenly doctrine through Scripture alone.[13] In spite of this trinitarian expansion, it seems strange to omit God from the definition of theology. Later theologians appeared gradually to make the implications of Ramus' definition clearer. Ames added the phrase, 'living to God' (*deo vivendi*) to explain what it meant to live well.[14] Most followed in his footsteps. As noted above, Mastricht added that theology was the doctrine of living to God 'through Christ' (*per Christum*). John Owen (1616–1683) brought the trinitarian implications of Reformed definitions of theology to their fullest expression by adding that we must live to God, through Christ, by the Spirit.[15]

---

10. Johannes Cloppenburg, *Exercitationes Super Locos Communes Theologicos* (Franekerae, 1653), p. 97. The original text is not paginated. The page listed here reflects the numbering in Google Books. The section comes from the first disputation on the Trinity, paragraph 18. For the common division of the Reformed doctrine of God in light of the three categories listed here, see Sebastian Rehnman, 'The Doctrine of God in Reformed Orthodoxy', in *A Companion to Reformed Orthodoxy*, ed. Herman J. Selderhuis, vol. 40, Brill's Companions to the Christian Tradition (Leiden: Brill, 2013), p. 386.

11. Ramus, *De Religione Christiana*, p. 6.

12. Ramus, *De Religione Christiana*, p. 7.

13. Ramus, *De Religione Christiana*, p. 9.

14. Ames, *Medulla*, p. 1.

15. John Owen, *Theologoumena Pantodapa, Sive, De Natura, Ortu, Progressu, Et Studio Veræ Theologiæ, Libri Sex Quibus Etiam Origines & Processus Veri & Falsi Cultus Religiosi, Casus & Instaurationes Ecclesiæ Illustiores Ab Ipsis Rerum Primordiis, Enarrantur* (Oxoniæ, 1661), pp. 5–6, 462–63. My description of Owen's trinitarian definition of theology is summary and conclusion primarily of books I and VI of this work. The pages cited are representative only.

The definitions of theology from which Puritan and Reformed orthodox authors drew were designed to address the whole person. Just as we need to be saved in all parts of our souls and bodies, so we must be subjected to God through faith and repentance in every part of our beings. The great insight of historic Reformed theology on this point is that theology is inherently experimental because it is trinitarian. This trinitarian and doxological definition of theology represents one of the best contributions of the movement to which Joel Beeke has dedicated so much of his life to studying, learning from, and spreading among others.

The Biblical Grounds of Puritan and Reformed Definitions of Theology

Now that we know what some older authors wrote about theology as a discipline, we can ask whether these formulations are biblical. Puritan and Reformed definitions of theology reflect well the teaching of Scripture regarding the knowledge of God. This is particularly true in relation to the trinitarian implications of these definitions. In many respects, such definitions of theology can be likened to building a three-step pyramid. The first and foundational level is that theology is the doctrine of living to God. The second step is that it is the doctrine of living to God through Christ. The third and final step is that it is the doctrine of living to God through Christ by the Spirit. Here is where I take off my historian's hat and put on my pastor's hat. By examining the implications of 1 Timothy 6:3-6, John 17:3, and 1 Corinthians 2:1-5 and 9-12, we will see that the older definitions of theology introduced above help make sense of the Bible.[16] They should also drive us to know God in Christ by the Spirit for ourselves and, in knowing Him, to have eternal life.

Theology is the Doctrine of Living to God (1 Tim. 6:3-5)

Biblical Christianity must include doctrine, but it must be more than doctrine. As the Lord saves us as whole people, so the

---

16. All Scripture quotations below are taken from the New King James Version.

knowledge of God involves both knowing about Him and trusting and loving Him with our whole beings. First Timothy 6:3-5 implies that theology is the doctrine of living to God.[17]

In the context, Paul was deeply concerned with personal godliness, which is the beauty and adornment of true believers. Earlier, he treated the necessity of godliness among pastors (4:6-16). Even the soundest instruction can poison souls if the streams that water them are polluted. Ministers must teach the truth that accords with godliness by exemplifying that truth through godliness. In the next section, Paul addressed the need for godliness with respect to age differences (5:1-2). In accord with the fifth commandment, we must learn to give the honor due to all persons in their several relations to us as superiors, inferiors, and equals.[18] It was a mark of godliness for Timothy to learn how to treat older and younger men as well as older and younger women. Paul next promoted godliness toward widows (5:3-16). In order to receive care from the church, widows must have a reputation for godliness and believers must exercise godliness in caring for their own households before burdening the church. Paul concluded the section preceding our text by illustrating how to exercise godliness toward the elders of the church (5:17-25) and how masters and servants should exercise godliness toward each other (6:1-2). It is clear that godliness must be one of the primary aims of Timothy's ministry. By implication, godliness should be a primary aim of any biblical ministry today.

What do these things have to do with the nature of theology? 1 Timothy 6:3-5 serves as a summary of the entire epistle up to this point. Paul observed that 'sound words' and sound living must be intertwined (6:3). Theology is doctrine, since it involves teaching and applying divine truth from Scripture. Such words are 'wholesome' and they are 'the words of our Lord Jesus Christ'. As such, we must receive sound biblical teaching from sound

---

17. Mastricht, *Theoretico-Practica Theologia*, p. 2. Mastricht ordered his chapter defining theology around an exposition of 1 Tim. 6:3-5.

18. See Westminster Shorter Catechism, Questions 64–65.

teachers as from Christ Himself. Yet sound words are not enough. This doctrine 'accords with godliness'. Those who profess to know God but in works deny Him (Titus 1:16) are false teachers because they have false lives, even if they speak the truth.

The rest of the section reinforces the fact that true theology, which aims at the true knowledge of God, must be practical as well as theoretical. Even if false teachers are concerned with doctrine, Paul's verdict was that they 'know nothing' if their doctrine is detached from godliness (1 Tim. 6:4 NKJV). False teachers can show their true colors through their personal qualities and the fruits of their labors as well as through the content of their teaching. In terms of character, Paul described such a person as, 'proud, knowing nothing, but is obsessed with disputes and arguments over words'. The sober warning embedded in these words is that it is not enough to be 'right' in our theological opinions. We must believe (and teach) the right things in the right way. Someone who teaches the Three Forms of Unity or the Westminster Standards to the letter, yet is prideful in their dealings with others, loves to get into the middle of every controversy, and argues more for words than for doctrines, according to Paul, knows 'nothing'. Rather than spreading the fragrance and beauty of Christ in every place, such teachers leave the stench and ugliness of Satan everywhere they go. The fruits of their labors are, 'envy, strife, reviling, evil suspicions, useless wranglings of men of corrupt minds and destitute of the truth, who suppose that godliness is a means of gain. From such withdraw yourself' (1 Tim. 6:4-5 NKJV). Teachers whom Christ is not making better men by the Spirit and who are not making men better through the Spirit's work in them can teach true doctrine, but they cannot attain true theology. Also referring to false teachers, Jude wrote, 'These are sensual persons, who cause divisions, not having the Spirit' (Jude 19 NKJV).

We learn from these things that sound doctrine must aim at sound living. This is why our forefathers defined theology as 'the doctrine of living to God'. Do you aim in Bible reading, in listening to sermons, in taking the sacraments, and in reading good books to love God better and to love your neighbor for God's sake? Jesus told us that we would know false teachers by their fruits (Matt. 7:16). In this light, is it not possible for Reformed Christians to act like false teachers by the wake of strife, anger, rudeness, and division that they leave behind them? It is just as important to hold our beliefs in the right way, as it is to hold right beliefs. This led the Puritan, William Bates (1626–1699), to say that sanctification 'equals if not excels our justification. For as the evil of sin in its own nature is worse than the evil of punishment, so the freeing us from its dominion is a greater blessing than mere impunity.'[19] Is your theology the doctrine of living to God that flows from the truth that accords with godliness?

Theology Is the Doctrine of Living to God through Christ (John 17:3)

If theology involves knowing God, then we must remember that Jesus is the way, the truth, and the life, and that no one comes to the Father but by Him (John 14:6). John 17:3 teaches us that we must know the right God ('that they may know You, the only true God' NKJV) in the right way ('and Jesus Christ whom You have sent' NKJV). Through this text we learn that theology is the doctrine of living to God through Christ.

John 17 represents what some have called the true Lord's Prayer. Christ here prayed for His own glory and for the salvation of His elect through His glorification. After praying for Himself (vv. 1-5), He prayed for His present disciples (vv. 6-19), and then for His future disciples (vv. 20-26). Concerning Christ's words, Anthony Burgess (1600–1664) wrote: 'Though all be gold, yet this is a pearl in the gold; though all be like the heavens, yet this is like the sun and the stars.'[20] In the context of John 14–16, Christ comforted His disciples, who were distressed at the prospect of His departure

---

19. William Bates, *The Harmony of the Divine Attributes in the Contrivance and Accomplishment of Man's Redemption*, in, *The Works of William Bates* (Harrisonburg, VA: Sprinkle Publications, 1990), 4:469.

20. Anthony Burgess, *CXLV Expository Sermons Upon the Whole 17th Chapter of the Gospel According to St. John, Or, Christs Prayer Before His Passion Explicated, and Both Practically and Polemically Improved* (London, 1656), p. 2.

from them, by promising the coming of the Spirit, through whom He would be present among them in greater glory and power than before. John 17 is Christ's prayer of application to this upper room discourse. 'Glorify me together with yourself, with the glory which I had with you before the world was' (John 17:5 NKJV) is the primary petition of the first part of His prayer. Verse three, which states: 'this is eternal life, that they may know you, the only true God, and Jesus Christ whom you have sent,' summarizes the result of the task that the Father committed to Christ. Jesus pleaded the completion of this work that the Father gave Him to do as the primary ground in the prayer for His own glorification. True theology finds biblical expression in living to God through Christ because Christ glorified the Father by securing our right to know the Father through Him.

The first thing that Jesus teaches in John 17:3 is that we need to know the right God. As is often the case in Scripture, the Father here represents the majesty of the entire Trinity. As Thomas Manton (1620–1677) wrote: 'Christ and the Spirit are true God, not without, but in the Father .... One person of the Trinity doth not exclude the rest.'[21] As Henry Scudder (1585–1652) observed, when we pray, we pray to God, 'in the name of Christ and by the Spirit.'[22] He added: 'But because of the indivisible essence of the Godhead, the naming of the Father doth necessarily imply the calling upon the Son and the Holy Ghost also.'[23] It is not enough to believe in a higher power or to worship a generic god or gods. We must know the only true God, who is the Father of our Lord Jesus Christ.

We must know the right God in the right way as well. First Timothy 2:5 is like a light shining on John 17:3, setting its beautiful features in greater relief. Paul wrote there: 'For there is one God and

---

21. Thomas Manton, *The Complete Works* (London: Nisbet, 1870), 10:141.

22. Henry Scudder, *A Key of Heaven: The Lord's Prayer Opened and so Applied, That a Christian May Learn How to Pray, and to Procure All Things Which May Make for the Glory of God, and the Good of Himself and of His Neighbor; Containing Likewise Such Doctrines of Faith and Godliness, as May Be Very Useful to All That Desire to Live Godly in Christ Jesus* (London, 1633), p. 41.

23. Scudder, *A Key of Heaven*, pp. 128–29.

one Mediator between God and men, the Man Christ Jesus' (NKJV). The reason why Christ is singled out in both of these passages is that He is the only person in the Trinity who became man in order to serve as the divine/human mediator between God and men. As a result, through His life God counts us righteous (Rom. 5:19), through His death we died to sin in its curse and its power (Rom. 6:2, 5), through His resurrection we walk in new life (Rom. 6:5), and through His ascension into heaven we have a place prepared in heaven for us (John 14:2-3). Faith is the empty hand by which we apprehend Christ, or rather in which we are apprehended by Him (Phil. 3:12). We know of Him through the preaching of the Scriptures (Rom. 10:14-17), but we know Him and God through Him by faith alone. As Manton wrote: 'The Scriptures are the picture of Christ, and Christ is the image of the Father.'[24] Concerning the omission of the Holy Spirit in the text, Burgess observed: 'the knowledge of the Spirit is necessarily implied in the knowledge of Christ. Christ was conceived by the Spirit and he left the Spirit to guide his apostles. No one can know Christ without knowing the Spirit as well.'[25] We must know the Father through the Son by the Spirit. To know Christ is also to love Christ, which demands keeping His commandments (John 14:15; 1 Cor. 16:22). This is why theology must be the doctrine of living to God through Christ.

Jesus concluded that knowing the right God in the right way is eternal life. Eternal life here describes the quality of life rather than the quantity or duration of life (for instance, see John chs. 3; 5, etc.). All people will exist forever, but some will do so in everlasting life while others will do so in eternal death (Dan. 12:2; John 5:29). Glorifying God and enjoying Him forever in Christ is alone worthy of the name life. This description of eternal life is like a mirror image of Puritan and Reformed definitions of true theology. If eternal life describes the quality of life as lived in God through Christ, then likewise theology is the doctrine of living to God through Christ. Is Christ the heart and soul

---

24. Manton, *The Complete Works*, 10:148.
25. Burgess, *CXLV Expository Sermons*, p. 100.

of your knowledge of God? Christ is not a tool that we use as a means of personal gain. He is a husband to whom we are wedded (2 Cor. 11:2). Is your greatest ambition in life to know Him? (See Phil. 3:10). As Manton noted: 'Christ is the living Bible; we may read much of the glory of God in the face of Jesus Christ. We shall study no other book when we come to heaven.'[26] Do we live to God through Christ now in connection with sound doctrine? We must do so now if we would hope to do so forever.

Theology Is the Doctrine of Living to God, through Christ, by the Spirit (1 Cor. 2:1-16)

Although theology is the doctrine of living to God through Christ, the question of how we come to know Christ remains. First Corinthians chapter two, particularly verses 13–16, completes our picture of true theology by reminding us that we can live to God through Christ by the Spirit only.

The theme of 1 Corinthians is the wisdom of God in Christ versus the wisdom of this world. As a wise pastor, instead of treating the multitude of pastoral problems in Corinth piecemeal, Paul illustrated that the root of their divisions, pride, sexual immorality, failures in church discipline, confusion over marriage and divorce, eating food offered to idols, abuses of the Lord's Supper, conduct in public worship, and instability over the resurrection was that they were acting according to the wisdom of this world rather than the wisdom of God in Christ. Christ is the wisdom and the power of God to salvation (1 Cor. 1:24). While Christ and His cross are foolishness to those who are perishing, to us He is the wisdom of God to salvation. Our relation to God through Christ reorders our priorities and reorients our thinking. Pride is transformed into humility, serving ourselves into serving others, and glorifying and enjoying ourselves forever into glorifying and enjoying God forever. First Corinthians 2:13-16 shows that the Spirit of God alone is our true and effective teacher, who is the author of our knowledge of God through Christ.

---

26. Manton, *The Complete Works*, 10:123.

The first part of this chapter ties the Spirit's ministry to Paul's preaching Christ. Jesus and Him crucified was both the primary content of Paul's preaching and the primary object of the Spirit's ministry (1 Cor. 2:1-5). Christ promised that when the Spirit of truth came, He would glorify Jesus by convincing the world of sin, righteousness, and judgment as these things related to Himself (John 16:8-11, 14). Since there is no knowledge of God apart from union and communion with Christ, we can only explain and apply our preaching in relation to Christ (Col. 1:28-29). For these reasons, a Christless sermon borders on being a Spiritless sermon.

This knowledge of Christ comes only through the Spirit of truth teaching us God's revealed truth (1 Cor. 2:6-12). The Spirit's revelation of God in Christ is the greatest thing that we can know. Eye has not seen, or ear heard, neither has it entered into the heart of man the things that God has prepared for those who love Him. But God has revealed them to us (presently) by His Spirit (2:9-11). This knowledge comes by the Spirit applying Christ to us through the Word of God. Theology is doctrine. Do we believe the content of what the Spirit teaches us concerning Christ and how we come to know God through Him?

The Spirit teaches us internally as well as externally. This stresses once again that theology is not doctrine only, but it is the doctrine of living to God. The Spirit's teaching is both necessary and sufficient for true theology. The natural man cannot know the things of the Spirit of God because they are spiritually discerned (2:13-14). The Spirit must reveal Christ to us twice: once in Scripture and again in our hearts. His latter work is an internal echo of His external call. We must receive those words 'which the Holy Spirit teaches' (v. 13) and we must discern them spiritually (v. 14) by being born of the Spirit (John 3:6). A person who understands and assents to sound doctrine without a sound heart and sound faith in Christ is not taught of God (John 6:45). He or she is like a runner with tied shoes but a broken leg. This is why theology is the doctrine of living to God, through Christ, by the Spirit. If the Spirit has taught us, then we will believe whatever Christ tells us in His Word and we will be willing to do whatever He requires us to do. In so believing and doing, we show that we are children of our heavenly Father. Are you a true theologian? Do you believe sound doctrine and do you live to God in light of it, through Christ, by the Spirit?

Conclusion: The Value of Puritan and Reformed Definitions of Theology

Definitions make a difference. Older Puritan and Reformed definitions of theology have several potential benefits for the church today. Treating theology as the doctrine of living to God, through Christ, by the Spirit fosters the following uses:

1. This definition of theology enables us to wed doctrine and piety in the Christian life more naturally. While some might think that experimental piety was a Puritan emphasis, in reality it characterized classic Reformed theology as a whole. Puritanism may have been distinctive in the extent to which it stressed personal piety, yet wedding personal piety with sound doctrine was one of the great strengths of Reformed theology as a whole.[27] Even Francis Turretin (1623–1687), who is recognized as a high orthodox scholastic theologian, acknowledged the vital importance of piety as an end of theology.[28] A Reformed theology that presses sound thinking without promoting sound hearts and sound living is not really Reformed in a historic sense. Does not the Bible address our minds, aim at our hearts and affections, and press our wills to respond to the teaching and commands of the triune God? Then should not theology include living to God as well as believing right doctrine?

2. This definition of theology promotes devotion to all three persons in the Trinity. Owen noted that the highest privilege

---

27. For the distinctiveness of Puritan piety, see Philip Benedict, *Christ's Churches Purely Reformed: A Social History of Calvinism* (New Haven: Yale University Press, 2002), pp. 317-19.

28. Francis Turretin, *Institutes of Elenctic Theology*, ed. James T. Dennison, trans. George Musgrave Giger, 3 vols. (Phillipsburg, N.J.: P&R Publishing, 1992), p. xli.

of believers under the new covenant was worshiping God as triune.[29] It is important for believers to love the Father who first loved them in their eternal election and in sending Christ to die for them. It is vital for them to esteem Christ to be greater than all riches who, though He was rich, became poor for their sakes (2 Cor. 8:9). Likewise it is necessary for Christians to cultivate fellowship with the Spirit joyfully, since He is the bond of communion between them and the Father through the Son. Believers need to depend more fully upon all three divine persons and to love the triune God more fervently. We must learn to confess with Hoornbeeck that the Trinity is the most eminently practical doctrine in the Bible because knowing God Himself subsumes all the teachings and exhortations found in Scripture.[30] If we are not devotionally trinitarians then we may run the risk of not remaining trinitarians in the future.[31]

3. This definition of theology equips preachers to weave theology naturally into their preaching. What sermon should not impart sound doctrine to those who hear it? What preacher who loves Jesus Christ does not desire to see Christ formed in his audience? Remembering that theology is the doctrine of living to God, through Christ, by the Spirit helps ministers preach the glory of God in the face of Jesus Christ for the transformation of sinners through the Spirit's power. In short, a biblical definition of theology reminds preachers that they must preach the gospel, which is too often reduced to a list of benefits rather than knowing the true God through Jesus Christ whom He has sent.

4. This definition of theology is a potential means of promoting the revival of the church. The greatest need of God's people

---

29. Owen, 'The Chamber of Imagery of the Church of Rome Laid Open,' *Works*, 8:555–56.

30. Hoornbeeck, *Theologia Practica*, 1:136.

31. Philip Dixon, *Nice and Hot Disputes: The Doctrine of the Trinity in the Seventeenth Century* (London; New York: T & T Clark, 2003), pp. 205–207.

is God Himself. This is why the summary of Isaiah's message of comfort was, 'behold your God' (Isa. 40:9). We 'see' Him primarily through the preaching of His Word and the administration of His sacraments. Yet we must not merely understand what man is to believe concerning God. We must know and submit to the duty that God requires of man.[32] Reformed churches today need to remember that theology is not merely doctrine. It is the truth that accords with godliness. Is it not easier to accept the five points of Calvinism than to deny ourselves in keeping the Sabbath? Is it not easier to take a position on infant baptism than to practice regular daily family and private worship? It is not easier to understand the Westminster Confession of Faith than to control anger and subdue lust? What would the effects be if Reformed churches today studied theology with the assumption that the goal of sound doctrine was sound practice as well as sound faith? Such examples highlight areas in which the church needs to be revived today. Such concerns are largely why Joel Beeke and I are co-editing the *Cultivating Biblical Godliness Series*. May the triune God grant us to learn from our forefathers in recovering theology as a theoretical and practical discipline. May we learn to study the doctrine of living to God, through Christ, by the Spirit.

---

32. Adapted from Westminster Shorter Catechism, question 3.

CHAPTER THREE

Christology and Piety in Puritan Thought

MARK JONES

READING the writings of the Puritans on Christology during the beginning of my doctoral studies was a perplexing time for me. Naturally, as a PhD student, I thought my theology was basically figured out—a naïve place for anyone to be, of course—with basically some fine-tuning left. But after reading Thomas Goodwin's (1600–1679) work, *The Heart of Christ in Heaven Towards Sinners on Earth*, I quickly realized that I had absolutely no clue what I was talking about when it came to the one who is not only 'chief among ten thousand' (Song 5:10), with 'grace poured upon [his] lips' (Ps. 45:2), but also the one who I supposedly intimately know, worship, love and desire to be with to see His glory (John 17:24). I quickly realized over the course of my theological studies that my preaching and personal piety were going to be enriched by the Christology of the Puritans. It gives me great honor to write on a topic that I know is very dear to Professor Beeke's heart.

Thomas Goodwin, along with other Puritan luminaries such as John Owen (1616–1683), John Arrowsmith (1602–1659), Stephen Charnock (1628–1680), Richard Sibbes (1577–1635), Isaac Ambrose (1604–1664), and others, sparked ideas in me concerning the person and work of Christ that, quite frankly, I had never seen anywhere else, not even in Calvin and his contemporaries.

Those who have spent time reading the Puritans cannot help but wonder in amazement at the claims made by scholars who have cast aspersions on the Puritans for suggesting they lacked a Christological focus in their writings. For example, Marshall Knappen in his well-known work, *Tudor Puritanism*, argued that the Puritans showed a 'surprising lack of Christological thought'.[1] John Eusden, in his introduction to William Ames' (1576–1633) *Marrow of Theology*, buttresses Knappen's point by arguing that the 'Christo-centrism of Martin Luther is not shared by most English Puritans.'[2] Having closely examined the writings of the Puritans it is hard to believe that these scholars have spent time reading the Puritans. There is not, to my mind, a period in church history where more Christologically devotional writing took place than in the Puritan era.

There are, obviously, hundreds of applications to Christian living that flow out of Christ's person and work. But in this essay I want to focus on three examples, offering a basic overview of the relationship of Puritan Christology to piety.

The Glory of Imitating Christ

Some in Reformed circles today appear to be uneasy at the idea that we should imitate our Savior. This may be a fear of losing the importance that Christ is principally our Redeemer. But the Puritans looked at the person of Christ during His time on earth as someone to be imitated in His deeds and words pertaining to the moral law of God. Thomas Manton (1620–1677), for example, will simply say: 'Christ must be imitated principally ... we look to any one that hath any good thing in him worth of imitation.'[3] Speaking of Christ's acts of kindness, Sibbes follows with this

1. M. M. Knappen, *Tudor Puritanism* (Chicago: University of Chicago Press, 1939), p. 376.

2. J. D. Eusden, introduction to *The Marrow of Theology*, by William Ames (Durham: Labyrinth Press, 1968), p. 20.

3. Thomas Manton, *Sermons Upon Philippians III*, in *The Complete Works of Thomas Manton, D.D.* (London: J. Nisber, 1870), 20:114.

exhortation to his readers: 'And because Christ is our pattern herein, let us labour to imitate Christ in the manner of relieving, and showing kindness, and communicating to others, that we may do it as Christ hath done.'[4]

There are, however, some points that need to be made so that we understand the difference between an orthodox, biblical understanding of the *imitatio Christi* and the moralistic version that can easily creep in.

Regarding God's holiness, for example, we must understand that the immediate motive to holy living is not God's essential holiness, but the holiness of God revealed in the person of Christ. If God chose to relate to us based on His essential holiness apart from mediation in the person of Christ, we would be utterly consumed. Consider whom Isaiah saw in chapter 6 (see John 12:41). As Owen notes: 'it is the holiness of God as he is in Christ, and as in Christ represented unto us, that gives us both the necessity and motive unto ours with God.'[5] Jesus is, morally considered, 'the most perfect, absolute, glorious pattern of all grace, holiness, virtue, obedience, to be chosen and preferred above all others, but he only is so; there is no other complete example of it.'[6] This is a fairly standard Christological reflection by Owen which could come from the pen of almost any of the Reformed Puritan theologians.

Whatever problems people may have with the concept of the *imitatio Christi*, we cannot escape the reality that if we have any interest in Christ, we must emulate Him in His holiness. Paul commands Christians to 'Have this mind among yourselves, which is yours in Christ Jesus' (Phil. 2:5 ESV) before setting before them the example of Christ's humility (Phil. 2:6–11).

Moreover, if we belong to Christ we will suffer with Him (Phil. 3:10; 1 Thess. 2:14–15). If we are in Christ we must walk as

---

4. Richard Sibbes, *The Works of Richard Sibbes* (repr., Edinburgh: Banner of Truth Trust, 2004), 4:523.

5. John Owen, *The Works of John Owen*, ed. William H. Goold (repr., Edinburgh: Banner of Truth Trust, 1965), 3:570.

6. Owen, *Works*, 3:510.

He did (1 John 2:6). This is why Owen, commenting on Hebrews 2:13, says:

> It was [Christ's] duty no less than it is theirs to depend on God in troubles and distresses .... And as such his duty it was, in all straits, to betake himself by faith unto the care and protection of God .... There was upon [Jesus] a confluence of every thing that is evil or troublesome unto human nature. And herein is he principally our example, at least so far that we should think no kind of suffering strange unto us .... [Jesus] is a precedent unto us in trusting as well as in suffering.[7]

Hence, Charnock's words are strong, but nevertheless appropriate: 'Those that lay claim to a relation to God, without imitation of him, are not children, but bastards. They may be of his family by instruction, not by descent. There is no implantation in Christ, without an imitation both of the Creator and Redeemer.'[8] Spiritually illegitimate children are those who desire to have Christ as their Redeemer, but not in any way as their example.

But there is an important point that must be made, which I wish had been more strongly emphasized by Thomas à Kempis in his famous work, *The Imitation of Christ*. Our faith in Christ for redemption (e.g., justification) is, according to John Owen, 'only half of our duty of faith'. He adds:

> Unto these ends, indeed, is [Christ] firstly and principally proposed unto us in the gospel, and with respect unto them are we exhorted to receive him and believe in him; but this is not all that is required of us. Christ in the gospel is proposed unto us as our pattern and example of holiness; and as it is a cursed imagination that this was the whole end of his life and death—namely, to exemplify and confirm the doctrine of holiness which he taught—so to neglect his so being our example, in considering him by faith to that end, and labouring after conformity to him, is evil and pernicious.[9]

---

7. Owen, *Works*, 19:429–30.

8. Stephen Charnock, *The Complete Works of Stephen Charnock*, 5 vols. (Edinburgh: James Nichol, 1864), 4:540.

9. Owen, *Works*, 3:513.

To deny the imitation of Christ is 'evil and pernicious', so long as we insist on the fact that Christ our redeemer is the principal focus of our faith. Far from entering into a dark realm of rigorous moralism or haunting legalism, the Christ-centered focus of Owen and his contemporaries is easy to see for the attentive reader.

Regarding a very specific point of imitation, Goodwin says that in the example of Christ's faith 'we have the highest instance of believing that ever was.'[10] Goodwin refers to Jesus as the greatest believer who ever lived. Our Lord trusted God's promises to Him, even in the midst of suffering. Should we not imitate Jesus in this instance?

Goodwin answers affirmatively:

> This example of Christ may teach and incite us to believe. For did Christ lay down all his glory, and empty himself, and leave himself worth nothing, but made a deed of surrendering all he had into his Father's hands, and this in a pure trust that God would 'justify many by him'? And shall not we lay down all we have, and part with whatever is dear unto us aforehand, with the like submission, in a dependence and hope of being ourselves justified by him?[11]

The imitation of Christ, when rightly understood in light of 'Christ for us', is a doctrine to be savored not jettisoned. The Puritans were not unaware of the potential pitfalls of legalism, which is why their pastoral ethic was firmly fixed on imitation of the one who is, first, our Savior and, second, our example.

The Glory of Christ's Sympathy in Heaven

Christ's affections, according to His manhood, are personal properties of His person in both His state of humiliation and His state of exaltation. The Puritans sometimes discussed the differences and similarities between His affections in these two states. Christ's resurrected body is termed a 'spiritual' body (1 Cor. 15:44). This does not mean that He lost His humanity upon His ascension, but

---

10. Thomas Goodwin, *The Works of Thomas Goodwin, D.D.*, 12 vols. (Edinburgh: James Nichol, 1861–1866), 4:9.

11. Goodwin, *Works*, 4:9.

that His body is now 'powerful' (Rom. 1:4). Not only Christ's body, but also His affections are 'spiritual'. According to Goodwin, Christ's affections do not, then, work in His soul only, but also in His body, 'as their seat and instrument'.[12]

However, the body is 'so framed to the soul that both itself and all the operations of all the powers in it are immediately and entirely at the arbitrary *imperium* and dominion of the soul.'[13] In other words, the infirmities in Christ's human nature on earth, experienced in terms of hunger and weakness, do not now affect His soul in heaven because His body is raised in power. Following from this, Goodwin notes that the affections of pity and sympathy move His 'bowels and affect his bodily heart' both in His states of humiliation and exaltation. But there is this difference: His affections in heaven 'do not afflict and perturb him in the least, nor become a burden and a load unto his Spirit, so as to make him sorrowful or heavy.' This is so because Christ's human nature is 'impassible' insofar as He cannot experience any hurt now that He is in His glorified state. Jesus is still compassionate and merciful, and thus His perfection does not destroy His affections, 'but only corrects and amends the imperfection of them.' Echoing the 'best of the schoolmen', Goodwin adds, '*Passiones perfectivas* to be now in him.'[14]

Goodwin contends that man has certain affections that are natural, and not the result of sin. In the Garden of Eden, Adam possessed natural affections that were governed not by sin, but by reason. Thus, Christ's affections of pity and compassion in His state of glory 'quicken and provoke him to our help and succour.'[15] That is to say, Christ is no longer a 'man of sorrows', but rather a 'man of succours' to His people! The church militant faces many difficult

---

12. Thomas Goodwin, *The Heart of Christ in Heaven Towards Sinners on Earth*, in *Works*, 4:144.

13. Goodwin, *The Heart of Christ in Heaven*, 4:144.

14. Goodwin, *The Heart of Christ in Heaven*, 4:145.

15. Goodwin, *The Heart of Christ in Heaven*, 4:145. To 'succour' is to give help, especially in times of difficulty.

trials on earth, not least because we possess indwelling sin. As a merciful high priest, Christ necessarily possesses affections suitable to their condition while He is in heaven. If heaven was suited only for Christ's personal happiness, then there is no need for Christ to possess the affections of sympathy and mercy. But, as Goodwin observes: 'Christ's relationship to his people is a part of his glory. Therefore, these types of affections are required to be in him if he is to be a good husband to his bride. Moreover, far from being a weakness, Christ's affections of pity and mercy are his strength; it is his glory to be truly and really, even as a man, sensible of all our miseries, yea, it were his imperfection if he were not.'[16]

The beauty of Goodwin's theology emerges precisely at this point. Though Christ has shed affections that were once a burden to Him and are thus not compatible or suitable to His state in heaven, there are nonetheless other affections that possess a 'greater capaciousness, vastness' that more than makes up for His lack of the former affections. In fact, Goodwin argues that just as Christ's knowledge was 'enlarged' in heaven, 'so his human affections of love and pity are enlarged in solidity, strength, and reality. ... Christ's affections of love are as large as his knowledge or his power.'[17] Another way to look at this would be to argue that, since Christ is freed from oppressive affections, it actually gives greater scope to His effective affections—being free from grief actually lets you be more compassionate. So, for example, when you yourself are desperately hungry, other people's problems don't receive your best attention. This can be applied to Christ based on the theology that Goodwin sets forth.

Where does this all lead Goodwin, one might ask? In his 'uses' section after writing so profoundly on the heart of Christ in heaven towards sinners on earth, he makes the following contention: 'Your very sins move him to pity more than to anger.'[18] Now, this statement might sound nice as a Tweet or a

---

16. Goodwin, *The Heart of Christ in Heaven*, 4:146.

17. Goodwin, *The Heart of Christ in Heaven*, 4:146.

18. Goodwin, *The Heart of Christ in Heaven*, 4:149.

Facebook post, but written in the context of what has gone before, the statement had a weight that crushes the Christian with God's overflowing mercy, love, and compassion towards us in Christ Jesus. Goodwin adds:

> The object of pity is one in misery whom we love; and the greater the misery is, the more is the pity when the party is beloved. Now of all miseries, sin is the greatest; and whilst yourselves look at it as such, Christ will look upon it as such only also in you. And he, loving your persons, and hating only the sin, his hatred shall all fall, and that only upon the sin, to free you of it by its ruin and destruction, but his bowels shall be the more drawn out to you; and this as much when you lie under sin as under any other affliction.[19]

Reading this for the first time made me feel like Pilgrim in Bunyan's classic work where the burden had finally been lifted. Good Christology leads to good practical theology. And in the case of this Puritan, there were few better, in all of church history so far, who have written on the heart of Christ in heaven towards sinners on earth.

Another example of the value of good Christology in relation to a believer's personal frailties comes from Stephen Charnock. Commenting on Hebrews 4:15, he argues that because of the incarnation 'an experimental compassion' was gained which the divine nature was not capable of because of divine impassibility.[20] As our sympathetic high priest, Christ 'reflects' back on His experiences in the world and so the 'greatest pity must reside in him' because the 'greatest misery was endured by him.' Christ is unable to forget above what He experienced below.[21] Charnock does not intend to say that Christ's human nature suffers in any way, which would contradict Goodwin. Instead, he is speaking about Christ's knowledge and memory of His sufferings as the means by which

---

19. Goodwin, *The Heart of Christ in Heaven*, 4:149.

20. Stephen Charnock, *A Discourse of Christ's Intercession*, in *The Complete Works of Stephen Charnock*, 5 vols. (Edinburgh: James Nichol, 1864), 5:106.

21. Charnock, *A Discourse of Christ's Intercession*, 5:106.

Christ is able to be sympathetic to His people in a way that would otherwise be impossible if the Son did not assume a human nature. Consequently, the value of an elaborate Reformed Christology for the advancement of biblical spirituality cannot be overstated.

The Glory of Christ's Face in Heaven

In all of my reading on Christology, I have not come across a theme in Puritan writing more exciting than the glory of Christ. The technical work to get to the place where we can discuss Christ's human and divine glory will, I pray, be worth it. The Puritans generally discoursed on Christ by either speaking of His divine glory, which the Son shares with the Father and the Holy Spirit, or by speaking of His human glory, which is a result of the incarnation (i.e., the hypostatic union).

Being a true human being, Christ's possesses a body and soul. He does so now, and will possess a body and soul forever. His exaltation, post-resurrection, was for Him a mighty transition from 'weakness' to 'strength'. Christ's entrance into glory was, for Himself, a major transition. Seated at the right hand of the Father, Ambrose writes: 'His soul was filled with all joy, solace, pleasure, which could possibly flow from the sight of an object so infinitely pleasing, as in the essence, majesty, and glory of God.'[22] His body was, says Ambrose, 'replenished with as much glory as was proportionable unto the most vast capacity of any creature; not only his soul, but his body is a glorious creature.'[23] Owen, Goodwin, and Ambrose, among others, gave copious attention to the exaltation of Christ's humanity not only because their Christology allowed for true exaltation, but also their Christology demanded a true exaltation of the human nature of Christ. Now, what is the pastoral benefit of the exaltation of Christ's human nature in glory? Ambrose lists several.

---

22. Isaac Ambrose, *Looking unto Jesus* (Pittsburgh: Luke Loomis & Col. 1832), p. 670.

23. Ambrose, *Looking unto Jesus*, p. 670.

First, like at the transfiguration, the 'lustre' of the divine nature now shines perfectly and unimpeded through the humanity, 'and that thereby our very bodily eyes may come to see God as much as is possible, for any creature to see him' (Job 19:27). Second, the redeemed in heaven shall see how God's power can be imparted or conveyed to a creature. As Ambrose says: 'I verily believe, that angels and men will be continually viewing Jesus Christ.'[24] This particular version of the beatific vision in Puritan writings is not uncommon. Other Puritans, such as Owen, Manton, and Goodwin, for example, could not conceive of a 'blessed vision' of God that did not have the humanity of Christ in full view. So, Ambrose will continue: 'In heaven there will be so much excellency in Christ, that we shall admire as much to all eternity, as we did at the very first moment; there will be no abatement in glory of our being taken with the sight of the glory, in Jesus.'[25] Third, following from this emphasis on the humanity of Christ, Ambrose adds that Christ, through His humanity, will 'converse more freely, and familiarly with his brethren in his Father's house: Oh! the intimacy that will be there betwixt Jesus and his Christian saints! ... The eye of the saints in glory can never be off Christ as Mediator and God.'[26]

For the saints in heaven, there shall be twofold manner of beholding Christ's glory: ocular and mental. Regarding the former, which has been briefly addressed above, God's people shall look upon Christ with their own eyes. Ambrose still affirms we shall behold the beauty of heaven and Christ's people, for example, but the chief delight of glorified saints will be Christ's glorious body. Is this glory too awesome for us? In our current state, because of the natural infirmities of our human nature particularly with the presence of indwelling sin, the answer is an unequivocal yes. But in heaven, according to Ambrose, the eye will be glorified.

Now glorification adds a singular excellency to the faculties, it advances the faculties, and raises them to a higher pitch of

---

24. Ambrose, *Looking unto Jesus*, p. 670–71.

25. Ambrose, *Looking unto Jesus*, p, 671.

26. Ambrose, *Looking unto Jesus*, p. 671.

excellency; glorification adds a great capacity to the eye than ever it had before … [in glory] it shall be enlarged exceedingly to take in objects which now it cannot receive; glorification adds strength to the faculties both internal and external, so that the eye shall be able to look on the glory of Christ, not with difficulty, but with contentment.'[27]

It appears to me that many Puritan theologians, including Ambrose, because of their Christology and the place they give to Christ in their theology, are willing to subject all things to the Lord of glory. In other words, why does God grant to His saints glorified bodies? His goodness may be a correct answer, but for the Puritans, it would not be sufficient. God desires to glorify His Son (John 17:1), and so God grants to us glorified eyes in order that we may properly see the glory of Christ in heaven. Naturally, we will not just be 'eyeballs' in the abstract, but we shall be true human beings with bodies that include parts that are all glorified. In heaven, we shall be stripped 'of all corruption and imperfections; so that there shall be no bar unto the influences of the glory of Christ which shall there be seen.'[28] As Owen says: 'Our eyes were made to see our Redeemer, and our other senses to receive impressions from him, according unto their capacity. As the bodies of wicked men shall be restored unto them to increase and complete their misery in their sufferings; so shall the bodies of the just be restored unto them, to heighten and consummate their blessedness.'[29]

As a true human being, Christ is both body and soul. Likewise, we shall have not only the blessing of physically glorified bodies, but also the blessing of spiritually glorified souls. Because of our glorified souls, when we look with our eyes upon Christ, we shall have the superadded advantage, which no man on earth now can have, of beholding the Lord of glory with our own glorified spirits illuminating our bodies to apprehend the true glory of the Lord.

27. Ambrose, *Looking unto Jesus*, pp. 672–73.
28. Ambrose, *Looking unto Jesus*, p. 673.
29. Owen, *Works*, 1:412.

This leads to the truth that we shall also have what Ambrose calls a 'mental vision', which is 'a sight of Christ by the eyes of our understandings'.[30] This is a great blessing. For, not only shall we see, but we shall see with an enlightened understanding.

Thus, for example, the doctrine that we believe on earth shall be clarified and confirmed in heaven. Regarding the beatific vision in relation to our better understanding of deep divine mysteries, Ambrose remarks:

> They shall see Christ as God, of the same essence with the Father, and the Holy Ghost, and yet a distinct person from them both; they shall see the unity in trinity, and trinity in unity; they shall see how the Son is begotten of the Father, and how the Holy Ghost proceeds from the Father, and the Son; they shall see the difference between the generation of the Son, and procession of the Spirit. These are mysteries in which we are blind, and know very little or nothing; but in seeing his face, we shall see all these.[31]

That is to say, the key to our fuller and better understanding of God and His truth is through the glorified Lord. Even when we behold the beauty, riches, and honor conferred upon those in heaven with us, we shall know that those graces are 'eminently, transcendently, and originally in Christ.'[32] As Goodwin would say: 'Now it is a certain rule, that whatsoever we receive from Christ, that he himself first receives in himself for us.'[33] His glorified body and our glorified bodies are an example of this principle.

There are many truths about heaven that we tend to take for granted. We believe God is good and able to do good things for us. Regarding heaven, we are frequently told that we shall never sin in heaven. With glorified bodies, we shall be free from sin, and we shall not sin. Yet, there is something Christologically lacking in such an account.

---

30. Ambrose, *Looking unto Jesus*, p. 673.
31. Ambrose, *Looking unto Jesus*, p. 674.
32. Ambrose, *Looking unto Jesus*, p. 674.
33. Goodwin, *Works*, 4:121.

This is a crucial point in Owen's own exposition on the beatific vision. Owen claims:

> In the vision which we shall have *above*, the whole glory of Christ will be at *once* and *always* represented unto us; and we shall be enabled in one act of the light of glory to comprehend it. Here, indeed, we are at a loss—our minds and understandings fail us in their contemplations. It will not yet enter into our hearts to conceive what is the beauty, what is the glory of this complete representation of Christ unto us. To have at once all the glory of what he is, what he was in his outward state and condition, what he did and suffered, what he is exalted unto—his love and condescension, his mystical union with the church, and the communication of himself unto it, with the recapitulation of all things in him—and the glory of God, even the Father, in his wisdom, righteousness, grace, love, goodness, power, shining forth eternally in him, in what he is, hath done, and doth—all presented unto us in *one view*, all comprehended by us at once, is that which at present we cannot conceive. We can long for it, pant after it, and have some foretastes of it—namely, of that state and season wherein our whole souls, in all their powers and faculties, shall constantly, inseparably, eternally cleave by love unto whole Christ, in the sight of the glory of his person and grace, until they are watered, dissolved, and inebriated in the waters of life and the rivers of pleasure that are above for evermore.[34]

Likewise, Ambrose claims the vision of Christ will be 'without interruption, and without intermission to all eternity. If once the eye be set on the face of Jesus Christ, it will never be taken off again.'[35] Now here is a most valuable Christological point about the glory of heaven, hinted at by Ambrose, which I think is most apt: 'Some conceive this to be the reason why the saints in heaven can never fall away, because they all have a continual view of Christ as God .... Turn them which way they will, they shall never turn aside the busied eyes of their understanding from off the Deity of Christ.'[36]

---

34. Owen, *Works*, 1:410.

35. Ambrose, *Looking unto Jesus*, p. 675.

36. Ambrose, *Looking unto Jesus*, p. 675.

This does not mean we shall in any way be 'idle spectators' in glory. We are not mere onlookers of His glory. What our salvation is here on earth shall be ten thousand times what we can now conceive. Christ is the Lord of heaven, but He also remains our Husband, our Savior, our Brother, and our Friend. We shall behold Him, but we shall also lay hold of Him. Ambrose makes a rich point for all of God's people to rejoice in:

> When once the spouse comes to behold Christ in his kingdom, she may then go boldly to her beloved, and say, 'All I see is my own, I had thee in hope, but now hope is vanished, and actual enjoyment comes into its place; lo! Now I have thee in my eye, and in my heart, and in my hands, and in my arms, and as nothing shall separate us now, for all our enemies are trodden under foot, so never will I part with thee, so far as to be out of my eye, I will still behold thee, and in beholding I will still possess thee, for thou art mine own.'[37]

Our communion on earth now is but a mere shadow compared to the communion we shall one day enjoy. The Puritans who spoke on this were, however, quite clear. No one could expect to have such enjoyments of the man, Christ Jesus, in heaven who did not, in some small measure, desire Him now on earth by faith.

Conclusion

The best theology is not to be hidden away in the 'ivory towers' of academia, but proclaimed simply and clearly from the pulpits. God desires that His Son permeate our Christian lives. This means that the Christian life is one of beholding the glory of God in the face of Jesus Christ, whether by imitation, meditation, worship, or reflection—all done through faith! We plant our eyes upon who He is, what He has done for us, what He continues to do for us, and what He shall be to us for all eternity. The Puritans were not perfect theologians by any means; but there is no question they did their best to draw us to a perfect Savior.

---

37. Ambrose, *Looking unto Jesus*, pp. 657–58.

CHAPTER FOUR

The Kingdom of God in the Theology of Jonathan Edwards

PAUL M. SMALLEY

ALL true piety is by the grace of God. The Puritans, in continuity with the broader Reformed tradition, set piety in the context of God's work of salvation. A central theme in the New Testament's teaching about God's saving intervention is the kingdom of God (Mark 1:15; Acts 28:31). This essay will explore the doctrine of God's kingdom in the theology of Jonathan Edwards (1703–1758) in order to provide some insights into the soteriological context of Puritan piety. Edwards has rightly been viewed as a Puritan theologian who lived after the Puritan era.

The doctrine of the kingdom pervades Edwards's writings, but receives no separate treatment in a treatise, nor even a separate category in his catalog of 'Miscellanies.'[1] However, he does give it extended attention in his historical-eschatological work, *The History of Redemption*. His view of the kingdom is intriguing because it is based on the triune nature of God, centered on the mediator-king, historically developed, practically executed in the application of salvation, relevant to his view of revival,

---

1. Thomas A. Schafer, editorial note in *The Works of Jonathan Edwards* (New Haven: Yale University Press, 1957–2008), 13:236. Henceforth cited as *WJE*.

and completed in eternal life. As such, the kingdom of God is a significant bridge between theology and piety in Edwards's thought.

The Kingdom and the Triune God

The kingdom of God arises from God's nature as King. At the center of Edwards's theology is the sovereignty of the triune God, and all of human history is a stage where God displays His glory.[2] Edwards's conversion revolved around the new sense of spiritual delight in God as revealed in 1 Timothy 1:17, 'Now unto the King eternal, immortal.'[3] Edwards's view of God was staggeringly majestic: He is the incomparable King of glory, all-sufficient, controlling life and death, infinitely holy, a boundless ocean of love. It is worth hearing Edwards extol at length the wonders of this God:

> Their God is a glorious God. There is none like him, who is infinite in glory and excellency: he is the most high God, glorious in holiness, fearful in praises, doing wonders: his name is excellent in all the earth, and his glory is above the earth and the heavens: among the gods there is none like unto him; there is none in heaven to be compared to him, nor are there any among the sons of the mighty, that can be likened unto him.
>
> Their God is the fountain of all good, and an inexhaustible fountain; he is an all-sufficient God; a God that is able to protect and defend them, and do all things for them: he is the King of Glory, the Lord strong and mighty, the Lord mighty in battle: a strong rock, and an high tower. There is none like the God of Jeshurun, who rideth on the heaven in their help, and in his excellency on the sky: the eternal God is their refuge, and underneath are everlasting arms: he is a God that hath all things in his hands, and does whatsoever he pleases: he killeth and maketh alive; he bringeth down to the grave, and bringeth up; he maketh poor and maketh rich: the pillars of the earth are the Lord's.

---

2. George M. Marsden, *Jonathan Edwards: A Life* (New Haven: Yale University Press, 2003), pp. 4, 88.

3. Marsden, *Jonathan Edwards*, p. 39.

Their God is an infinitely holy God: there is none holy as the Lord. And he is infinitely good and merciful. Many that others worship and serve as gods, are cruel beings, spirits that seek the ruin of souls; but this is a God that delighteth in mercy; his grace is infinite, and endures for ever: he is love itself, an infinite fountain and ocean of it.

Such a God is their God! Such is the excellency of Jacob! Such is the God of them, who have forsaken their sins and are converted! They have made a wise choice, who have chosen this God for their God. They have made an happy exchange indeed, that have exchanged sin, and the world, for such a God![4]

The kingdom is rooted in the Father's eternal covenant with His Son. God created the universe for the purpose of performing and displaying the work of redemption. All of Christ's redeeming work as prophet, priest, and king executes the plan formed by the triune God in the eternal covenant of redemption.[5] Edwards said: 'The persons of the Trinity were as it were confederated in a design and a covenant of redemption, in which covenant the Father appointed the Son and the Son had undertaken their work, and all things to be accomplished in their work were stipulated and agreed.'[6] The Father leads in this arrangement, for He is the head of the Trinity.[7]

The kingdom of God is the goal of all creation and history. God's goal in His plan of creation and redemption is Himself, that is, His glory, His name, and His praise.[8] God glorifies Himself by sharing His fullness with His creatures for their joy in esteeming

---

4. Edwards, 'Ruth's Resolution,' in *WJE*, 19:310. Paragraph breaks added for ease of reading.

5. Edwards, 'A History of the Work of Redemption,' in *WJE*, 9:117.

6. Edwards, 'A History of the Work of Redemption,' in *WJE*, 9:118. See also his sermon on Heb. 13:8 in *The Works of Jonathan Edwards* (Edinburgh: Banner of Truth, 1974) 2:950. Henceforth cited as *Works* (Banner).

7. Unpublished ms. sermon on 1 Cor. 11:3. Quoted in John H. Gerstner, *The Rational Biblical Theology of Jonathan Edwards, Volume II* (Orlando: Ligonier, 1992), p. 91. Also cited in *WJE*, 13:131n4.

8. Edwards, 'Concerning the End for which God Created the World,' in *WJE*, 8:467, 475–92.

and loving Him.[9] He aimed to glorify each person in the triune Godhead by triumphing over His enemy Satan, restoring the ruins of the fall by His Son, placing all elect creatures under the headship of Christ, and advancing the elect to inconceivable glory and joy in Christ.[10] Thus God created the world in order to make a kingdom for His Son. Edwards wrote: 'The end of God's creating this world was to provide a kingdom for his Son in it; for he is appointed the heir of the world, and that he might have the possession of it and kingdom in it to all eternity.'[11] Edwards said: 'God created the world to provide a spouse and kingdom for his Son. And the setting up the kingdom of Christ, and the spiritual marriage of the spouse to him, is what the whole creation labors and travails in pain to bring to pass.'[12]

The Christ-Centered Kingdom

God promises to bring His kingdom through the mediatorial kingship of Christ. Edwards followed the classic Reformed formulation of Christ's office as prophet, priest, and king.[13] Christ is the prince of life (Acts 3:15), possessing the divine life and having authority to grant it to His people by right of His purchase.[14] The Son of God is the heir of the world, and therefore His mediatorial kingdom will gather all nations together through the gospel. Edwards said:

> It is natural and reasonable to suppose, that the whole world should finally be given to Christ, as one whose right it is to reign, as the proper heir of him, who is originally the king of all nations, and the possessor of heaven and earth: and the Scripture teaches us, that God the Father hath constituted his Son, as God-man, and in his kingdom of grace, or mediatorial

---

9. *WJE*, 8:526–31; 14:146.

10. *WJE*, 9:123–25.

11. Edwards, 'A History of the Work of Redemption,' in *WJE*, 9:349.

12. Edwards, 'A History of the Work of Redemption,' in *WJE*, 9:513.

13. See *WJE*, 9:117, pp. 210–211.

14. See *WJE* 53, #498b.

kingdom, to be 'the heir of the world,' that he might in this kingdom have 'the heathen for his inheritance, and the utmost ends of the earth for his possession' (Heb. 1:2 and Heb. 2:8; Pss. 2:6–8) ... . God has appointed Christ to be the heir of the world in his kingdom of grace, and to possess and reign over all nations, through the propagation of his gospel, and the power of his Spirit communicating the blessings of it.[15]

Since Christ's exaltation, the Father has entrusted His entire government of the world to the Mediator-King, who reigns as absolute ruler. Edwards said: 'Christ as Mediator has now the kingdom and government of the world so committed [to] him, that he is to all intents and purposes in the room of his Father. He is to be respected as God himself is, as supreme, and absolute, and sovereign Ruler. God has left the government in his hands wholly, now since his exaltation, that he may himself have the accomplishment and finishing of those great things for which he died.'[16] Christ directs 'the motion of every atom' in the universe to serve His purpose of bringing His church to her glorious marriage with Him.[17]

The kingdom of God is shaped by the character of the incarnate Son. Here Edwards found a beautiful paradox, for the King is both a lion and a lamb (Rev. 5:5–6), infinite majesty before whom all nations and angels are nothing, joined with infinite lowliness exercised in Christ's tender attention to children, beggars, and the worst of sinners.[18] This is grounded in Christ's voluntary humiliation. The King over heaven and earth became the least and lowest of all. The kingdom of Christ is founded upon humility, not pride and ambition for personal glory. Yet the Father is pleased to make His humble Son preeminent, so that after all other kingdoms fall, Christ's kingdom will persevere and prevail.[19]

---

15. Edwards, *Humble Attempt*, in *WJE*, 5:330.

16. Edwards, 'Notes on Scripture,' in *WJE*, 15:95.

17. Edwards, Miscellanies no. 86, in *WJE*, 13:251.

18. Edwards, 'The Excellency of Christ,' in *WJE*, 19:565–66.

19. See *WJE*, 9:154, 321–22, 518.

The Kingdom Developed through History

Christ brings His kingdom step-by-step in history. God's promises of the universal extension of Christ's kingdom (e.g. Dan. 7:13–14) are realized through progressive fulfillment every time Christ acts in the world to save His people and destroy His enemies.[20] J. I. Packer writes: 'A universal dominion is pledged to Christ, and in the interim before the final consummation the Father implements this pledge in part by successive outpourings of the Spirit, which prove the reality of Christ's kingdom to a skeptical world and serve to extend its bounds among Christ's erstwhile enemies.'[21]

Every drop of mercy falling upon sinners came through the Mediator, and so Christ took up His offices immediately upon the fall of man. Whenever God appeared to men, it was the Son who came.[22] But all the great events of the Old Testament were preparations for the arrival of the kingdom, when the great King and Savior came in the flesh. John the Baptist and Christ announced the coming of the kingdom of heaven. The kingdom officially began after Christ's resurrection. The triumphant ministry of the apostles, the destruction of Christ's enemies in Jerusalem, the breaking of paganism's power in the time of Constantine, the overthrow of Antichrist, and the coming of Christ with glory are all examples of Christ's kingdom breaking into history.[23]

The kingdom of Christ opposes and overcomes the kingdom of Satan in the world and in the individual soul of the believer.[24] Edwards said: 'The visible kingdom of Satan shall be overthrown and the kingdom of Christ set up on the ruins of it everywhere, throughout the whole habitable globe. Now shall the promise made to Abraham be fulfilled, that 'In him and in his seed all the

---

20. Edwards, 'History of the Work of Redemption,' in *WJE*, 9:144, p. 353.

21. J. I. Packer, *A Quest for Godliness: The Puritan Vision of the Christian Life* (Wheaton: Crossway Books, 1990), pp. 322–23.

22. See *WJE*, 9:129–31.

23. See *WJE*, 9:244, pp. 350–53.

24. See *WJE*, 5:25; 16:136.

families [of the earth shall be blessed]."[25] Satan had attempted to set up a rival kingdom, usurping the Creator's dominion on earth.[26] Conversion delivers a sinner out of the kingdom of the devil and translates him into the kingdom of Christ.[27]

The true Christian is a soldier in Christ's kingdom at war with the kingdom of the devil. Edwards said: 'This every true Christian doth. He makes Jesus Christ the highest end of his actions …. He greatly rejoices when he sees or hears of anything done that is signally to his honor and the advancement of his kingdom. His principal endeavor is to do something towards the destruction of the kingdom of Satan, and the setting up [of] the kingdom of Christ in his own soul and in the world, and gladly lays hold on all opportunities so to do.'[28] Yet in this age the influences of Satan continue in the hearts of believers alongside the influences of the devil, so that both kingdoms may in some sense be said to reside in the regenerated heart. Edwards wrote: 'Yea, the same persons may be the subjects of much of the influences of the Spirit of God, and yet in some things be led away by the delusions of the Devil; and this be no more of a paradox than many other things that are true of real saints, in the present state, where grace dwells with so much corruption, and the new man and the old man subsist together in the same person; and the kingdom of God and the kingdom of the Devil remain for a while together in the same heart.'[29]

The Kingdom and the Application of Salvation

Christ applies as king what He purchased as priest. Christ's humiliation was the climax of redemptive history and the focal point of the covenant of redemption, for then He made the purchase of redemption. Christ conquered the powers of evil when Satan's

---

25. Edwards, 'A History of the Work of Redemption,' in *WJE*, 9:473.

26. Edwards, 'A History of the Work of Redemption,' in *WJE*, 9:123.

27. Edwards, 'Lectures on the Qualifications for Full Communion in the Church of Christ' in *WJE*, 25:357.

28. Edwards, 'Living to Christ and Dying to Gain,' in *WJE*, 10:572.

29. Edwards, *The Distinguishing Marks*, in *WJE*, 4:244.

visible kingdom was at its greatest strength and glory in the Roman Empire. Christ slew the spiritual Goliath with His own weapon— death, and that on the cross.[30] Yet Edwards did not view Christ's redemption primarily as victory over Satan, but as a purchase, in which His humiliation was the price necessary to satisfy God's law both by suffering its penalties and obeying its precepts. The greatest act of His public ministry on earth was when as a priest He offered Himself up to God as a sacrifice, purchasing heaven for His people.[31] Though the work of redemption continues, the purchase of redemption began and ended with Christ's humiliation, and so 'it is finished.'[32]

Christ's present work as the heavenly king does not add to His purchase of redemption, but applies the results of His purchase; what He bought as priest He applies as king. Edwards said:

> His resurrection ... was necessary in order to Christ's obtaining the end and effect of his purchase of redemption that he should rise from the dead; for God the Father had committed the whole affair of redemption, not only the purchasing of it but the bestowment of the blessings purchased, that he should not only purchase it as priest but actually bring it about as king, and that he should do this as God-man. For God the Father would have nothing to do with fallen man in a way of mercy but by a mediator .... Therefore Christ, after he had finished this purchase by death and by continuing for a time under the power of death, rises from the dead to fulfill the end of his purchase and himself to bring about that which he died for.[33]

The context of the kingdom is the church. Christ is the head of the kingdom of grace, and His kingdom is His people. He rules them externally through His Word and the officers, and internally by the influences of His grace. His kingdom is within them, and He rules not by coercion like rulers of this world, but by making

---

30. See *WJE*, 9:206, 279, 295.

31. See *WJE*, 9:304–305, 318.

32. See *WJE*, 9:117, 331.

33. Edwards, 'History of the Work of Redemption,' in *WJE*, 9:358.

His people willing to obey by His power.[34] The Christian church is Christ's kingdom because they are the people who have Christ as their king, just as King George's kingdom consists of the people who have him as their king. But not all in the visible kingdom of Christ, the church, belong there; some are like bad fish in the net that will be thrown away in the final judgment.[35]

The essence of the Christ's kingdom is the saving work of the Spirit. The ministry of the Holy Spirit is the sum of all spiritual good that Christ purchased. Thus, the Father gives the Redeemer, the Son purchases redemption, and the Spirit is the blessing purchased—trinitarian redemption. Michael Haykin says: 'One of God's major purposes in the atoning work of Christ was to secure the blessed presence of the Spirit of Christ for his people.'[36] Edwards wrote:

> The sum of the blessings Christ sought, by what he did and suffered in the work of redemption, was the Holy Spirit. So is the affair of our redemption constituted; the Father provides and gives the Redeemer, and the price of redemption is offered to him, and he grants the benefit purchased; the Son is the Redeemer that gives the price, and also is the price offered; and the Holy Spirit is the grand blessing, obtained by the price offered, and bestowed on the redeemed. The Holy Spirit, in his indwelling, his influences and fruits, is the sum of all grace, holiness, comfort and joy, or in one word, of all the spiritual good Christ purchased for men in this world: and is also the sum of all perfection, glory and eternal joy, that he purchased for them in another world. The Holy Spirit is that great benefit, that is the subject matter of the promises, both of the eternal covenant of redemption, and also of the covenant of grace; the grand subject of the promises of the Old Testament, in the prophecies of the blessings of the Messiah's kingdom; and the chief subject of the promises of the New Testament.[37]

---

34. Edwards, 'The Threefold Work of the Holy Ghost,' in *WJE*, 14:420–22.

35. Edwards, 'Heaven's Dragnet,' in *WJE*, 25:577–78.

36. Michael A. G. Haykin, *Jonathan Edwards: The Holy Spirit in Revival* (Darlington, England: Evangelical Press, 2005), p. 32.

37. Edwards, *Humble Attempt*, in *WJE*, 5:341.

The immediate fruit of Christ's exaltation is the outpouring of the Holy Spirit at Pentecost, for the King came in His kingdom to His people through the Spirit and struck a mighty blow against Satan's dominion.[38] Haykin comments: 'The exaltation of the God-man in his kingly office, whereby he gives eternal life to the elect by sending them the Holy Spirit from the Father, is seen as the result of Christ's priestly work of having fully satisfied the justice of his Father.'[39] Partaking of the Spirit, they share in the fullness of Christ. Christ becomes their life by the indwelling Spirit, a fountain of living water within the soul.[40] In His Spirit, the exalted King is conquering the devil already on earth, especially in converting and sanctifying the elect.[41]

However, despite the militaristic language of conquest, the Spirit brings the kingdom in the gracious love and gentleness of Christ, for such is the power of a soldier of Jesus Christ to fight in the spiritual war. Edwards said: 'Truly gracious affections differ from those affections that are false and delusive, in that they tend to, and are attended with the lamblike, dovelike spirit and temper of Jesus Christ; or in other words, they naturally beget and promote such a spirit of love, meekness, quietness, forgiveness and mercy, as appeared in Christ.'[42] Edwards proceeded to wax lyrical about the power of Christian meekness:

> The whole Christian life is compared to a warfare, and fitly so. And the most eminent Christians are the best soldiers, endowed with the greatest degrees of Christian fortitude. And it is the duty of God's people to be steadfast, and vigorous in their opposition to the designs and ways of such, as are endeavoring to overthrow the kingdom of Christ, and the interest of religion.

---

38. Edwards, 'History of the Work of Redemption,' in *WJE*, 9:375.

39. Haykin, *Jonathan Edwards: The Holy Spirit in Revival*, p. 34.

40. See *WJE*, 2:200; 17:209.

41. See *WJE Online*, 53, #485. Cf. 'Christ Exalted: or, Jesus Christ Glorious Exalted above All Evil in the Work of Redemption,' in *Works* (Banner), 2:215.

42. Edwards, *Religious Affections*, in *WJE*, 2:344–45.

But yet many persons seem to be quite mistaken concerning the nature of Christian fortitude. 'Tis an exceeding diverse thing from a brutal fierceness, or the boldness of beasts of prey. True Christian fortitude consists in strength of mind, through grace, exerted in two things; in ruling and suppressing the evil and unruly passions and affections of the mind; and in steadfastly and freely exerting and following good affections and dispositions, without being hindered by sinful fear, or the opposition of enemies. But the passions that are restrained and kept under, in the exercise of this Christian strength and fortitude, are those very passions that are vigorously and violently exerted, in a false boldness for Christ. And those affections that are vigorously exerted in true fortitude, are those Christian holy affections, that are directly contrary to 'em.

Though Christian fortitude appears, in withstanding and counteracting the enemies that are without us; yet it much more appears, in resisting and suppressing the enemies that are within us; because they are our worst and strongest enemies, and have greatest advantage against us. The strength of the good soldier of Jesus Christ, appears in nothing more, than in steadfastly maintaining the holy calm, meekness, sweetness, and benevolence of his mind, amidst all the storms, injuries, strange behavior, and surprising acts and events of this evil and unreasonable world.[43]

The Kingdom and Revival

God accelerates the advance of His kingdom through revival. In revival, God is especially present with His people by His Spirit.[44] The kingdom of Christ flourishes in an extraordinary manner because God comes to the church as its covenant king; as He manifests His glory and strengthens their graces, they rejoice to see the goings of their God and king in His sanctuary (Ps. 68:24; Isa. 33:22).[45] Revival is like the public coronation of a king, or when a sovereign rides forth in battle against his enemies, thus calling

---

43. Edwards, *Religious Affections*, in *WJE*, 2:350. I have added paragraph breaks for the ease of the reader.

44. Edwards, 'Continuing God's Presence,' in *WJE*, 19:393.

45. Edwards, 'God Amongst His People' in *WJE*, 19:453, 455, 457.

all men to submit to his dominion or face his wrath. Revival is an open manifestation of God's eternal purpose to glorify His Son and give Him the kingdom.[46]

God will extend Christ's kingdom over every nation in the latter-day glory. Edwards believed that God's promises implied a remarkable advance of the kingdom of Christ by an outpouring of the Spirit in the future. He cited the promises to the patriarchs that 'in thee shall all families of the earth be blessed' (Gen. 12:3; cf. 18:18; 22:18; 26:4; 28:14), the promises to the Messiah that 'all nations' shall serve Him (Ps. 72:11, 17), the prophecies that 'all nations' will come to the Lord (Isa. 2:2; Jer. 3:17), the prophecies that true religion will prevail throughout the world (Ps. 22:27; 65:5, 8; 67:7; 98:3; 113:3; Isa. 11:9; 54:1, 2, 5; Mal. 1:11), the warnings that idols and idolatrous nations will perish from the earth (Isa. 60:12; Jer. 10:11, 15), and the promise that the fullness of the Jews and the Gentiles will be saved (Rom. 11:12, 25).[47] Edwards made an eschatological connection between revival by the Spirit and the universal kingdom of Christ. Alan Heimert noted: 'The crux of Edwardean theology was the inherent and necessary relation of the regenerating work of the Spirit to the "erection, establishment, and universal extent of the Kingdom of the Messiah."'[48] John Gerstner said: 'The idea of the latter days was a controlling concept in Edwards' thinking.'[49]

He believed that God would pour out the Spirit and raise up mighty preachers, so that the gospel would be propagated throughout the world and many converted.[50] Satan's kingdom will put forth a mighty effort to defeat Christ's kingdom, but this resistance will fail and Satan's visible kingdom will fall—Christian

---

46. Edwards, *Some Thoughts Concerning the Revival*, in *WJE*, 4:349–50.

47. Edwards, *Humble Attempt*, in *WJE*, 5:329.

48. Alan Heimert, *Religion and the American Mind: From the Great Awakening to the Revolution* (Eugene, OR: Wipf & Stock Publishers, 1966), p. 62.

49. John H. Gerstner, *Jonathan Edwards: A Mini-Theology* (Morgan, PA: Soli Deo Gloria, 1996), p. 95.

50. Edwards, 'History of Redemption,' in *WJE*, 9:460.

heresies, the Roman Catholic Antichrist, Islam, unbelief among the Jews, and idol-worshiping paganism. Christ, though not yet physically appearing, will nevertheless show His power as 'King of kings and Lord of lords' (Rev. 19:16) by overcoming His enemies.[51] Next comes the era known in Revelation 20 as the 'thousand years' where the Christian religion reigns on earth and mankind enjoys great peace and love.[52] It is the church's latter-day glory when it enjoys the fulfillment of the promises by the great outpouring of the Spirit on earth.[53] Sadly, it will end with a large-scale apostasy led by Satan which Christ will destroy by His coming with visible glory.[54]

Edwards indicated in 1740 that he hoped the present revival was the dawning of this day of Christ's kingdom casting down the kingdom of Satan.[55] However, in 1744 he denied that he ever said the millennium was beginning, but instead asserted that he had hoped that the revivals were the open salvos of the great conflict leading up to the latter-day glory.[56]

The Kingdom and Eternity Life

The kingdom of God will find its completion in eternal glory. Though the kingdom of heaven consists of the church on earth, it finds its ultimate reality in that state of happiness and holiness in heaven itself. Edwards said: "'Tis called the kingdom of heaven because Christ the King is from heaven, and the laws of his kingdom are all from heaven, and the new heart and new nature that his people have given them is holy and heavenly, and the country they are to live in forever with Christ, their king, is heaven.'[57]

In one sense Christ's mediatorial work will be done and He will hand over the kingdom to His Father (1 Cor. 15:28), but in another

---

51. Edwards, 'History of Redemption,' in *WJE*, 9:462–72.

52. Edwards, 'History of Redemption,' in *WJE*, 9:482.

53. See *WJE*, 25:183, 241.

54. See *WJE*, 9:488, 494.

55. Edwards, Letter to George Whitefield, in *WJE* 16:80–81.

56. Edwards, Letter to William McCulloch, *WJE*, 16:135–36.

57. Edwards, 'Heaven's Dragnet,' in *WJE*, 25:577.

sense He will be the mediator as never before and will reign as absolute king in the hearts of His people. Edwards wrote:

> But when the end shall be entirely accomplished and the church is brought to the consummation of glory, there will be no more need of this governing and ordering of all things to this end; there will be no more need of a mediatorial government of the universe, inasmuch [as] all will be accomplished, all enemies will be put under his feet. Then Christ Jesus shall govern the universe no more as Mediator, but shall deliver up the kingdom to the Father, having accomplished fully all the ends of his government, and nothing else will remain to be done that is proper to a Mediator.
>
> Christ then shall present the church before his Father, having redeemed those whom his Father gave him to be redeemed by him. Not but that Christ will still remain as highly exalted as ever, yea in some respects as Mediator more glorious; being now complete, being married to her who is the fullness of him who filleth all in all, being yet sovereign King in their souls, reigning with them for ever and ever, being the eternal object of the joyful praises of all the hosts of heaven.[58]

In this age God reigns through Christ, and in the next age the Son will reign alongside His Father. Christ must reign forever, for He is God the Son and the heir of all things; furthermore, by His work of redemption He is ever worthy of ruling.[59] Indeed, Christ will enjoy more fully than ever the crown and kingdom He won by redemption, and His people will be with Him to behold His glory. Edwards said: 'Christ will to all eternity continue the medium of communication between God and the saints. That God, who gathers all the things in heaven together in Christ, will doubtless continue him, as an everlasting bond of union, and medium of communion, betwixt himself and the glorified saints.'[60] Through their marriage to Christ, God will communicate His glory to them for their eternal delight.

---

58. Edwards, Miscellanies no. 86, in *WJE*, 15:250–51, paragraph break added.

59. Edwards, Miscellanies no. 609, in *WJE*, 18:143–45.

60. Edwards, Miscellanies no. 736, in *WJE*, 18:363.

Conclusion

Edwards's doctrine of the kingdom illuminates the larger theological framework that creates and sustains Christian piety. Consequently, it enriches our understanding of piety itself. Piety is God-centered, the human echo of God's thunderous sovereignty and majesty. Piety is trinitarian, effected by the decree of the triune God and involving communion with each person of the Trinity. Piety depends upon Christ as the only Mediator between God and men, the King who rules in Christians on the gracious basis of His lamb-like work for them. Piety is not an abstract concept or privatized mysticism, but an historical reality implemented by God's works in nations and individual lives. Piety is not humanly generated, but the work of God's Spirit as He applies the redemption purchased by Christ. Piety has its differing seasons, and at times God advances the piety of His church in extraordinary ways by revival. Piety is eschatological, awaiting its completion when Christ returns to gather His bride in His arms. In a word, the divine gift of piety is the vast riches of the gospel of Jesus Christ brought home to the human heart.

Part 2: Means of Grace and Puritan Piety

CHAPTER FIVE

Calvin the Preacher and the Puritans

JOSEPH PIPA

TODAY, the church faces a crisis of major proportions with respect to the task of preaching. Neil Postman has documented that, by its very nature, the medium of television has created a generation of people who are unable to listen to or think through the carefully reasoned statements or arguments of any sustained, logical discourse. People respond much better to visual, emotionally oriented messages.[1] Herein lies our crisis. We have been taught that preaching is the primary means of grace. But, in this present culture, are we to continue to employ a medium that television has rendered antiquated?

Calvin's theology and practice of preaching is a useful model for us who live in a day when many have lost faith in preaching as God's great means of grace. From him, we can learn what is necessary to continue to preach.

In this chapter, I will examine Calvin's theology of preaching, derive some essential elements, and show how these elements characterized Puritan preaching as well.

---

1. Neil Postman, *Amusing Ourselves to Death* (New York: Penguin Books, 1986).

Theology

Steven Lawson states: 'Every preacher who expounds God's word brings a body of core values with him into the pulpit. These foundational commitments inevitably shape his preaching. His pulpit ministry is governed by what he believes Scripture to be, what place he assigns to preaching, and how he believes his preaching ought to be conducted. Calvin was no exception.'[2]

What were Calvin's core commitments that shaped his preaching?

First, Calvin's theology of preaching began with his theology of the Word of God. He believed that the sixty-six books of the Bible were God's inspired, infallible word: 'Scripture is from God … it has flowed to us from the very mouth of God by the ministry of men.'[3]

Second, preaching possesses a unique authority. This authority entailed two things. Calvin believed that when the minister preached the Word of God, he preached with God's authority: 'This was the unshakable foundation of Calvin's preaching—the authority of divinely inspired Scripture. He firmly believed that when the Bible speaks, God speaks.'[4]

But, more to the point, Calvin taught that when a commissioned, ordained preacher proclaims the word of Christ, it is Christ who speaks through him. He wrote in the *Institutes* that God 'deigns to consecrate to himself the mouths and tongues of men in order that his voice may resound in them.'[5] In his commentary on Isaiah, he stated: 'Christ acts by his ministers in such a manner that he wishes their mouth to be reckoned as his mouth, and their lips as his lips.'[6]

---

2. Steven J. Lawson, *The Expository Genius of John Calvin* (Orlando: Reformation Trust, 2007), p. 24. See T.H.L. Parker, *Calvin's Preaching* (Louisville, KY: Westminster/John Knox, 1992), p. 1. See also John Calvin, *Sermons on Ephesians* (Edinburgh: Banner of Truth, 1973), p. 10.

3. John Calvin, *The Institutes of the Christian Religion*, trans. Ford Lewis Battles, ed. John T. McNeill, 2 vols. (Philadelphia: Westminster, 1960), 1.7.5; 1.8.1, 2.

4. Lawson, *Expository Genius*, p. 27.

5. Calvin, *Institutes*, 4.1.5.

6. John Calvin, *Commentaries* (Grand Rapids: Baker, 1974), on Isaiah 11:14.

Paul taught this truth in Romans 10:14: 'How shall they believe in Him of whom they have not heard?' (NKJV). We should note that it is not 'of whom they have not heard' but 'whom they have not heard.'[7] How shall they hear (hear Christ) without a preacher? When the lawfully ordained preacher proclaims the word, Christ speaks through him.

Therefore, when a commissioned man preaches the infallible Word of God, God the Spirit takes the spoken proclamation of the divine, inerrant Word of God and speaks uniquely through him.

Third, preaching is God's primary means of grace. Calvin's theology of preaching led him to place the primary emphasis in the worship service on preaching. By no means was his service bare—it was liturgically rich; however, he devoted usually an hour of the Lord's Day service to preaching. According to the Geneva Ordinances, 'their office is to proclaim the Word of God for the purpose of instructing, admonishing, exhorting, and reproving.'[8]

Moreover, Calvin's commitment to preaching is seen in his preaching schedule. He preached on an average 200 times a year (about one hour in length), in addition to about 200 expository lectures, which were the basis of his commentaries. Early on, he preached twice on Sundays and each weekday every week. Later he alternated weeks, preaching one week twice on Sundays, but not during the week, while, the next week, he preached then each day.

These theological commitments also shaped the Puritans' approach to preaching. The Puritan theology of preaching was that of John Calvin.[9] Like him, they exalted preaching as the supreme work of a pastor. For the Puritans, preaching was their chief work

---

7. The Greek verb *akouō* often takes the genitive as the direct object. Cf. John 3:29; Mark 9:7; 1 John 4:5-6.

8. 'The Ecclesiastical Ordinances,' in *The Register of the Company of Pastors of Geneva in the Time of Calvin*, trans. and ed. Philip Edgcumbe Hughes (Grand Rapids: Eerdmans, 1966), p. 36. See also Lawson, *Expository Genius*, p. 31; John Calvin, *Calvin's New Testament Commentaries: First Corinthians* (Grand Rapids: Eerdmans, 1973), p. 176. Henceforth cited as Calvin, *First Corinthians* (NTC).

9. For an excellent study of Calvin's theology of preaching, see Pierre Marcel, *The Relevance of Preaching.*

because it was the chief work of Christ and His apostles.[10] William Gouge wrote in his learned commentary on Hebrews:

> If Christ the Lord vouchsafed to be a minister of the gospel, who shall scorn this function? The pope, cardinals, sundry bishops, and others that pretend to be Christ's vicars, are far from performing that which Christ did in this kind; and many that lay claim to Peter's keys, are far from observing the advice which he, for the right use of them, thus gave: 'Feed the flock of God which is among you, taking the oversight thereof, not by constraint, but willingly; not for lucre, but of a ready mind; neither as being lords over God's heritage, but being ensamples to the flock,' 1 Peter v. 2, 3.[11]

The Puritans believed with Calvin that when the lawfully ordained man preached God's word, God Himself spoke. Gouge affirmed this truth: 'He who is sent of God, that is, set apart, according to the rule of God's word, to be a minister of the gospel, doth himself understand the mysteries thereof, and is enabled to make them known to others; he also standeth in God's room, and in God's name makes offer of salvation, 2 Corinthians, verse 20. This moves men to believe and to be saved.'[12]

Thus, for the Puritans, the preaching of God's word was the primary means of grace. The Westminster Larger Catechism (Q. 155) points out the primacy of preaching:

> *How is the word made effectual to salvation?*
> The Spirit of God maketh the reading, but especially the preaching of the word, an effectual means of enlightening, convincing, and humbling sinners; of driving them out of themselves, and drawing them unto Christ; of conforming them to his image, and subduing them to his will; of strengthening them against temptations and corruptions; of building them up in grace, and

---

10. Horton Davies, *The Worship of the English Puritans* (London: Dacre Press, 1948), p. 183.

11. William Gouge, Commentary on Hebrews (Grand Rapids: Kregel Publications, 1980), p. 101.

12. Gouge, *Commentary on Hebrews*, p. 101.

establishing their hearts in holiness and comfort through faith unto salvation.[13]

Essential Elements

How, then, did Calvin work out his theology in his preaching? I will examine six essential elements of Calvin's preaching.

Exegetical/Expositional

According to Calvin, the work of preaching consisted in the exposition and application of the Word of God. He maintained that the content of a sermon should be the Word of God explained and then applied: 'The subject to be taught is the Word of God, and the best way to teach it … was by steady and methodical exposition, book after book.'[14] Calvin expounded the text by explaining what the writer was saying and what it meant. Therefore, he sought to preach exactly what the writer of Scripture expressed:

> Since it is almost his only task to unfold the mind of the writer whom he has undertaken to expound, he misses the mark, or at least strays outside his limits, by the extent to which he leads his readers away from the meaning of his author …. It is … presumptuous and almost blasphemous to turn the meaning of Scripture around without due care, as though it were some game that we were playing. And yet many scholars have done this at one time.[15]

To accomplish this purpose, Calvin employed the historico-grammatical method of exegesis. The preaching method he chose was consecutive, expository preaching (*lectio continua*); at times, he preached through extended passages like Psalm 119, but, most often, he preached through entire books of the Bible. During his

---

13. Quotations from The Larger Catechism and The Directory for Publick Worship are both taken from *Westminster Confession of Faith* (Glasgow: Free Presbyterian, 1994).

14. Publisher's introduction to Calvin, *Sermons on Ephesians*, xiv.

15. John Calvin, *Calvin's New Testament Commentaries: Romans* (Grand Rapids: Wm. B. Eerdmans Publishing Company, 1973), p. 1.

ministry in Geneva, he preached on the great majority of the books of the Bible.[16]

Moreover, he usually expounded each verse in order: 'Whether the biblical book was long and extensive, such as Genesis or Job, or brief and short, such as the New Testament epistles, Calvin was determined to preach every verse.'[17] Lawson commented: 'This verse-by-verse style—*lectio continua*, the 'continuous expositions' —guaranteed that Calvin would preach the full counsel of God. Difficult and controversial subjects were unavoidable. Hard sayings could not be skipped. Difficult doctrines could not be overlooked. The full counsel of God could be heard.'[18]

Calvin shaped his sermons by what is called the 'ancient' form of preaching. In the development of preaching before the Reformation, there were two forms of sermon structure: the 'ancient' form and the 'modern' form. The 'ancient' form, which is the homily, originated with the church fathers. J. W. Blench wrote: 'The "ancient", which was descended from the homilies of the Fathers, is without any elaborate scheme of arrangement peculiar to sermons, and consists either of the explication and application of a passage of Scripture (often the Gospel or Epistle of the Day), *secundum ordinem textus* [according to the order of the text]; or of the topical treatment of any subject, according to reason and Scripture.'[19]

Calvin, and many of the early English reformers, used the 'ancient' form. He used it with great skill. The 'ancient' form could degenerate into a running commentary, with no coherence or momentum. Calvin's sermons, however, were marked by coherence

---

16. Lawson, *Expository Genius*, p. 33.

17. Lawson, *Expository Genius*, p. 34.

18. Lawson, *Expository Genius*, p. 32. For a thorough discussion of Calvin's preaching program, see Elsie Anne McKee, *The Pastoral Ministry and Worship in Calvin's Geneva* (Geneva: Librairie Droz, 2016), pp. 460–523; Scott M. Manetsch, *Calvin's Company of Pastors* (Oxford: Oxford University Press, 2013), pp. 145–64.

19. J. W. Blench, *Preaching in England in the Late Fifteenth and Sixteenth Centuries: A Study of English Sermons 1450–1600* (Oxford: Basil Blackwell, 1964), pp. 71–72.

and momentum. One safeguard was the division of the portion that he had selected to be preached. He labored to divide the text according to its inherent unity. Lawson concluded: 'The point is that Calvin always had a carefully chosen and specifically defined section of Scripture to exposit for his people.'[20]

His sermon structure was fairly consistent. After reading his portion from the text, he usually began with a brief introduction and review of the previous sermon. At times, he would state a theme that held the section together and then would proceed through the text verse-by-verse; although, occasionally, he would omit a verse or skip it and return to it later. He would use the theme of the section to maintain unity: 'It [the sermon] is saved from being rambling by his capacity for keeping to the point and breaking the material up into short sections, usually with some such formula as "So much for that point", or "So you see what the prophet [or apostle] meant to say".'[21]

Parker pointed out that Calvin often had an unspoken outline that served to give unity to his remarks. He gave an example from Calvin's sermon on Job 21:13-15.[22] Occasionally, the structure was more evident, as in the sermon on 2 Timothy 3:16-17. He introduced this sermon by explaining what Paul means by Scripture and teaching that great reverence is due to the word of God. Then, he divided the first part of this text into two parts: 'Now let us come to those two points which are touched here. He saith first of all, *That the holy Scripture is given by inspiration of God.* And then he addeth, *that it is profitable.* These are two commendations which S. Paul giveth to the holy Scripture; to make us in love with it, and show it is worthy to be received with all humbleness.'[23]

---

20. Lawson, *Expository Genius,* p. 67.

21. T. H. L. Parker, *John Calvin: A Biography* (Louisville, KY: Westminster/ John Knox, 2007), p. 92.

22. Parker, *Preaching,* The numbered headings are not in the sermon, but easily supplied to mark the logical flow of thought.

23. John Calvin, *Sermons on Timothy and Titus: Facsimile of 1579 Edition* (Edinburgh: Banner of Truth, 1983), p. 934.

A further way he structured his sermon was by the use of technical terms to highlight important truths and application. As he made his way through the text, he often would use the term 'doctrine' to highlight a biblical truth he derived from the text and the terms 'use' or 'lesson' to delineate his application.

In making application, Calvin frequently used the term 'use'. We find a number of examples of his setting out his application with the term 'use': 'What must we then do? We must apply the word of God to our *use,* we must be awaked, whereas we were too fast asleep before, we must begin to take better heed to ourselves that we forget God no more, nor the salvation of our souls, but give good heed to it.'[24]

Admittedly, Calvin does not use this language consistently. Nevertheless, it is found throughout his sermons.

By his employing the terms 'doctrine' and 'use' and by the structure noted in 2 Timothy 3:16–17 of division, explanation, and application, it would seem that Calvin probably influenced the Puritans in the development of the 'new Reformed method' that was popularized by William Perkins. Blench says: 'The sermons of those who use this scheme proceed according to the order of the text, to give Doctrines, Uses, Objections and Answers, marked as such in the margin, with no attempt at the formal symmetry of the classical scheme.'[25] A 'doctrine' is the statement of a truth found in the text. The 'proofs' are Scripture references and arguments that confirm the truth of the 'doctrine'. 'Uses' are the application made from the 'doctrine'. Sometimes, there would be a number of 'doctrines' as the preacher worked through the text, much in the same way that Calvin did in 2 Timothy 3:16–17, while, other times, the preacher would derive one doctrine from the text, which he would prove and then give his 'uses'. This tripartite division of 'doctrine', 'proofs', and 'uses' was called the triple schema.[26]

---

24. Calvin, *Sermons on Timothy and Titus,* p. 940 (emphasis mine).

25. Blench, *Preaching in England,* p. 102.

26. See Joseph Pipa, 'William Perkins and the Development of Puritan Preaching' (PhD Dissertation, Westminster Theological Seminary, 1985).

Moreover, the Puritans preferred the expository method, as noted in the Westminster Directory: '[H]e may go on in some chapter, psalm, or book of holy scripture, as he shall see fit.'[27] Oftentimes, their method was more textual-topical than purely expository, and they would, at times, miss the main point of the text. Yet what they were attempting to do was to bring order to Calvin's expository method.

Applicatory

A sermon, however, must do more than expound the truth. According to Calvin, every sermon must include application. In the introduction to Calvin's sermons on Ephesians, the publisher wrote: 'But if we assumed from a reading of Calvin's commentaries that we know what he means by pulpit teaching, we should be greatly mistaken. Explanation and interpretation is enough for students, but it not enough for the pulpit. Exhortation and practical application are essential parts of pulpit teaching and are to be present in every sermon.'[28] In the sermon on 2 Timothy 3:16-17, he preached:

> Now we may judge hereby, whether it be enough for a man when he would expound the holy scripture, to devise and discourse upon it, as though it were a bare history, for if it were so, that which Saint Paul giveth there to holy scripture, were unprofitable .... Seeing the office of a good and faithful shepherd is not barely to expound the scripture, to say, This it is, but he must use earnestness therewithal, and sharpness to give force and virtue to the word of God, for this cause saint Paul saith in the other place, that the shepherds of the church must be earnest, even to be importunate saith he, and not only show them what is good, but reprehend and reprove.[29]

Usually, at least half of Calvin's sermons consisted in application.

---

27. *Westminster Confession of Faith*, p. 379.

28. Publisher's introduction to Calvin, *Sermons on Ephesians*, xiv.

29. Calvin, *Sermons on Timothy and Titus*, p. 941. See p. 959 for another example.

Calvin derived his types of application from 2 Timothy 3:16. He used four main categories: rebuke, exhortation, examination, and polemical. An example of rebuke is found in the sermon on Job 34:21–26: 'Seeing that God doth so much and so often warn us, that we must in the end come to the great light. Let us not still shut our eyes willfully, nor wittingly be blinded when he sendeth us his word to discover our filthiness, and to shew us that we cannot hide ourselves from his sight.'[30]

His sermons were full of exhortations. One example is in the conclusion of the sermon on 2 Timothy 3:16–17 in which he developed the types of application: 'If we will profit well in the holy scripture we must employ our study to holiness of life, and know that God will be served or our fantasies, but he hath given us a certain rule, which we must take as a perfect rule, and such an one as cannot be found fault withal.'[31]

He regularly called his hearers to self-examination with expressions such as, '[L]et us learn to examine ourselves in this way'; 'If each of us were to examine himself carefully'; or, 'We must all, therefore, carefully examine our lives.'[32]

The sermons were rich with polemical application. The primary target was the Roman Catholic Church and its hierarchy. In a sermon on Job 9:1-6, dealing with 'the righteousness of faith', he declared: 'The papist cannot be persuaded of this that we say, namely that we become righteous through the mere favour of God in our Lord Jesus Christ. And why? What shall become of the merits (say they) and of the good works wherein the salvation of men consisteth? And why do the Papists stand so upon their merits, and why are they so besotted with them, but because they look not up to God?'[33]

---

30. John Calvin, *Sermons on Job* (Edinburgh: Banner of Truth, 1993), p. 622. See also Lawson, *Expository Genius*, p. 109. See John Calvin, *Sermons on the Book of Micah*, trans. and ed. Benjamin Wirt Farley (Phillipsburg, NJ: P&R, 2003), p. 101.

31. Calvin, *Pastoral Sermons*, pp. 944–45.

32. For specific examples see Lawson, *Expository Genius*, pp. 108–109.

33. Calvin, *Sermons on Job*, p. 152. See also Calvin, *Pastorals*, p. 35, for polemical application to situations in Geneva.

With respect to placement, the applications were scattered throughout the sermon, following the exposition. Sometimes, he would not have a conclusion to the whole. He simply applied the last point. At times, his concluding exhortation was found in the bidding prayer at the end of the sermon. For example, the conclusion to the sermon on Job 9:1-6:

> And now let us fall flat before the presence of our good God with acknowledgment of our faults, praying him to make us so to enter in the examination of our sins, as when we shall have known them thoroughly, we may not doubt but that he hath us at a great advantage, and thereupon humble ourselves to be indebted to that great judge. And if that during this mortal life, he handle us more roughly than we would, and send us afflictions that are over sore and contrary to the flesh: let us beseech him to assuage them, and that although he abate them not at the first dash, yet nevertheless he will always hold us up with a strong hand, and not suffer Satan to inveigle [entice] us to blasphemy, but that we may acknowledge his righteousness and honor it, until he make us feel his goodness in giving us full fruition of our salvation: to the end we may not send up our sighs to him while we be here beneath, but also cry out unto him with open mouth as to our father.[34]

Calvin also believed that application needed to be addressed to different classes of people. With respect to the importance of discriminating application, Calvin preached:

> We must, then, show wisdom by accommodating the message to those whom God has placed in our charge, for he places us under obligation to his people when he establishes us as his messengers. He unites us to his church, and we must have an adequate and true perspective. If we cast our words to the wind, closing our eyes and having no consideration for those to whom we speak, we unjustly and excessively abuse the word of God. For this reason let us note well that they who have this charge to teach, when they speak to a people, are to decide which teaching will be good and

---

34. Calvin, *Sermons on Job*, p. 165.

profitable so that they will be able to disseminate it faithfully and with discretion to the usefulness of everyone individually.[35]

The Puritans shared Calvin's commitment to applicatory preaching. The holy practicality of truth was one of the trademarks of Puritan piety. The Westminster Directory for Worship summarizes the Puritan commitment to application:

> He [the preacher] is not to rest in general doctrine, although never so much cleared and confirmed, but to bring it home to special use, by application to his hearers: which albeit it prove a work of great difficulty to himself, requiring much prudence, zeal, and meditation, and to the natural and corrupt man will be very unpleasant; yet he is to endeavour to perform it in such a manner, that his auditors may feel the word of God to be quick and powerful, and a discerner of the thoughts and intents of the heart; and that, if any unbeliever or ignorant person be present, he may have the secrets of his heart made manifest, and give glory to God.[36]

The Plain Style

A third characteristic of Calvin's preaching was his commitment to the plain style. The plain style was the predominant style of all Protestant preaching, with the exception of the high Anglicans in England.

The plain style was a philosophy of communication that sought to address the people in a way that they could readily grasp the truth of the sermon. A. F. Herr stated: 'The plain style is sober, simple in expression, as direct as possible, and free from ornamentation of either fantastic ideas or verbiage .... It appears, on the whole, to be the spontaneous creation of the spirit of the Reformation.'[37]

---

35. Marcel's translation of Calvin on Job, Sermon XCV, 446; Marcel, *The Relevance of Preaching*, pp. 70–71.

36. 'The Directory for the Publick Worship of God', in *Westminster Confession of Faith*, p. 380. For a thorough development of Puritan approach to application see William Perkins, *The Art of Prophesying* (Edinburgh: Banner of Truth, 1996), p. 79.

37. A. F. Herr, *The Elizabethan Sermon* (New York: Octagon Books, 1969), pp. 89-90.

Calvin spoke plainly and simply in order to be understood by the common people. Commenting on 1 Corinthians 2:13, he wrote:

> By the words 'taught by human wisdom', Paul means those which savour of human learning, and are polished according to the rules of the rhetoricians; or are purposely and proudly overloaded with philosophy in order to rush hearers into admiration. But the words 'taught by the Spirit' are suitable for a style which is sincere and simple, rather than empty and ostentatious, and one more in keeping with the dignity of the Spirit.[38]

Calvin's commitment to a plain style manifested itself in a number of features in his sermons. First, he used simple sentences: 'Rather than using long, prosaic sentences, as did some Puritans, the Reformer mainly used simple subject-verb-predicate sentence constructions that were easy to digest …. Even the longer sentences in the English translations of his sermons were probably shorter in the original language. As he preached, Calvin's towering intellect nearly always lay 'concealed, behind [his] deceptively simple explanations of his author's meaning.'[39]

Second, he spoke with a simple vocabulary. With respect to Calvin's language, Parker stated:

> His language was clear and easy. He spoke in a way that the Genevese could understand, even, it would seem, to the point of using some of their idiosyncrasies of French, some of which may still be encountered today. To clarity of sense and diction he paid great attention, carefully explaining unusual or technical words in the Biblical text. There is a remarkable little passage where he is afraid that the people will confuse two words with similar sounds and so lose his meaning: 'let us note that the Gospel is like *un van* [a winnowing fan] in two ways. (I do not mean *le vent* which blows, but *un van*

---

38. Calvin, *First Corinthians* (NTC), p. 60. For a full discussion of Calvin's style see Parker, *Preaching*, pp. 139, 140; McKee, *The Pastoral Ministry and Worship in Calvin's Geneva*, pp. 523–33.

39. Parker, as quoted by Lawson, *Expository Genius*, p. 87.

to winnow, or a sieve—which many of you will understand better).'[40]

Calvin's simple style, however, did not deter him from using biblical and theological language. Parker has noted: 'Calvin's terminology in this respect hardly moves outside the Bible. Common words are "justify", "elect", "redeem", "sin", "repentance", "grace", "prayer", "judgment"—in fact, all the familiar language of the Old and New Testaments.'[41] However, he firmly believed that the pulpit was not the place for abstract theological discussion or display of learning. He did not use Greek or Hebrew terms.[42]

Third, Calvin used pithy and concrete language, with many similes and metaphors. Of Calvin's style, Hughes Oliphant Old commented: 'Calvin had ... clarity of thought and expression. He knew how to use the language ... his vocabulary was brilliant. Words are used with the greatest precision. His vocabulary is rich but never obscure or esoteric. It is never vain or contrived .... He often presents us with marvelous similes and metaphors.'[43]

Fourth, he made ready use of familiar proverbs: 'There is nothing worse than to be hasty: we know that these ordinary proverbs are continually put in use among us, namely that haste maketh waste.'[44] Or, in Micah 1:1-3: 'For as the saying goes, "What comes in one ear, goes out the other."'[45]

One other thing about Calvin's style was his use of illustrations. His illustrations were primarily scriptural, but he gathered many from everyday life. He did not use anecdotes and rarely quoted non-inspired authors.

---

40. Parker, *Biography*, p. 93.

41. Parker, *Preaching*, p. 141.

42. Parker, *Preaching*, p. 88.

43. Hughes Oliphant Old, *The Reading and Preaching of the Scriptures in the Worship of the Christian Church*, vol. 4: *The Age of the Reformation* (Grand Rapids: Eerdmans, 2002), p. 129. See Lawson, *Expository Genius*, p. 89.

44. Calvin, *Sermons on Job*, p. 559.

45. Calvin, *Sermons on the Book of Micah*, p. 6.

Of course, one of the hallmarks of Puritan preaching was the plain style. The commitment to a plain style is found in the Westminster Directory's instruction on preaching: 'Plainly, that the meanest may understand; delivering the truth not in the enticing words of man's wisdom, but in demonstration of the Spirit and of power, lest the cross of Christ should be made of none effect; abstaining also from an unprofitable use of unknown tongues, strange phrases, and cadences of sounds and words; sparingly citing sentences of ecclesiastical or other human writers, ancient or modern, be they never so elegant.'[46]

Unction

Calvin was conscious of his dependence upon the Holy Spirit in the act of preaching. Lawson wrote: 'The Holy Spirit, Calvin said, is actively at work in the preaching of the Word, and this powerful ministry of the Spirit was the *sine qua non* of Calvin's expository ministry. He stated that during public proclamation, "when the minister executes his commission faithfully, by speaking only what God puts into his mouth, the inward power of the Holy Spirit is joined with his outward voice." In fact, in all preaching, he affirmed, there must be an "inward efficacy of the Holy Spirit when He sheds forth His power upon hearers, that they may embrace a discourse by faith."'[47]

This dependect efficace is called unction. Marcel defines unction:

> When, in preaching, a man abandons himself to the freedom of the Spirit, he discovers that his faculties are developed above normal: freedom is given not only to the soul but also to the tongue, his mental penetration is deeper; his ability to picture things in his mind is greater; truth works a greater power in his soul; his faith is more intense; he feels himself involved in a living and compact reality. His feelings are much more sensitive and spontaneously permeate his heart. He comes to think the thoughts of Christ, to experience the feelings and emotions of Christ.... The Spirit

---

46. *Westminster Confession of Faith*, p. 381.
47. Lawson, *Expository Genius*, pp. 28–29.

endows his word, his expression, with a natural freshness and vitality which gives the word a new and original appearance *and which belong only to the spoken style.*[48]

Perkins related unction to plain style: 'To preach in the demonstration of God's Spirit is to preach with such plainness, and yet with such power, that even the least intellectually gifted recognize that it is not man but God himself who is teaching them. Yet at the same time, the conscience of the mightiest may feel not man but God reproving them through the power of the Spirit.'[49]

Delivery

This commitment to preaching in dependence upon the Holy Spirit led Calvin to preach extemporaneously. By extemporaneous preaching, I mean that he did not rely on prepared notes or a manuscript for the expression of the sermon. In Calvin's case, he preached without notes. One is not to infer from this commitment that he was ill-prepared. He believed that to be effective the minister prepared carefully. He stated: 'If I should enter the pulpit without deigning to look at a book and should frivolously think to myself, 'Oh, well, when I preach, God will give me enough to say,' and come here without troubling to read or think what I ought to declare, and do not carefully consider how I must apply Holy Scripture to the edification of the people, then I should be an arrogant upstart.'[50]

Moreover, Calvin preached extemporaneously because he believed it contributed to a lively style. He wrote Lord Somerset:

> What I have thus suggested as to the manner of instruction is only that the people be so taught as to be touched to the quick, and
> - that they may feel that what the Apostle says is true (Heb. iv.) that 'the word of God is a two-edged sword, piercing even through the thoughts and affections to the very marrow of the bones.' I speak

---

48. Marcel, *Relevance of Preaching,* pp. 100–101.
49. Marcel, *The Relevance of Preaching,* p. 86.
50. Quoted in Parker, p. 81.

thus, Monseigneur, because it appears to me that there is very little preaching of a lively kind in the kingdom (England), but that the greater part deliver it by way of reading from a written discourse.... But all these considerations ought not to hinder the ordinance of Jesus Christ from having free course in the preaching of the Gospel. Now, this preaching ought not to be lifeless, but lively, to teach, to exhort, to reprove, as Saint Paul says in speaking thereof to Timothy (2 Tim. iii.) ... but that the Spirit of God ought to sound forth by their voice, so as to work with mighty energy.[51]

Calvin's delivery was forceful and lively. Parker explained: 'His manner of delivery was lively, passionate, intimate, direct, and clear .... He could be furiously and coarsely angry and he could be gentle and compassionate. Now like a judge of the old cast, now like a father or mother.'[52]

Preaching on Deuteronomy 1:42-46, Calvin declared:

Preaching is more than speaking in dead images. It is, in substance, the image of God which appears to us, indeed with such power that we are transformed by it. That is why they whose duty it is to proclaim God's word take care to proceed soberly, so that they may always be able to affirm that it is God who has put the instruction in their mouth. They are to try to make every hearer feel the power of God which is, in a manner of speaking, enclosed in his word, so that it may be received and submitted to as it deserves to be, with the view to glorying God and serving him with unanimity.[53]

The Puritans emphasized that the one who enjoys the unction of the Spirit will preach with zeal and passion; when the Spirit is upon a man there will be an obvious zeal in his preaching. This

---

51. John Calvin, *Calvin's Selected Works,* ed. Jules Bonnet, trans. David Constable (Grand Rapids: Baker, 1983), 5:190.

52. Parker, *Biography,* p. 93. See also Calvin, *Sermons on Timothy and Titus,* p. 941; Lawson, *Expository Genius,* p. 98.

53. John Calvin, *Sermons on Deuteronomy* (Edinburgh: Banner of Truth, 1988), on Deuteronomy 1:42–46.

zeal will manifest itself in each man differently, according to his gifts and personality, but each man must preach with a passion. Richard Baxter insisted on the need to have one's heart stirred up:

> O sirs, how plainly, how closely, how earnestly, should we deliver a message of such moment as ours, when the everlasting life or everlasting death of our fellow-men is involved in it! Methinks we are in nothing so wanting as in this seriousness; yet is there nothing more unsuitable to such a business, than to be slight and dull. What! Speak coldly for God, and for men's salvation? Can we believe that our people must be converted or condemned, and yet speak in a drowsy tone? In the name of God, brethren, labour to awaken your own hearts, before you go to the pulpit, that you may be fit to awaken the hearts of sinners. Remember they must be awakened or damned, and that a sleepy preacher will hardly awaken drowsy sinners. Though you give the holy things of God the highest praise in words, yet, if you do it coldly, you will seem by your manner to unsay what you said in the matter .... The manner, as well as the words, must set them forth.... Though I move you not to constant loudness in your delivery (for that will make your fervency contemptible), yet see that you have a constant seriousness; and when the matter requireth it (as it should do, in the application at least), then lift up your voice, and spare not your spirits, Speak to your people as to men that must be awakened, whether here or in hell.[54]

Theocentric

Calvin's preaching was more theocentric than Christ-centered in the sense of historical-redemptive preaching. After surveying the Christological references in the Job sermons, Derek Thomas concluded: Calvin is primarily concerned to explain the text within the boundaries of historico-grammatical exegesis; the need to see Christ was given second place.'[55]

---

54. Richard Baxter, *The Reformed Pastor* (Edinburgh: Banner of Truth, 1974), pp. 147–48.

55. Derek Thomas, *Proclaiming the Incomprehensible God: Calvin's Teaching on Job* (Ross-shire, Scotland: Christian Focus, 2004), p. 334.

The overall thrust of his preaching, however, focused on Christ as the object of hope and power. He concluded his comments on 1 Corinthians 2:2 as follows: 'This is a beautiful verse, and from it we may learn what faithful ministers ought to teach, and what we must be learning throughout our life; and in comparison with that everything else is to be counted as *dung*.'[56]

Parker summarized Calvin's position:

> In sum, then, the redemption of God in Christ and the believer's life of obedience are the themes that are daily preached in Saint Pierre. All that is negative in the sermons is but the converse of this positive preaching; it does not exist in its own right. Not the threats of perdition, but the promises of eternal life; not the wrath of God, but his goodness and mercy; not the denial of man's merits, but the assertion of Christ's merits; not the attacks on current superstitions, but the urging of obedient service and self-sacrifice; not the rejection of the sacrament of penance, but the preaching of the two glorious Sacraments of the Gospel.[57]

The Puritans also reveled in preaching Christ. Perkins concluded *The Art of Prophesying* with these words: 'The heart of the matter is this: Preach one Christ, by Christ, to the praise of Christ.'[58]

Conclusion

Calvin's preaching transformed not only a city, but the Protestant church. To this day, his sermons are used by God to teach and edify serious Christians. If we are to see our churches revived and reformed and our culture transformed, we need to be gripped by Calvin's theology and take the characteristics of Calvin's preaching and apply them to ours.

Most of what made Calvin and his Puritan descendants effective is easily accomplished by those who preach today. You do not need Calvin's prodigious intellect to be able to preach like him or

---

56. Calvin, *First Corinthians* (NTC), p. 49.

57. Parker, *Biography*, pp. 94–95.

58. Perkins, *Art of Prophesying*, p. 79.

his Puritan descendants and homiletically to build on them; go beyond Calvin in the area of structure; but learn from him and the Puritans.

CHAPTER SIX

The Highway of Holiness: Puritan Moral Reform in the English Revolution

CHAD VAN DIXHOORN

I N May 1644, the Westminster Assembly wrote to the General Assembly of the Church of Scotland: 'We walk in paths that have hitherto been untrodden by any Assembly in this Church. We therefore are inforced to spend more time in our inquiries, and in seeking of God a right way for us, that at length we may put into that highway, the way of holinesse, wherein wayfaring men, though fools, shall not erre.'[1] Unlike previous assemblies in the Church of England, this new synod had built a new path, constructing a highway of holiness.

Like most endeavors of the Assembly meeting at Westminster Abbey, the highway project was government-sponsored. The Assembly itself was bankrolled by England's Long Parliament, which also directed and oversaw the Assembly's work. As with many government endeavors, it was running behind schedule. To be fair, the delays were caused in part by the scope of the religious

---

1. C. Van Dixhoorn, ed., *The Minutes and Papers of the Westminster Assembly, 1643–1653* (Oxford: Oxford University Press, 2013), 5:194 (Document 21). Hereafter, *MPWA*.

engineering feat being undertaken. The beneficiaries of this joint-effort between Parliament and the Assembly were English, Scottish and Irish, and theologians from all three locations labored together in Westminster Abbey with thirty members of Parliament.

Contracted through a solemn league and covenant designed to unify the three nations ecclesiastically, the Assembly's multi-year project was supposed to bridge the churches on both banks of the Tweed and all sides of the Irish Sea. Nonetheless, almost from the beginning it was clear that the project would involve the destruction of important elements of the existing church in each nation. Liturgies would be removed. Disciplinary and ecclesiastical structures were to be completely revamped. It was decided that even a review of the Church of England's doctrine could not be bypassed. The process would be time-consuming, requiring in-depth inquiries and much time in prayer.

The Westminster Assembly was writing to the General Assembly in May of 1644 because the men working in the Abbey recognized that the presbyterian Scots, some of the most loyal supporters of the synod, were disappointed at the lack of movement in England. The truth was that leaders in the Assembly could not agree about the design of the new church, especially in matters of discipline and government. The Assembly had also assumed additional tasks not specified in the original contract, including extensive examinations of ministers and candidates for pastoral ministry. And there was the difficult fact, candidly mentioned in the letter to the General Assembly, that those who needed to journey along the highway of holiness tended to be fools.

The Assembly never specified who these 'fools' were and it is an epithet the gathering almost never used. Nonetheless it appears to be a strikingly inclusive reference, well in keeping with the Assembly's insistence that all wayfarers tend to be wanderers, and thus needed sturdy ethical guardrails to keep them from erring.

Error was everywhere in the 1640s, as Assembly members saw it, not least in the worship, government, and teaching of the Church of England. But problems did not only lurk behind church pillars—they were also to be found in homes throughout the three nations. The early 1640s were marked by a near hysteria about social disorder. As John Morrill has noted, while on the one hand it is nearly impossible to measure actual disorder, it is also the case that, on the other hand, the collapse of the censorship process, the increase of correspondence between propertied men in London and their families, and parliament's increased involvement in prosecuting crime made the dissemination and documentation of immorality tales much easier.[2] Similar complaints of rampant iniquity were issued by preachers at the monthly fast sermons sponsored and hosted by Parliament—bully pulpits alleging the same set of national sins mourned by godly preachers in preceding decades, but now with a new prominence.

For moralists the current decade is always the worst. Thus, historians have always been obliged to dispute the distance between perceptions and realities of moral decline. They have also contested the relevance of religion to those episodic bursts of moral reform in the British Isles which can be found in both the pre-modern and early-modern periods. This author acknowledges that one did not need to be a card-carrying member of a godly elite to oppose theft, adultery, or even Sabbath-breaking in pre-Civil War Britain or Ireland. And yet it is hard to deny that the reformation of manners conducted during the mid-century upheavals of society achieved notoriety in part because of its religious character. The Long Parliament's legislative reforms are synonymous, even in modern public memory, with an oppressively strict Puritan moral code. And contemporaries targeted the Long Parliament's assembly of divines for its efforts to promote personal holiness. Assembly members were 'the holy fatherhoods', the synod was 'the reverend and most sanctified assembly'.[3] Attempts were made to show just how depraved these warriors of righteousness really were, and

---

2. J. S. Morrill, 'Order and disorder in the English Revolution', in *The Nature of the English Revolution* (London: Longman, 1993), pp. 359–60, 371.

3. *Mercurius mercuriorum, stultissimus. Written for the use of the assembly of divines* (N.P., 1647), pp. 3, 8.

tales were told and printed of drunken assembly members making passes at barmaids.[4]

In spite of its attention to moral praxis, the synod's contributions have typically been measured according to the gathering's mandate of ecclesiastical reform. And yet already in July of 1643 the Assembly was looking for ways to stamp out sin. The first document that the gathering penned was an urgent call to action both to 'speedily set up CHRIST more gloriously in all his Ordinances' and to 'reforme all things amisse throughout the Land, wherein God is more specially and more immediately dishonoured'. Ten categories of examples of things amiss were offered by the Assembly.[5] In August the Assembly was even more explicit about its plan for a reform of ethics in the nation, for in the first of the Assembly's nine letters to the General Assembly of the Church of Scotland, the Assembly in London supplemented Parliament's own mandate with an additional objective: the Assembly indicated that it expected to be 'vindicating of [God's] pretious Truth', 'seeking out of a right way of worshiping', 'laying forth ... a Discipline', *and* 'promoting the power of godlinesse'.[6]

A substantial literature exists on the reformation of manners (a movement, as in this essay, often anachronistically applied to early- and mid-seventeenth century attempts at moral reform) including a body of literature examining that part of the reform owned by godly clergy. This essay introduces for the first time the Westminster Assembly's effort to promote a form of godliness that would keep foolish wayfarers on the moral high road. Intended as a footnote to John Morrill's extensive work on the relationship between politics and religion, it outlines aspects of cooperation between the different forces at Westminster as well as the eventual parting of ways between the Long Parliament and its Assembly,

---

4. *A Fraction in the Assembly: or, the Synod in Armes, being a punctuall relation of their set meeting, upon the 25. of Aprill ... 1648, at a tavern in London* (London, 1648).

5. *MPWA*, 5:10 (Doc. 1).

6. *MPWA*, 5:19 (Doc. 3).

as road maps for creating the highway of holiness eventually diverged, with each party offering a different route to a similar endpoint.

Seeking of God a Right Way for Us

The Assembly often resorted to prayer and fasting as it sought from God the right way forward, and the future presbyterian elder, Nehemiah Wallington, was one of those eager to join his prayers with those of the Assembly. Imagining himself as representative of a world of avid supporters, Wallington wrote to an Assembly scribe, assuring him that Assembly members 'have the prayrs (as of me so) of all Gods children throughout the world for to blesse them in this great worke that they have under tooke in the Casting out of all the filth and Garbish and all things that are offensive'. Wallington was all the more confident because the Assembly sought 'God in an extraordinary manner, as in Fasting & prayre for direction in this great worke: which right Fasting and prayr God hath promised to accept'.[7]

While in full dependence on God, leading Assembly members did not arrive at the gathering's meetings without a plan. Certainly the Assembly's opening petition for moral reform was premeditated, and members came prepared to the opening plenary session of the Assembly with a proposal to call a fast to grieve the ills of the nation.[8] Parliament had not, in fact, asked the Assembly to add the reform of manners to its agenda and never requested the gathering's advice on the subject. But nor did it need to. The godly had turned to moral reform as an outlet for their energies and hopes during the personal rule of Charles I and their opinions were well known. John White had transformed Dorchester into England's Geneva.[9] From Wiltshire, Henry Scudder had publicized what a private life of piety could look like with his runaway best

---

7. British Library, Sloane MS 922, fol. 140v

8. British Library, Harleian MS 165, fol. 105b.

9. D. Underdown, *Fire from Heaven: Life in an English Town in the Seventeenth Century* (London: Pimlico, 2003).

seller, the *Christian's Daily Walk*—a sustained attempt to show what life could look like with no moment of the day untouched and thus unsanctified.[10] Between these visions of social and personal transformation lay a great variety of expressions of godliness, all of them intense and most of them invasive.

Advice for moral reform was not solicited by Parliament but there is no indication that the gathering anticipated resistance to its expansive self-presentation of its mission. Not only were the hopes of the godly members clearly articulated prior to summoning the Assembly, but members of Parliament also proved themselves willing to believe complaints about moral deprivation and hear proposals for change. The Westminster Assembly was not so much pushing a moral reform as being pulled along: the Assembly did issue a dozen or more communications to one or both houses on moral or spiritual error,[11] and fast-day preachers, including Assembly members, kept these vices in view; but it was the Long Parliament itself which initiated the legislative campaign against iniquity—perhaps the only government campaign sustained without reprieve throughout the 1640s and early 1650s.

The Assembly's own crusade against societal decline lasted for five years. Initially the Assembly found its voice in petitions to Parliament, pleas of the moment requesting immediate action against an urgent concern. These petitions contain the clearest expressions of the Assembly's fervor against national mis-demeanors. Here the synod bewailed the huge range of sin that obtained across the country, as in the December 1643 warning to Parliament about the 'dayly increase & growth of all manner of outragious and intollerable abominations, such as are drunkennes, swearing, uncleanenes, & other crying sinnes in very many places of this Kingdome'.[12] Here and elsewhere the Assembly urged the containment of a wide range of sins, from private vices to socially disruptive abuses, from careless steps toward sin, such as immodesty

---

10. H. Scudder, *The Christian's Daily Walk with God* (London, 1631).

11. *MPWA*, vol. 5, Docs 1, 4, 7, 8, 11, 12, 31, 61, 64, 74, 93 and 107.

12. *MPWA*, 5:27 (Doc. 12).

or laziness, to direct violations of the law of God, such as adultery or theft. The need to halt the slide of society into sin was a note sounded frequently in the Abbey, and with increasing volume to the end of 1646. In fact some of the most detailed exposés of the sins of the nation are found in the assembly's correspondence with Parliament about church discipline between 1645 and 1646.

In spite of the many petitions to Parliament, the Assembly's long-term plan was to educate the public. The Assembly's practical orientation was always more educational than regulatory. At its most basic level the Assembly saw its task to be one of convincing people that their sin was more dangerous than they supposed (an opinion often expressed in petitions to Parliament) and their holiness more imagined than real (an idea often explained in Assembly texts and in sermons before Parliament). To that end, extensive lists of Scripture-prohibited sins were offered in memos to Parliament, expositions of the Decalogue, and in direction to other ministers.

Yet these were merely lists of sins and never detailed descriptions. So drawn are people to wrongdoing and wrong-thinking that the Assembly warned preachers on one occasion not to be so explicit in their denunciations as to 'rayse an old heresy from the grave' or give parishioners bad ideas they had not considered themselves.[13] On the other hand, some people were so blind to sin that the Assembly also encouraged pastors to use opportunities, such as that provided by severe sickness, to help people see more clearly the 'filth & pollution' which they had contracted in their guilty souls.[14] The gathering urged the problem of sin in its 1645 Directory for Public Worship, its 1646 confession, and its 1647 catechisms. The Assembly spent more time on its treatment of the moral law than most other subjects discussed in the catechisms, but since the synod's theological writings were never issued as official ecclesiastical texts for England, the impact of these texts was both delayed and limited.

---

13. *MPWA*, 5:101 (Doc. 36).
14. *MPWA*, 5:139 (Doc. 46).

The synod's effort to expose and to crush sin persisted through the years 1643 to 1647, but it was one of a handful of causes championed by the Assembly. In addition to the reformation of manners the Assembly had five other key concerns: the promotion of biblical literacy, the purge and reform of preachers and teachers in the church and university, and the reform of worship, government and doctrine. What sets apart the gathering's anxieties and convictions about moral reform is the tendency to address the issue in so many forms and contexts. It finds a prominent place in every major text of the Assembly except the translation of the Psalter and the polemical pamphlets exchanged with the Congregationalists on the subject of church governance (but appears even there). It is the subject of independent position papers. And it is an important underlying concern in the Assembly's contest with Parliament about discipline, discussed below. The very fact that this theme threads through so many Assembly documents is testimony to its importance to the men in the Abbey. Thus a paper explaining why ordination was an ordinance of Christ almost inevitably contains a solemn warning that people are stooping 'to vilify not only the persons of Ministers, but their very office & calling'.[15] These types of comments about common transgressions were not randomly placed; they were organically integrated in Assembly texts. Danger was everywhere, the nation was asleep, and the self-designated 'watchmen upon the walls' saw the need to sound the alarm.[16]

Putting into the Highway

When the Assembly did join the fray, the only thing more impressive than the number of Assembly documents that addressed moral reform was the amount of support initially offered by the two houses of Parliament. The Assembly was commanded to print both its initial call for a solemn fast and its first letter to the Scottish kirk, each of which set out an agenda for fighting sin.[17] Parliament's

---

15. *MPWA*, 5:85 (Doc. 30).

16. *MPWA*, 5:233; see also 5:10 (Docs. 83 and 1).

17. *Journal of the House of Lords* (London: His Majesty's Stationery Office,

appointed Assembly was 'putting into' the highway of holiness, and it could only do good for the image of the two houses to let the world know that they approved of the Assembly's strong moral stand.

It is hard to imagine that there would not have been a corresponding appreciation from Assembly members for supportive legislation of the two houses. Many peers and MPs retained close, even intimate, friendships with Assembly members and maintained frequent contact with them. What is more, some of the ordinances against the rise of lay preaching and the spread of heresy were prompted by petitions from the Assembly. Nonetheless, in the Assembly's surviving minutes and papers, there is a puzzling lack of positive reinforcement in the assembly's communications to parliament. Whatever thanks might have been offered must have been private and not public. The obsequious phrases which litter fast sermons before Parliament are absent in all surviving Assembly texts to Parliament. The Assembly's simple acknowledgement of the 'honourable' houses stands in striking contrast to the lavish praises found in the Assembly's letters both to the Scottish General Assembly and to foreign churches.

Only six of the Assembly's surviving petitions contain any praise and thanks for Parliament. The first four petitions offered pats on the back, mentioning Parliament's 'integrity and zeale', 'pious endeavors', 'wisdome and zeale', 'care & indeavour', and 'pious care'.[18] Two further communications, each of them treating a particularly delicate topic, extended something more substantial. One took the time to thank the two houses for their 'fidelity, constancy & indefatiguible diligence'. The other for being 'singularly usefull towards the saving of these three Nations from the bondage of Tyranny & Idolatry'.[19] Nonetheless, although the Assembly would admit that Parliament took 'off many yoakes &

[1767–1830]), 6:138 (hereafter, *LJ*); *Journal of the House of Commons* (London: His Majesty's Stationery Office, 1802), 3:237 (hereafter, *CJ*).

18. *MPWA*, 5:11, 28, 177 and 224 (Docs 1, 12, 61 and 80).

19. *MPWA*, 5:229 and 301 (Docs 81 and 104).

burdens, both in matters of Religion & of civill concernment', the synod had the gall to add that the houses were only 'laying the foundations & beginnings of a positive Reformation'. The best thing the two houses had accomplished was their 'ingaging this Kingdom in that solemn & sacred League & Covenant'.[20] It was a backhanded compliment about Parliament's zeal in addressing evil. It suggested nothing about the government's ability to do any positive good.

This tone is all the more striking—almost bewildering—given the extent of Parliament's efforts and the correlation between these reforms and the Assembly's expressed complaints and hopes. Any one of Parliament's calls for public fasting, pushes for improved observance of occasions for humiliation,[21] or summonses to deeper sorrow on account of the nation's profound sins could have been ghost-written by members of the Assembly. Perhaps some were. What is more, not only in the sheer volume of their ordinances, but also in the manner of their attempts to persuade the nation of their sins, the two houses shared a common vision with the Assembly. In one theologically creative attempt to convict England of a need to change, Parliament invoked the idea of a 'treasury of wrath' accumulated by the nation, a dark play on words with the Roman Catholic idea of a treasury of merit. It was all the more powerful when coupled, as it was, with the reminder of the national debt for idolatry and murder amassed during the reign of Mary Tudor.[22]

The monthly fast was only one of Parliament's weapons deployed in its war for righteousness, nor was the pursuit of righteousness conceived of narrowly. There was probably no clear line between regulating social behaviour and the advocacy of iconoclasm,[23] the

---

20. *MPWA*, 5:301 (Doc. 104).

21. *LJ*, 5:320; C. H. Firth and R. S. Rait, eds, *Acts and Ordinances of the Interregnum* (London: H.M. Stationery Office, 1911), 1:22. (Hereafter, *AOI*.)

22. *LJ*, 5:607; *AOI*, 1:80. John Calvin, *Concerning the Eternal Predestination of God*, trans. J. K. S. Reid (Cambridge: James Clarke, 1961), 90.

23. *LJ*, 6:184–85, *AOI*, 1:249; *LJ*, 6:546, *AOI*, 1:425.

destruction of William Laud, the removal of his episcopal offices, and the redistribution of church property. Protestants perceived remote but significant social benefits to any action that widened the gap between the Church of England and the Church of Rome. Thus, there were liturgical revisions too: taking away the Book of Common Prayer, putting in the Directory for Public Worship; the task of threatening those too fond of the old forms, and penalizing those so willing to promote the new forms that they were tempted to print illegal copies.[24] All of these reforms were close to the heart of the godly men in the Assembly; some of them were preparatory for, or extensions of, the Assembly's own work.

Parliament's concern with the cultus of the nation also dovetailed with the Assembly's ambitions, extending to the termination of not only saints' days but also holidays. The Christmas celebration was really an occasion of fasting, all the more because people were commonly 'pretending the memory of Christ into an extreame forgetfulnesse of him, by giving liberty to carnall and sensuall delights, being contrary to the life which Christ himselfe led here upon earth'.[25] Similar logic lay behind the April 1645 condemnation of children scrambling for treats on Easter day.[26] Parliament's attempt to change the calendar was manifestly a vehicle for social control and social change that the majority in the Assembly endorsed. Holidays were abolished first. Two years later monthly days of recreation took their place (a net gain in terms of employee vacation benefits),[27] followed by an ordinance penalizing masters who worked scholars or apprentices on a recreation day.[28] The abolishment of a 'Christian' calendar appeared to be a step towards secularization, but was really intended to promote an even earlier calendar: that of the schedule of one day of rest and six days of work. Days of recreation were

---

24. *LJ*, 7:125, *AOI*, 1:582–607; *LJ*, 7:273; *LJ*, 7:551–52, *AOI*, 1:755.
25. *LJ*, 7:106, *AOI*, 1:580.
26. *LJ*, 7:300.
27. *LJ*, 9:248, *AOI*, 1:954.
28. *LJ*, 9:301, *AOI*, 1:985.

a necessary concession for those who missed their holidays; they were also to provide a relief valve for those who struggled to keep a Sabbath day without sports.

Sabbath-keeping illustrates how a line between worship reform and ethical reform is thin, in some cases almost arbitrary. Parliament produced copious legislation for the Lord's Day, culminating in a comprehensive act in April 1650. Throughout the 1640s the two houses required the Book of Sports to be burned, insisted that the sale of milk be restricted to the hours before morning and after evening worship, and urged inns, 'victualing houses', and homes preparing meals on the Sabbath to keep dinner simple.[29] Even the reform of the cult and the calendar of the English church had strong ethical implications.

While reformation of worship and liturgy had moral dimensions not always immediately obvious, Parliament also implemented many reforms that fit any conventional definition of a reformation of manners. The two houses used the conflict with Charles as a reason to limit games and shows, since 'Public sports do not well agree with Public Calamaties, nor Public Stage-plays with the seasons of humiliation'.[30] But when the war was later won, it was because the theatre proved a context and vehicle for 'lascivious mirth and levity' that plays and interludes were suppressed, playhouses gutted, players treated as rogues, and audiences fined (with proceeds going to the poor).[31]

Morality, like theology, could be employed as a cloak to dignify politics and legislation to prevent the printing and dissemination of 'scandalous' pamphlets offers a case in point, for the scandal in view was usually sedition, not lewdness.[32] Nonetheless, Parliament could be tough on crime. Kidnapping, especially the abduction of children, was targeted in 1645.[33] Harsh penalties—

---

29. E.g., *LJ*, 6:507–508, *AOI*, 1:420; *CJ*, 6:400–401, *AOI*, 2:383.

30. *LJ*, 5:336, *AOI*, 1:26.

31. *LJ*, 5:336, *AOI*, 1:26; *LJ*, 10:41–42, *AOI*, 1:1070.

32. *LJ*, 9:457–8, *AOI*, 1:1027; *CJ*, 6:298, *AOI*, 2:245; *CJ*, 7:245, *AOI*, 2:696.

33. *LJ*, 7:361, *AOI*, 1:681.

including whipping, branding, a term in a house of correction, or even death—were implemented for pimps and brothel owners. Capital punishment was required for both incest and adultery, and three months imprisonment for fornication.[34] In the later 1640s ordinances were passed for the relief and the employment of the poor and for punishing vagrants, along with the erection of workhouses for the former, and houses of correction for the latter.[35] Acts passed in the early 1650s ranged from efforts to forbid extortionist interest to attempts to better prevent swearing and cursing. Legislation was passed affirming prior legislation and prescribing punishments for error, heresy and blasphemy—punishments including, until August 1650, the death penalty.[36] Not all of these measures were new to the Long Parliament, and these are but a fraction of the whole, but there can be no doubt that the affirmation, reaffirmation, and reinforcement of godly laws was designed to strengthen the godly cause in London and the localities.

Wayfaring Men

These measures bear repetition here because many of them were effected in the 1640s and yet the Assembly held back from a full-throated approval of Parliament's efforts. The Assembly was first to assume, and then to announce, that the benefits of legislated morality were limited in at least four ways. An understanding of these limitations was hardly unique to the synod; members of parliament would themselves acknowledge three of the four.

The most obvious limit to the effectiveness of parliamentary legislation, often mentioned by historians, was the ability to execute it. As the Assembly saw it, the wayfaring people of Britain

---

34. *CJ*, 6:410–11, *AOI*, 2:387.

35. *LJ*, 9:580–81, *AOI*, 1:1042; *CJ*, 6:202, *AOI*, 2:104.

36. For profanity see *CJ*, 6:433, *AOI*, 2:393; for usury *CJ*, 6:618, *AOI*, 2:548. For error, heresy, and blasphemy see the 4 February 1647 call for a Day of Humiliation *LJ*, 8:706–7, a 2 May 1648 (*LJ*, 10:240–1, *AOI*, 1:1133) and a 9 August 1650 act (*CJ*, 6:453–4, *AOI*, 2:409). This latter act substituted banishment in place of the death penalty.

tended to travel toward sin, no matter how many warning signs were posted. The Assembly was not inclined to remind Parliament that ethical standards slipped, in part, because the prior system of courts had been permitted by Parliament to lapse before a new system was in place—a truly staggering misstep for the nation's legislative body. It was much easier to say that so long as the nation suffered from an insufficient number of reform-minded magistrates that Parliament's ethically advanced ordinances would do little good. One reason why antinomians and Anabaptists were thought to have such a chilling effect on the moral order of the nation was because they openly argued that authority cannot suppress error.[37] The Assembly, on the other hand, was convinced that governors of the church should 'implore the ayde of the Civill Magistrate; who ought to use his coercive power' to suppress heresy and crime.[38] The Dutch churches in England were to be admired for recognizing that 'conspiracies, treasons, murthers, robberies, rapes' and particularly ugly or abominable sins should be punished by the magistrate.[39] One problem with the two houses, it appeared, was that they had not made the appointment of godly officials a priority task. In late November 1643 the Assembly urged the Commons to find 'Godly and zealous Magistrates to represse' rampant iniquity lest it 'render fruitlesse all your pious endeavors for Reformation & the Weale of the Kingdome'.[40] Two weeks later it sent the same message to the Lords, in the same words.

Enforcement was not the only limitation to legislative moral reform. There were many other evils which laws could not reach but which still required repentance: sins of the heart, sins too private or too small to deserve the attention of the civil magistrate. Here the remedy was education. People needed to be informed about the penetrating depth of the law and the many ways in which they were found guilty by it. This kind of instruction needed to start at home,

37. *MPWA*, 5:87–88 (Doc. 31).
38. *MPWA*, 5:217 (Doc. 77).
39. *MPWA*, 5:240 (Doc. 88).
40. *MPWA*, 5:27–28 (Doc. 12).

because saints were sinners too. The Assembly's members regularly focused on the iniquities of the godly. In its own fasts, the Assembly elicited embarrassing confessions of its own faults,[41] and documents the Assembly provided for the reformed church called worshippers to acknowledge 'their owne vilenesse & unworthynes'.[42] A pastoral prayer of confession before the sermon recommended that congregants 'bewaile' not only their 'blindnes of mind, hardnes of hart, unbeliefe, impenitency, security, lukewarmnes, [and] barrennes', but also their 'not endeavouring after mortification & newnes of life, nor after the exercise of Godlines in the power therof'. The prayer assumed that some people might be behave better than others, but even 'the best of us have not soe stedfastly walked with god, kept our garments soe unspotted, nor bene soe zealous of his glory & the good of others, as we ought'.[43] Indeed, these sorts of sins could creep into the worship service itself, where preachers spotted 'private whisperings, conferences, salutations, or doeing reverence to any persons present, or coming in, as alsoe from all gazing, sleeping, & other undecent behaviour'. Individuals tended to 'disturbe the minister or people, or hind[e]r themselves or others in the service of god'.[44]

The conviction that there was bound to be iniquity in every place and person was rooted in a theology of sin articulated by the Assembly in its confession of faith. In an egalitarian statement appearing to blame the fall and communication of sin on both parents of the human race, the Assembly explained that 'They being the root of all man-kinde, the guilt of this sin was imputed, and the same death in sin and corrupted nature conveied to all their posterity'.[45] This fall in turn necessitated an historic

---

41. *MPWA*, 3:280–87, 289 (Sess. 282; 10 Sept. 1644).

42. *MPWA*, 5:95 (Doc. 36, Of the Assembling of the Congregation).

43. *MPWA*, 5:97 (Doc. 36, Of Publique Prayer before the Sermon).

44. *MPWA*, 5:95 (Doc. 36, Of the Assembling of the Congregation).

45. *The Humble Advice of the Assembly of Divines, Now by Authority of Parliament Sitting at Westminster, Concerning a Confession of Faith, with the Quotations and Texts of Scripture* (London, [1647]), 6.3. Hereafter *CF*.

republication of the law in the Ten Commandments, a text which required detailed explication by the Assembly, especially in its two catechisms.

The Assembly's Shorter Catechism contained only the core of the Assembly's educational curriculum. The Larger Catechism presented a far deeper analysis of the Decalogue. Questions and answers opened for each commandment a detailed list of the related duties required and sins forbidden. The seventh commandment, forbidding adultery, required 'chastity in body, mind, affections, words, and behaviour; and the preservation of it in ourselves and others'.[46] The eighth commandment, forbidding theft, forbade 'vexatious law-suits, unjust inclosures, and depopulations' and 'ingrossing commodities to inhance the price'.[47] The importance given to reflection on the Decalogue in the Larger Catechism is testified by the fact that the Assembly appointed eleven committees to treat the Ten Commandments and provide rules for their interpretation.[48]

Characteristic of the Assembly's effort to educate others is their instance that this duty to correct and admonish belongs to every Christian. Moral instruction begins at home, but cannot stop there. Hence 'what is forbidden or commanded to our selves, we are bound, according to our places, to endeavour that it may be avoided or performed by others, according to, the duty of their places'. And 'in what is commanded to others, we are bound according to our places and callings to be helpful to them; and to take heed of partaking with others in what is forbidden them'.[49] Thus not only is 'chastity' to be preserved 'in our selves' but also in 'others'.[50] Not only are readers of the catechism obligated to

---

46. *MPWA*, vol. 5, Doc. 127. Citation from J. Bower, ed., *The Larger Catechism: A Critical Text and Introduction* (Grand Rapids: Reformation Heritage Books, 2010), Q & A, 138 (hereafter, *LC*).

47. *LC*, Q & A, 142.

48. J. Bower, introduction to *The Larger Catechism*, p. 33.

49. *LC*, Q & A, 99.

50. *LC*, Q & A, 138.

'the disapproving, detesting, [and] opposing, all false worship' but also 'according to each one's place and calling, removing it, and all monuments of idolatry'.[51] Injunctions of this kind are found in the assembly's exposition of the second, third, fourth, sixth, seventh, eighth and ninth commandments.[52] On this view 'tolerating' a sin or an error is tantamount to committing it.

Characteristic, too, of the Assembly's exposition of the Decalogue is a sustained effort not merely to list duties and misdemeanours, but to go further and identify the root cause of external sin with the intermediate (often mental) steps toward sins of word or deed. In considering a good conscience and the problem of concupiscence, the Assembly was saying nothing that could have surprised their contemporaries. This kind of probing was what a catechism was good for, and when Parliament called the Assembly to complete its catechism it must have expected an exposition of the Decalogue, for that is what standard catechisms provided.[53] Thus taking a cue from the Sermon on the Mount, where Jesus preaches that name-calling is a step toward murder and the impulse to murder is located in the deeper problem of hate, the Larger Catechism is as pre-occupied with the seeds and the development of sin as much as with the sin itself. So often is this evident in the gathering's treatment of the first nine commandments that the Assembly's treatment of the tenth—the one precept that explicitly addresses the motivations of the heart—is uncharacteristically brief.[54]

Moral change could not be effected by enforced legislation. But nor was it enough for the Assembly to offer a solid education in the extensive depravity of humanity. Knowledge of sin did not contain the power to remove it. It was a godly axiom, inherited

---

51. *LC,* Q & A, 108.

52. *LC,* Q & A, 108, 112 (perhaps), 118, 135, 136, 138, 139, 141 and 145.

53. For the presence of the Ten Commandments in early-modern catechisms, see I. Green, *The Christian's ABC: Catechisms and Catechizing in England c. 1530–1740* (Oxford: Oxford University Press, 2004), pp. 422–78.

54. *LC,* Q & A, 146-148.

from Martin Luther, that good laws and a good understanding of fallen human nature were incapable of addressing the root cause of sin; it could only offer a guide, perhaps restrain sin's effects, and expose the need for a Savior. [55] Understanding, almost as a reflex, this third limitation to a moral reform by law only, both Parliament and the Assembly were committed to the idea of supplementing good laws with a teaching ministry that would apply the law and preach the gospel.

Already in 1641 the House of Commons declared that preaching 'is even the way to bring People into a state of Salvation; it is the way to save their souls'. A minister is sent from God 'as an ambassador, to publish and spread abroad the mind and message of God touching Man's duty, and salvation, and to instruct the Church of God'.[56] These principles too were enforced by legislation. The two houses tried to regulate preaching, removing lay preachers, reducing the numbers of scandalous fellows in the universities and ministers in the church, and introducing numerous measures to maintain financially those who were preaching faithfully.[57] A major part of Parliament's religious reformation consisted of appointing ministers for churches and chaplains for the armed forces, eventually effecting a clerical disruption in the 1640s that was, although for a shorter duration, far greater than that of the 'Great Ejection' of the early 1660s. The House of Commons' committee for scandalous ministers in monitoring, ejecting, and ratifying ministers, and the assembly in examining ministers, offered a time-intensive overhaul of the preachers of the Church of England. Together they took strides towards educating England not only in the ways of godliness, but in the power required for a renovation in life.

---

55. *LC*, Q & A, 95.

56. P. Seaver, *The Puritan Lectureships* (Stanford: Stanford University Press, 1970), p. 20.

57. E.g., *LJ*, 8:165, *AOI*, 1:830; *LJ*, 7:97, *AOI*, 1:579; *LJ*, 7:337, *AOI*, 1:677. One measure included the decision to exclude all appeals regarding tithes until the tithe had been paid (*LJ*, 9:380, *AOI*, 1:996).

In combination with actions putting godly preachers into churches, legislation forced rogues and beggars to go to church, ordered masters to order their servants to attend worship services, and required them to remain orderly while they were there.[58] In attending services they could be exposed to the reading, explanation, and application of the moral law. As the Assembly explained: 'The Morall Law is of use to all men, to inform them of the holy nature and will of God, and of their duty, binding them to walk accordingly'. But what is more, the law could also 'convince them of their disability to keep it, and of the sinfull pollution of their nature, hearts, and lives; to humble them in sense of their sin and misery, and thereby help them to a clearer sight of the need they have of Christ, and of the perfection of his obedience'.[59]

Laws bringing the unregenerate to church were hardly part of the moral law itself. Nor were they unique to the Long Parliament. However, when enforced, they increased opportunities for corrupt men to be exposed to the law and to the gospel. The Assembly asserted in its confession that 'Repentance unto life, is an evangelicall grace, the Doctrine whereof is to be preached by every Minister of the Gospel, as well as that of faith in Christ'.[60] People needed this preaching: the Assembly explained that 'the Spirit of God maketh the Reading, but especially the Preaching of the word, an effectual means of enlightning, convincing, and humbling sinners'.[61] It was, in part, to keep preaching about repentance and faith from being muddied that the assembly petitioned against erring preachers and on behalf of orthodox ones.[62]

Where Fools Shall Not Err

With the two Houses of Parliament legislating, the Westminster Assembly educating, and both parties promoting godly preaching,

---

58. *LJ*, 6:507–8, *AOI*, 1:420.

59. *LC*, Q & A, 95.

60. *CF*, 15.1.

61. *LC*, Q & A, 155.

62. E.g., *MPWA*, vol. 5, Docs 4, 8, 31 and 61.

a co-ordinated godly reform should have advanced inexorably over the objections of the 'Edomites and Philistines' that opposed it.[63] But the Westminster Assembly was convinced that there was a fourth hindrance to moral reform: a lack of effective church discipline. This was a key step that Presbyterians at the Assembly demanded and Parliament resisted, with the House of Commons insisting on a pastorally insensitive legislated solution that the assembly could not accept. Every other Reformed church had been employing elder-administered excommunication to fight the cancer of sin. Parliament needed to take this last step if they were to build a road where fools would no longer err—or at least not so often. Discipline was, after all, intended to guide the traveller and recall the wanderer. It warned those who followed foolish examples, and may themselves be led astray. And church discipline honored Christ by keeping the Table pure. As the Assembly saw it, if ministers were forced to give the Lord's Supper to everyone, they were 'prostituting' the very 'Sacrament of the Body & Bloud of Christ'.[64]

To the consternation of members of both houses, but especially the House of Commons, every avenue to moral reformation was considered incomplete by the presbyterian majority in the Assembly unless ministers were enabled, not only to talk about sin and forgiveness, but to hold in their own hands the keys of the kingdom for locking out stubborn sinners from communion with the church of God or opening the door to admit the repentant into fellowship with the faithful. Ministers and other church governors wanted the freedom not only to exercise the office of teaching but also of ruling. Unless the church was given freedom to exclude ignorant and scandalous people from the Lord's supper, the moral reformation of Church and nation would remain unfinished.[65]

---

63. *MPWA*, 5:15 (Doc. 2).

64. *MPWA*, 5:233 (Doc. 83).

65. See C. Van Dixhoorn, 'Politics and Religion in the Westminster Assembly and the "Grand Debate"; in *Alternative Establishments in Early Modern Britain and Ireland: Catholic and Presbyterian*, ed. R. Armstrong and T. O'hAnnrachain (Manchester: University of Manchester Press, 2013), pp. 129–48.

The Path Not Followed

Famously, at least for historians of the civil war and Puritanism, the Westminster Assembly and the Long Parliament clashed repeatedly throughout 1646. The Assembly fired a volley of protests over the ordinance for the Lord's Supper, insisting on the divine right of self-contained church government; the House of Commons charged the Assembly with a breach of privilege.

Traditionally, and quite understandably, this conflict has been narrated in exclusively ecclesiological terms. Disciplinary action in the church is an application of a form of governance, whatever form that governance might take. Nonetheless, if the Assembly's intransigent opposition to Parliament's legislative offerings on the subject of discipline is to be fully understood, and Parliament's mistrust and disillusionment is to be properly appreciated, the exchange also needs to be placed in the context of a co-operative moral reform. For those loyal to Parliament but critical of the Assembly, the gathering appeared to be unreasonable precisely because Parliament had effected so many changes in church government and had made so much progress in the reform of manners. Nonetheless, this essay has endeavoured to show that when ecclesiastical discipline is read as a final chapter in the Assembly's own endeavours for moral reformation, the heat generated over this exchange is more intelligible than when it is not. The conflict was intense, in part, because the houses of politicians and house of theologians had worked so closely and so effectively in other attempts to suppress iniquity throughout the 1640s. Parliament in particular felt betrayed. The houses had passed numerous reform laws, they had flung open the door to sound preachers, they had urged the assembly to haste the catechisms. And yet as the Assembly explained in 1645, 'the Corruptions of men, & the severall waies of mens scandalous manifestations of them, are innumerable'.[66] The creativity of sinners meant that the one-size-fits-all solutions offered by lawmakers could not pastorally address the problem of sinful hearts. It offered a way for wayfaring men, who are fools, to err too easily.

---

66. *MPWA*, 5:202 (Doc. 74).

As the Assembly wound down, its members, most of them no longer actively participating in the gathering's remaining work, watched as the Rump Parliament (what was left of the Long Parliament) reduced the severity of England's religious penal code.[67] Beginning in the summer of 1649, the Rump aggressively pursued ecclesiastical 'education' in a series of Acts for the propagation of the gospel.[68] Ironically, by this time most Assembly members appear to have made peace with Parliament's form of Presbyterianism, functionally accepting it as the best that the state had to offer. By the 1650s Presbyterians (and Congregationalists) were heavy involved in the system of discipline the Assembly had so vigourously opposed in the 1640s.

The Westminster Assembly had attempted to build a narrow road from which wayfaring men, though fools, would not wander. But the form that this reformation took was a path untrodden by any previous assembly in the English church, not least in the disciplinary dimension of its moral reform. Ultimately, to the grave disappointment of English Presbyterians, its path of pastor-led moral reformation would not be followed by Parliament; its highway of holiness would not be paved with any public success. The Puritan dream of transforming a culture would wait for another day.

---

67. See above, and note the 27 September 1650 'Act for the relief of the religious and peaceable from the Rigour of former Acts of Parliament, in matters of Religion', where laws against recusants were revoked for the sake of other godly people (*CJ*, 6:474; *AOI*, 2:423).

68. Acts for the propagation of the gospel begin in 27 July 1649 (*CJ*, 6:271; *AOI*, 2:197).

CHAPTER SEVEN

John Cotton and the Spiritual Value of Psalm-singing

W. ROBERT GODFREY

ONE foundational aspect of the Reformation was a return to the Scriptures. The Reformers studied, taught, preached, and wrote on the Bible. They also sang the Word. It was one of the ways in which the people of God could hide the Word of God in their hearts (Ps. 119:11).

John Calvin (1509–1564) in particular was passionate about psalm-singing. He seemed to have a special affinity for the Psalms, identifying with both the trials and triumphs of David. Early in his career he versified some psalms for singing, making singing an important part of worship. Even in his years of exile in Strasbourg, the singing in his congregation was remarkable. One visitor wrote of it:

> No creature could believe the joy one feels at singing the praises and marvels of God in one's native tongue. I had been there only five or six days when I saw this small assembly, which had been expelled from every country for having maintained the honor of God and the Gospel. I began to cry, not from sadness but for joy, on hearing them sing with such a good heart as they did. You could not hear any voice interfere with another; each had a music book in his hand, men and women, and each praised the Lord ....

113

And here one's conscience is at rest when one is where the Word of God is purely preached and the sacraments purely distributed.[1]

One of the remarkable achievements of Calvin's ministry was the completion in the last year of his life of a complete Psalter for singing. The work of versifying every psalm and finding composers for the tunes had taken many years as the book for singing had gradually grown. The labor had been demanding, but the fruit was invaluable.

Reformed churches throughout Europe made extensive use of the Genevan Psalter, from Hungary, to the Netherlands, to France. The importance of the Psalter can hardly be overstated. For example of French Calvinists it has been said: 'The psalter *was* the French Reformation . . . . The singing of psalms was to the French Reformation what the chorale was to the German Reformation. Music was an intimate part of Calvinist culture.'[2] The Psalms became a treasured part of the spiritual lives of Calvinists for centuries. Calvin's passion for psalm-singing, if not the Genevan Psalter, was also taken up among the Scottish Presbyterians and the English Puritans.

The Ministry of John Cotton

One leading Puritan minister in the first half of the seventeenth century, John Cotton (1584–1652), wrote a significant defense of that practice. While Cotton was one of the most respected and influential Puritans of the first half of the seventeenth century, he is relatively little-known today. If he is remembered, it is probably either for his involvement in the antinomian controversy that surrounded Anne Hutchinson or his rather famous grandson, Cotton Mather. He wrote less than many of his contemporary Puritans and wrote much more succinctly. Yet what he wrote clearly and effectively presented the Puritan ideal of church and society.

Cotton was born in England in 1584 and studied at Trinity College, Cambridge, receiving his AB in 1603. He excelled in classical languages laying down a foundation for careful,

---

1. Cited in Bernard Cottret, *Calvin* (Grand Rapids: Eerdmans, 2000), pp. 134–35.
2. Cottret, *Calvin*, p. 172.

thoughtful scholarship. He continued his studies at Emmanuel College, Cambridge coming under increasing Puritan influence. He later said that he was regenerated in 1609. He was ordained in the Church of England in 1610 and in 1612 was called to serve in Boston, Lincolnshire. He ministered there humbly, faithfully, and effectively for twenty years, seeking to follow a Puritan approach without offending non-Puritan church authorities. His preaching followed the plain style taught by William Perkins. By 1632 William Laud, then Bishop of London and the next year elevated to be Archbishop of Canterbury, turned his anti-Puritan campaign against Cotton. Knowing Laud's ruthlessness, Cotton went into hiding and in 1633 sailed to New England. He was already known to John Winthrop, the governor, and was soon called to pastor the First Church in Boston, Massachusetts. His clear preaching of grace led to an unusual number of conversions.

Already in the seventeenth century Cotton's significance was well recognized. As one scholar put it, Cotton's son-in-law, Increase Mather, recognized 'that John Cotton, more than any other man, gave New England its name and being. His son [Cotton Mather] repeated this judgment, explaining that John Cotton had pro-vided the most exact statement of the New England way of life by the founders in his *The Keys of the Kingdom of Heaven*.'[3] Later historians have expressed similar judgments. Larzer Ziff observed: 'He was undeniably the greatest preacher in the first decades of New England history, and he was, for his contemporaries, a greater theologian than he was a polemicist.'[4] Horton Davies concluded, that Cotton was the 'leading New England Independent of his day.'[5]

In addition to his notable preaching he wrote a number of theological works. He particularly engaged in defending

---

3. Robert Middlekauff, *The Mathers* (Oxford: Oxford University Press, 1971), p. 196.

4. *John Cotton on the Churches of New England*, ed. Larzer Ziff (Cambridge, MA: Harvard University Press, 1968), p. 35.

5. Horton Davies, *The Worship of the English Puritans* (Morgan, PA: Soli Deo Gloria Publications, 1997), p. 224.

congregational church polity. John Owen wrote that he was drawn from Presbyterianism to Congregationalism by reading Cotton.[6] He was also one of the leading figures in the antinomian controversy in New England, initially defending Anne Hutchinson, but then turning away from her as the radical nature of her views became clear.

Cotton on Psalm-singing

John Cotton was so committed to psalm-singing that he was one of the key participants in the preparation of *The Whole Booke of Psalmes Faithfully Translated into English Metre* (1640), commonly known as *The Bay Psalm Book*, the first book ever printed in North America. The Preface to the Bay Psalter of which Cotton seems to have been the author[7] presents arguments for the value of the Psalter for the Christian community.

The first sentence of the Preface acknowledges the spiritual forces that oppose the singing of Psalms: 'The singing of Psalmes, though it breath forth nothing but holy harmony, and melody: yet such is the subtilty of the enemie, and the enmity of our nature against the Lord, and his ways, that our hearts can finde matter of discord in this harmony, and crotchets of division in this holy melody.'[8] Satan and our human nature resist the blessing of the Psalter. That is why Cotton writes an explanation and defense of the practice.

---

6. Larzer Ziff, *The Career of John Cotton* (Princeton, NJ: Princeton University Press, 1962), pp. 30–31. For other works on Cotton, see Everett H. Emerson, *John Cotton* (New Haven, CN: College and University Press 1965); Lisa M. Gordis, *Opening Scripture, Bible Reading and Interpretive Authority in Puritan New England* (Chicago: University of Chicago Press, 2003); Charles E. Hambrick-Stowe, '*Christ the Fountaine of Life* by John Cotton (1584–1652),' in *The Devoted Life*, ed. Kelly M. Kapic and Randall C. Gleason (Downers Grove, IL: InterVarsity Press, 2004); Paul R. Schaefer Jr., *The Spiritual Brotherhood: Cambridge Puritans and the Nature of Christian Piety* (Grand Rapids: Reformation Heritage Books, 2011).

7. Emerson, *John Cotton*, p. 27.

8. *The Bay Psalm Book*, facsimile edition (Oxford: Bodleian Library, 2014), preface, p. 1.

He stresses the divine inspiration of the Psalter as the foundation of its distinctive value. While some delight in hymns of uninspired authorship, the superiority of David should be recognized: 'Must the ordinary gifts of a private man quench the spirit still speaking to us by the extraordinary gifts of his servant David?'[9] What sense does it make to prefer the uninspired to the inspired?

He also addresses the most frequent complaint against the Psalter which argued that it could not fully meet the needs of worship in the new covenant. While the Psalter is not a complete systematic theology, he insists that it does provide a complete range of responses for Christians to all the works of God:

> Because the booke of the psalms is so compleat a System of psalms, which the Holy Ghost himself in infinite wisdom hath made to suit all conditions, necessityes, temptations, affections, etc. of men in all ages; (as most of all our interpreters on the psalms have fully and perticularly cleared) therefore by this the Lord seemeth to stoppe all mens mouths and mindes ordinarily to compile or sing any other psalms (under colour that the ocasions and conditions of the Church are new) etc. for the publick use of the Church, seing, let our condition be what it will, the Lord himself hath supplied us with farre better.[10]

He is convinced that the Reformed have shown the sufficiency of the Psalter for the church and stresses its spiritual strength and completeness.

Near the end of the Preface Cotton recognizes that these metrical Psalms may not be the most eloquent:

> If therefore the verses are not alwayes so smooth and elegant as some may desire or expect, let them consider that Gods Altar needs not our pollishings: Ex. 20. For wee have respected rather a plaine translation, then to smooth our verses with the sweetnes of any paraphrase, and soe have attended Conscience rather then

---

9. *The Bay Psalm Book*, p. 4.
10. *The Bay Psalm Book*, pp. 4–5.

Elegance, fidelity rather then poetry, in translating the hebrew words into english language, and Davids poetry into english meetre.[11]

We can see this lack of eloquence, for example, in *The Bay Psalm Book*'s metrical version of Psalm 105:1–5,

> O Prayse the Lord, call on his Name.
> 'mong people shew his facts.
> Sing unto him, sing psalms to him:
> talk of all's wondrous acts.
> Let their hearts joy, that seek the Lord:
> boast in his Holy-Name.
> The Lord seek, and his strength: his face
> always seek yee *the same.*
> Those admirable works that hee
> hath done remember you:
> his wonders, and the judgements which
> doe from his mouth *issue.*

The attempt at a literal rendering has resulted in a very wooden translation and shows why *The Bay Psalm Book* did not become one of the most popular Psalters.

The topics, which Cotton briefly introduced in the Preface, he develops in a longer treatise, 'On the Singing of Psalms', which carefully, yet concisely summarizes typical arguments of many Puritans. To be sure questions had been raised about the practice of psalm-singing from outside and inside the Reformed movement. Cotton's treatise in particular responds to certain Puritan critics who challenged the Bible foundations of the psalm-singing done by most Puritans. Cotton begins in the Puritan plain style, without any literary introduction, simply plunging into the substance of the issue. He is so confident in the propriety of Puritan psalm-singing, that he immediately labels criticisms of the practice as the work of Satan, just as he did at the beginning of the Preface of *The Bay Psalm Book*: 'To prevent the godly-minded

---

11. *The Bay Psalm Book*, p. 12.

from making melody to the Lord in singing His praises with one accord (I mean with one heart, and one voice) Satan hath mightily bestirred himself to breed a discord in the hearts of some by filling their heads with four heads of scruples about the duty.'[12] He then plunges into addressing those four issues.

The four specific topics or questions discussed in the treatise are: 1) Are we to sing audibly with our voices or only in our hearts? 2) Are we to sing only divinely inspired psalms or also hymns of uninspired composition? 3) Are we all to sing or only some? 4) How are we to sing in terms of versification and tunes? Rather than simply follow Cotton's line of thought in these four areas, however, we will step back and look at the convictions that underlie what he writes, namely that psalm-singing is required, inspired, and desired.

Psalm-singing Required

Cotton stresses that psalm-singing is a duty to which Christians are called by the Lord. This duty is the same as the duty to pray: 'As in prayer, though spiritual gifts be requisite to make it acceptable; yet the duty of praying lyeth upon all men.'[13] Against this duty Cotton recognizes certain 'Antipsalmists' among the Puritans.[14] He writes: 'In opposition to this, there be some *Antipsalmists*, who do not acknowledge any singing at all with the voice in the New Testament, but only spiritual songs of joy and comfort in the heart in the word of Christ.'[15] This position seems very similar to that of Ulrich Zwingli in Zurich with which the Puritans were probably familiar.

In response Cotton shows with careful exegetical arguments that the New Testament continued the duty for Christians to

---

12. John Cotton, 'On the Singing of Psalms,' in *John Cotton on Psalmody and the Sabbath*, ed. Greg Fox (Edinburgh, IN: Puritan Reprints, 2006), p. 1.

13. Cotton, 'On the Singing,' p. 55.

14. These Puritans and their specific objections are discussed by Davies, *The Worship of the English Puritans*, pp. 168–72.

15. Cotton, 'On the Singing,' p. 2.

sing to the Lord. For example, he writes, regarding Ephesians 5:19 and Colossians 3:16, 'Now what reason can be given why the Apostle should direct us in our singing to the very titles of David's Psalms, if it were not his meaning that we should sing them?'[16] He summarizes the character of this duty: 'It must needs be that the Lord alloweth us to sing them in any such grave, and solemn, and plain tunes, as do fitly suit the gravity of the matter, the solemnity of God's worship, and the capacity of a plain people.'[17] Psalms carry the serious content of praise, fit the character of public worship, and speak to God's people.

Psalm-singing Inspired

The extraordinary value of the Psalms for Cotton derives from their inspiration by the Holy Spirit, necessarily superior to un-inspired compositions:

> The *Psalms of David*, and Asaph, and the rest, are as full of holy and lively, spiritual, and evangelical meditations, and affections, instruments, prayers, and praises, as any that we can expect to be indited by an officer or member of the Christian Churches now. Yea it is to be feared that the psalms compiled by the devoutest Christians now, would fall short of those of David and Asaph, in spirit and life. How then can we make the Psalms of David and Asaph, ceremonial types of the spiritual songs of the faithful of the New Testament, when as types are wont to be more carnal, and worldly, and literal, and less spiritual and lively, then the antitypes? But here the antitypes are less spiritual and lively then the types.[18]

The Psalms are not shadows waiting to be fulfilled, but are true and living spiritual reality already given to the people of God in the old covenant, but equally vital in the new covenant.

---

16. Cotton, 'On the Singing,' p. 21. Here Cotton refers to the fact that in the titles of various psalms in the Septuagint the words psalms, hymns, and songs are used of the canonical psalms. For example, these three words can be found in the titles of Psalm 66 and 67 (65 and 66 in the Septuagintal numbering.)

17. Cotton, 'On the Singing,' p. 69.

18. Cotton, 'On the Singing,' p. 31.

He reiterates the superiority of inspired song in several ways very forcefully. For example, 'Neither is it credible, that Christ would take us off from singing the Psalms of David and Asaph, which were of divine and infallible inspiration, and leave us to an uncertain and common gift of private brethren.'[19] Here he highlights the confidence that singers can have in the content of inspired texts over uninspired ones.

Cotton is also confident that the Holy Spirit through the Psalms provides for all the needs of Christians in their sung responses to God:

> There is no estate and condition that ever befell the Church and the people of God, or can befall them, but the Holy Ghost, as He did foresee the same, so He hath provided and recorded some Scripture-Psalm, suitable thereunto. And these Psalms being chosen out suitably to the new occasions and new conditions of God's people, and sung by them with new hearts and renewed affections, will ever be found new songs. Words of eternal truth and grace, are ever old (as the Gospel is an eternal Gospel) and ever new; as the commandment of love is a new commandment as well as old.[20]

In particular he sees the Psalms as full of Christ: 'the *Psalms*, (which is full of Christ, as other Scriptures).... Singing of Psalms holdeth forth as much of Christ externally, as reading of the Word, or as the hearing of it read or preached....'[21] Not to see Christ filling the Psalms is to misunderstand the Psalms completely.

Psalm-singing Desired

The singing of Psalms should be eagerly desired by the people of God because of the blessings that accompany such singing. When God appoints a duty for His people, that duty is also a blessing:

> It is an honor to Christ, and to His grace, not only when we hold forth spiritual gifts, but also when we perform Christian duties.

19. Cotton, 'On the Singing,' p. 46.
20. Cotton, 'On the Singing,' p. 33.
21. Cotton, 'On the Singing,' p. 4.

And duties performed in faith (without which prayer itself is not accepted) they go not without a spiritual blessing, though nature and art might perform the same for the outward work .... When the people of God do perform the same in the faith of Christ, and in the obedience of God's command, they find a gracious blessing of God.[22]

Faith is necessary for duty to become a blessing in every area of the Christian life including psalm-singing.

This blessing has been experienced in the church where the duty is faithfully performed throughout the ages:

God is not wont to honor and bless the ways of superstition, with the reward of sincere devotion. But surely God hath delighted to bless the singing of His holy Psalms, with gracious and spiritual affections, not only in Augustine's time, and in Justin Martyr's before him, but from age to age to His Saints, usually, generally, and abundantly: so that doubtless the servants of God defraud their souls of much spiritual good, and comfort, who defraud themselves of the fellowship of this ordinance.'[23]

Christians must not deprive themselves of the blessing by failing to fulfill their duty.

This singing stirs the emotions in the worship and service of God: 'The translating of the Psalms into verse, in number, measure, and meter, and suiting the ditty with apt tunes, do help to stir up the affection: And the singing of Psalms being appointed of God, they tend to make a gracious melody to the praise of God and edification of His people. The sound of Aaron's bell, and the blast of the silver trumpets, and the workmanship of Hiram.'[24] The singing of Psalms properly moves the emotions in the service of God. Truly, singing 'allayeth the passions of melancholy and choler ....'[25]

---

22. Cotton, 'On the Singing,' pp. 6–7.
23. Cotton, 'On the Singing,' p. 90.
24. Cotton, 'On the Singing,' p. 74.
25. Cotton, 'On the Singing,' p. 5.

Cotton specifies the kinds of blessings that the singing of Psalms brings to the church. He summarizes those blessings in three ways: 'The Psalms of David and Asaph, and the like, were written for a threefold end, as we see expressed by the Apostle, *Colossians 3:16.* To wit,

1. For instruction, or teaching.
2. For admonition.
3. For singing praise and thanksgiving to the Lord.'[26]

At various points in the treatise he seems to expand on or amplify these three points. He writes that through the Psalms Christians '... employ and improve their holy mirth and joy, to the singing of *Psalms and Hymns and Spiritual Songs,* for their own mutual edification and consolation, and for holy thanksgiving and praise unto the Lord.'[27] More specifically he argues:

> For every Psalm setteth forth either the attributes and works of God and His Christ, and this yieldeth me matter of holy reverence, blessing, and praise: Or else it describeth the estate and ways of the Church and the people of God, and this affecteth me with compassion, instruction, or imitation: Or else it deciphereth the estate and ways of the wicked, and this holdeth forth to me a word of admonition: Or else it doth lively express mine own affections and afflictions, temptations and comforts, and then it furnisheth me with fit matter and words to present mine own condition before the Lord.[28]

Here he shows that the Psalms provide both reflection on the objective work of God in Christ and words for the believer's subjective response to God.

To be sure the singing of Psalms can degenerate into a formal, lifeless activity: 'It requires a good measure of the indwelling Spirit, and word of God to pray in the Spirit; but much more to sing in the Spirit, wherein our senses delighted with the

---

26. Cotton, 'On the Singing,' p. 45.
27. Cotton, 'On the Singing,' p. 26.
28. Cotton, 'On the Singing,' p. 66.

melody are apt to steal away our hearts from spiritual fervency.'[29] Properly pursed, however, it is enlivening, '... the quickening and edifying of the Spirit of one another, by singing together Psalms of instruction, admonition, consolation to themselves, and prayers and praises to the Lord.'[30] It blesses God, and the singer, and others: 'The end of singing is to praise the Lord for His goodness, and to stir up ourselves and others to serve the Lord with cheerfulness and glad hearts.'[31]

Scriptural Foundations

The blessings which Cotton finds in the Psalms remarkably reflects what we find taught in the Psalter itself and in the teaching of the Apostle Paul in Ephesians and Colossians. We can see such teaching clearly, for example, in the first five verses of Psalm 105 which repeat the opening words of David's song celebrating the arrival of the ark in Jerusalem (recorded in 1 Chron. 16:8–12), Here David as the sweet psalmist of Israel (2 Sam. 23:1) sets the foundation and pattern of the Psalter. While the Psalter is called in Hebrew, 'The Book of Praises', it contains a broader variety of elements. Psalm 105 shows several important elements that characterize the Psalms and the blessing they bring to the people of God.

These few verses of Psalm 105 point to various activities for the people of God: give thanks to God, call on Him, make known His deeds, sing praises, seek the Lord, and remember Him. These activities, of course, are directed primarily to God, but are also directed to others and to our own hearts. These multiple directions are part of the distinctiveness of the praise of the Psalms. We direct our praise and petition to God (Ps. 105:1–4) and at the same time we tell others about our God (vv. 1–2) and speak to our own hearts remembering God (v. 5).These activities and directions in many ways are united in the call to 'seek the Lord' (Ps. 105:4). The action of seeking is directed to the Lord in praise and petition. The

---

29. Cotton, 'On the Singing,' p. 27.
30. Cotton, 'On the Singing,' p. 52.
31. Cotton, 'On the Singing,' p. 56.

imperative to seek is addressed to others and to the self. Calvin saw the importance of seeking the Lord in the Christian life: 'Seeking God, it is true, is the mark by which all genuine saints are particularly distinguished from the men of the world; but they come far short of seeking him with due ardour; and, accordingly, they have always need of incitements, to urge them on to this exercise.'[32] He saw that the Psalms themselves incite us to seek the Lord. Seeking the Lord in the covenant community of song rests on remembering His works and leads on to praise and prayer.

Does this pattern of praise that we find in the Psalter continue in the New Testament or is there a new pattern established in the new covenant? As we look at the New Testament to answer that question, we see several points.

First, the New Testament tells us relatively little about music or song in the life of Christians, the church, and worship. For some Christians this limited amount of information has meant that they have great freedom to make whatever use of music that seems best to them for the cause of Christ. For Reformed Christians this approach to the New Testament and to worship is not acceptable. Since we believe that we may do in worship only what God has commanded in His Word, we must examine, in the spirit of John Cotton, what revelation there is about music very carefully and limit ourselves to what it teaches.

Second, the limited discussion of song in the New Testament needs to be considered carefully. Two basic texts for this examination are Ephesians 5:19 and Colossians 3:16. In these two places Paul uses three terms usually translated 'psalm', 'hymn' and 'song.'[33] These terms also have a verbal form. All of these words for song and singing are used only about thirty times in the New Testament. How are they used and to what do they refer?

The nominal and verbal forms of 'psalm' are clearly used in several places to refer to the canonical Psalms of the Old Testament:

---

32. John Calvin, *Commentary on the Book of Psalms* (Grand Rapids: Baker, 2003), 4:173 (on Ps. 105:4).

33. For Cotton's understanding of these terms see footnote 15.

Luke 20:42; 24:44; Acts 1:20; 13:33, Romans 15:9. The word is also used in 1 Corinthians 14:15 twice apparently to refer to inspired songs given as a spiritual gift. The word is also used in Ephesians 5:19, Colossians 3:16, and James 5:13 without any further definition.

The use of the nominal and verbal forms of 'hymn' three times refer to canonical Psalms: Hebrews 2:12, Matthew 26:30, and Mark 14:26 (the hymn Jesus sang at the end of the Passover meal with His disciples was certainly Ps. 118.) This word is used of Paul and Silas singing in prison (Acts 16:25), which may have been canonical Psalms. The word is also used without any further definition in Ephesians 5:19 and Colossians 3:16.

The use of word 'song' is used five times in the Revelation to refer to inspired songs (Rev. 5:9, 14:3 twice, 15:3 twice). The word is also used without any further definition in Ephesians 5:19 and Colossians 3:16.

Clearly these three word-groups are mostly used in the New Testament to refer to divinely inspired songs. In three or four places the words might refer to uninspired song, but in none of the cases is that clear or certain.

Third, the cases of 1 Corinthians 14 and Revelation 5, 14, 15 as songs inspired in the New Testament might imply the need for new songs to carry the meaning of the new covenant. But is that conclusion consistent with the character of the new covenant songs that we actually have in the New Testament? We know nothing of the content of the song in I Corinthians 14. By contrast we have the words of two inspired songs in Revelation 5 and 15. These two songs are the only poems in the New Testament explicitly called songs. The church at times has referred to some New Testament poems as songs, such as the song of Mary, the song of Zechariah, and the song of Simeon. But none of these poems are called songs in the Bible or are even likely to have been songs.

Perhaps the most notable feature of the two inspired songs that we have in the Revelation is that neither of them are distinctively new covenant in content. For example, neither names the name of Jesus, but rather uses Old Testament language such as lamb, blood, priest, and king. The 'new song' of Revelation 5:9 is not a phrase original to the New Testament, but is used in several Psalms (e.g., Ps. 98). The 'new song' is the song of redemption in distinction from the old song of creation. That is clear from the Psalms themselves, but is even clearer in the Revelation where the 'new song' of Revelation 5:9–10 is preceded by the old song of creation, Revelation 4:11.

Fourth, as we turn to Ephesians 5:19 and Colossians 3:16, we may ask if the context gives us any help in knowing more particularly the meaning of 'psalms, hymns, and spiritual songs' there. In Ephesians and Colossians Paul moves from his foundational doctrinal teaching (Eph. 1–3 and Col. 1–2) to his application of these truths to the lives of Christians. Some aspects of his application are closely parallel to one another, while others are somewhat diverse. While Paul uses the three terms together in both letters, he uses them in somewhat different ways.

In Ephesians 4:1 Paul calls Christians to *walk* worthy of their calling. He returns repeatedly to that theme (Eph. 4:17, 5:15). When he calls for careful walking—still implicitly contrasting such living with the life of Gentiles—he describes what that walk is in terms of contrasts: the Christian walks in wisdom, not in the folly of the Gentiles, the Christian redeems the time, not living in the evil of current days, the Christian is filled with the Holy Spirit, not being drunk and immoral. Next Paul seems to show how the Christian can pursue wisdom, redeeming the time, and being filled with the Holy Spirit, namely through psalms and hymns and spiritual songs. He is of course not speaking comprehensively of all the ways in which Christians walk, but is showing some of the ways for the Christian to live and grow.

Similarly, in Colossians 3:1 Paul calls on Christians, rather than to walk (although he does write of walking in Col. 1:10 and 2:6), to seek what is above in Christ. One way to seek things above is by letting the Word of Christ dwell in us richly through psalms and hymns and spiritual songs (Col. 3:16).

While the images of walking and seeking differ, the substance is very much to same: what it means to live for Jesus. As we seek to live for Jesus, Paul shows that psalms, hymns, and spiritual songs

127

will help. He shows their value in ways exactly parallel to what we have found in Psalm 105. The direction of song is to God in praise (Eph. 5:19, 20; Col. 3:16, 17)[34] and in petition (Eph. 6:18; Col. 4:3).[35] It is also directed to others (Eph. 5:19 and Col. 3:16).[36] It also speaks to our own heart (Eph. 5:17 and Col. 3:16).[37] So we see a remarkable agreement in the teaching of David, Paul, and Cotton on the value and blessing of psalm-singing.

John Cotton spoke for most in the Reformed churches in the seventeenth century when he wrote about the duty, the character, and the blessing of psalm-singing. Today some Reformed Christians seem to have forgotten their heritage and missed the blessing. Yet as we have looked at the Scriptures we have seen that Cotton's call to sing Psalms is not just an old-fashioned tradition or an ill-considered conviction. It is a strong position. Even those not persuaded by Cotton's case for exclusive psalmody, should be convinced that the singing of Psalms should be increased among us as a vital path to seeking the Lord and receiving His blessing.

---

34. Ephesians 5:19, 20: 'singing and making melody in your heart to the Lord, giving thanks always for all things to God the Father in the name of our Lord Jesus Christ ... .' Colossians 3:16, 17: 'singing with grace in your hearts to the Lord ... giving thanks to God the Father through Him' (NKJV).

35. Ephesians 6:18: 'praying always with all prayer and supplication for all the saints ... .' Col. 4:3: 'praying also for us ...' (NKJV).

36. Ephesians 5:19: 'speaking to one another ... .' Col. 3:16: 'teaching and admonishing one another ...' (NKJV).

37. Ephesians 5:17: 'understand what the will of God is.' Colossians 3:16: 'Let the word of Christ dwell in you richly in all wisdom ...' (NKJV).

CHAPTER EIGHT

John Owen and the Lord's Supper

SINCLAIR B. FERGUSON

THE works of John Owen (1616–1683) are more widely disseminated and read today than at any period since he first penned them. What has made him particularly attractive to modern readers—despite the challenges of his Latinate style—is his remarkable combination of Reformed theology and profound spirituality. On the one hand he was the author of powerful polemical books like *The Death of Death in the Death of Christ,* and of major works on the doctrine of the Trinity and the person of Christ. On the other hand, he gave detailed attention to spiritual psychology and to the cure of souls. He ranks among those to whom we rightly accord the titles, *theologicus pastorum* (theologian of pastors) and *pastor pastorum* (pastor of pastors).

In a variety of ways Owen gives the lie to various caricatures of the Puritan movement of which he was such a significant part. For one thing he dressed well; for another, he was involved in the great issues of his day in the body politic. He also gives the lie to a caricature sometimes drawn by scholars, namely that like other Puritans (but unlike Calvin) he had no interest in the sacraments except to polemicize concerning them (in an anti-Roman fashion).

But quite apart from the fact that the Puritans had a broader theological perspective than simply mimicking Calvin (they tended to refer to Augustine three or four times more frequently than to Calvin), in Owen's case the accusation is demonstrably false. In fact, he gave considerable attention to the significance of the Lord's Supper. But he did so largely within the context in which that is most essential—not in the schoolroom where the Supper was not celebrated, but in his instruction to his own congregations, where it *was*.

Here, while he does not follow Calvin in some of his unique formulations of how Christ is present to and received by the believer, he nevertheless provides a richness and depth of instruction that few congregations anywhere in the world today are likely to enjoy. Indeed, it could be said that we find something better in Owen than in Calvin, namely the brief addresses he gave to his congregation during the table service itself. To that extent his published work on the Lord's Supper not only provides theological formulations, but pastoral instruction that still has the power to nourish Christians today. It also, incidentally, provides ministers with an example of serving Christ and His people in their conduct of the Lord's Supper. This (so it seems to the present writer) is especially valuable in our contemporary evangelical subculture. For anyone looking for help in this area of church life, John Owen serves as a thoughtful and profoundly Christ-centred guide.

Owen published little on eucharistic theology during his lifetime. The bulk of his extant teaching comes from the closing period of his life when he ministered in London. His collected *Works* as a whole contain catechetical instruction, theological expositions, and pastoral teaching given at specific celebrations of the Supper. Here we will attempt to build up a picture of Owen's theology in that order.

Two Catechisms

One of Owen's earliest publications, *Two Short Catechisms wherein the Principles of the Doctrine of Christ are Unfolded and Explained* (1645),[1] was an expression of his concern for the spiritual well-being

---

1. John Owen, *The Works of John Owen,* ed. W. H. Goold (1850-55, reprinted Banner of Truth Trust, 1965-68; *Hebrews* 1991), 1:463–94.

of both the children and adults in his Stadhampton parish. Both catechisms contained instruction on the Lord's Supper.

Here he set down his earliest views of the theology of the Supper, although he wrote 'I have been sparing in the doctrine of the Sacraments, because I have already been so frequent in examinations about them.'[2] In his *Lesser Catechism*, intended for children, five of thirty-three questions touch on the Lord's Supper. It is one of six privileges enjoyed by believers and one of the two 'visible seals of God's spiritual promises, made unto us in the blood of Jesus Christ.' In *The Greater Catechism* he addressed the subject in yet greater detail:

Chap. XXIV. —OF THE LORD'S SUPPER

Q. 1. What is the Lord's supper?

A. An holy action instituted and appointed by Christ, to set forth his death, and communicate unto us spiritually his body and blood by faith, being represented by bread and wine, blessed by his word, and prayer, broken, poured out, and received of believers.

Q. 2. When did Christ appoint this sacrament?

A. On the night wherein he was betrayed to suffer.

Q. 3. Whence is the right use of it to be learned?

A. From the word, practice, and actions of our Saviour, at its institution.

Q. 4. What were the actions of our Saviour to be imitated by us?

A. First, blessing the elements by prayer; secondly, breaking the bread, and pouring out the wine; thirdly, distributing them to the receivers, sitting in a table-gesture.

Q. 5. What were the words of Christ?

A. First, of command, 'Take, eat'; secondly, of promise, 'This is my body'; thirdly, of institution for perpetual use, 'This do,' &c.

---

2. Owen, *Works*, 1:466.

Q. **6.** Who are to be receivers of this sacrament?

A. Those only have a true right to the signs who by faith have an holy interest in Christ, the thing signified.

Q. **7.** Do the elements remain bread and wine still, after the blessing of them?

A. Yes; all the spiritual change is wrought by the faith of the receiver, not the words of the giver: to them that believe, they are the body and blood of Christ.[3]

Owen was not yet thirty when he wrote these catechisms. It is no criticism of him to say that they do not have the rich depth and balance of his later exposition—this he himself recognized. For example, while he frames his comments on sacraments in general in terms of them being 'seals of the New Testament' and states that they are 'visible seals and pledges' by which 'God confirmeth the covenant' he omits any reference to this obsignation in his exposition of the Supper, and focusses only on communication and representation.[4]

A Morning Exercise

Fast forward to 1682. Now, within a few months of his death, we find Owen preaching one of the Morning Exercises at St Giles in the Fields, Cripplegate. His topic is polemical: 'How is the practical love of truth the best preservative against Popery?' His basic argument is that the best defence against error is the exposition of the truth. So, over against the Roman criticism that Protestants demeaned the Supper by denying the 'real' presence of Christ in it, Owen marks out his view in these confident terms: 'It is a *universal*, unimpeachable

---

3. Owen, *Works*, 1:491–92.

4. This said, his later statements place less emphasis on sealing than they do on other aspects of the Supper. But see Owen, *Works*, 9:575 for an example of his teaching on this theme. It is noticeable however that even in the later material, there is a lacuna in Owen's teaching—on proclaiming the Lord's death '*until he comes*' (1 Cor. 11:26). Given our present access to Owen's preaching we have no way of knowing whether such an emphasis was present on other occasions.

persuasion among all Christians, that there is a *near, intimate communion with Christ, and participation of him, in the supper of the Lord.* He is no Christian who is otherwise minded.'[5] Christ Himself is present to believers. And to the extent that this is true, the supper is 'the principle mystery in the *agenda* of the church.'[6]

There is then for Owen something unique to be experienced in the Lord's Supper, distinct from what is experienced in either prayer or preaching, namely, '*an eating and drinking of the body and blood of Christ,* with a spiritual *incorporation* thence ensuing.'[7] This, he stresses, is not carnal, but spiritual and mystical—as Christ's discourse on the bread of life makes clear (John 6). It is implicit that eating the flesh and drinking the blood of the Son of man (6:53) must be understood within the context of the limiting principle provided later in the same passage, namely that flesh cannot profit spiritually; only the Spirit can give life (6:63). What is in view then is a faith-communion with Christ that involves not the digestion of body and blood through the mouth but the 'actings' of faith.

'Acting faith' is not a common notion in contemporary evangelicalism where faith tends to be seen as either a decision of the will or as passively receptive rather than active. The former is the pitfall of Arminianism, the latter a distortion of Calvinism. By contrast, the Reformed idea of 'acting faith' involves the believer engaging the promises of the gospel and the person of Jesus Christ Himself. Thus, at the Lord's Table the believer does not sit passively, or mindlessly, but rather actively engages the following four dimensions of the Lord's Supper:

1: Obedience. We celebrate the supper in obedience to Christ, and so our coming to it is an act of explicit obedience to Him.

2: Representation. In the supper the love and grace of Christ in His sufferings and atoning death are represented in a visible

---

5. Owen, *Works,* 8:560. This sermon, 'The Chamber of Imagery in the Church of Rome Laid Open' was preached in October 1682.

6. Owen, *Works,* 8:560.

7. Owen, *Works,* 8:560.

way. While the words of Scripture set forth the gospel in large and discursive manner what is set before us visually here is the gospel in a specifically focused form. Christ is represented to our sight and engaged by us specifically *as crucified* (Gal. 3:1—a favorite text for Owen in this context).

3: Communication. Christ communicates with us and is communicated to us and received by us through the preaching of the word (to which Gal. 3:1 refers in the first instance). But in the Supper the communication is, as it were, made by means that appeal to the senses of sight, touch, smell, and taste as well as hearing. Here the wisdom and sovereignty of Christ come into view. If the method of communication were, for example, an image or a crucifix that obviously portrayed Christ there would have been a *natural* connection between the sign and what it signified and we could easily be deceived into thinking that sight alone could make this connection. But here it requires the activity of faith to grasp the sacramental union, and enjoy authentic participation in Christ.

4: Exhibition. The bread and wine do not *contain* the body and blood of Christ. Nevertheless, Owen argues, they *exhibit* Christ to those who believe, so that they may receive *Him* as they receive *them* in active faith.

Owen's summary here is, of course, set specifically within an apologetic-polemical context. In the face of the century-and-a-half old canard that the rejection of transubstantiation implied the denial of the 'real' presence of Christ at the Supper, Owen argues that Rome is guilty of turning the spiritual into the carnal. She has substituted a physical, localised 'Host'—the body and the blood of Christ enclosed in the bread and wine—for the dynamic presence of the true personal Host, Jesus Christ. He is exalted at the right hand of God, but is also present with and communicates Himself to His people in the power of the Holy Spirit. Here, towards the close of his ministry (Owen would die within a few months of preaching this sermon), he was simply summarizing a eucharistic theology which he had taught virtually from the beginning of his ministry.

It is, however, from sermons Owen later preached in London that we learn most about his mature understanding of the Supper.

Posthumous Sermons

We owe a great deal to Sir John Hartopp (1637–1722), a member of Owen's congregation in London and transcriber of Owen's sermons, without whose Christian diligence we would have a very impoverished sense of how experientially and pastorally important the Lord's Supper was to him. The eucharistic sermons were posthumously published under the direction of Revd Richard Winter.

The transcripts are clearly the work of an eye (or better, ear) witness. Neither Sir John Hartopp nor Richard Winter made any attempt to edit out of the text the spoken form. Here, then, we come closest to the 'real' John Owen, his *vox vivens* and *ipsissima verba*.[8] Thus for example despite a time gap, he will refer to, or even continue, a previous Table address—even, on one occasion, when almost two months had intervened![9] Reading them one can almost see the good Doctor quietly instructing his little flock. There is often an unusual simplicity and directness here. There is also, at the Table service, a brevity that bespeaks his pastoral concern that if communicants are to 'act faith,' they cannot afford that their minds should be empty; but by the same token, if they are to benefit from the Supper their minds should not be overburdened to the point where they cannot see that the whole drama is focused on and is about Jesus Christ Himself.

Spanning the period between October 1669 and September 1682, these sermons afford a remarkable insight into Owen the pastor-teacher. Here we find him employing 'I-thou' and 'we' forms of address. He is speaking to people he knows and loves, conscious of

---

8. See, for example, the tenor of Owen's second 'use' in Discourse IV, Owen, *Works*, 9:544, or his words when speaking on self-examination: 'Friends, let us not be afraid of calling ourselves to a strict account' (p. 562).

9. Discourse XVI in Owen, *Works*, 9:594. This message was preached on October 31, 1675 and continued his exposition of John 12:32 on September 5 of the same year. In Discourse III he refers to Discourse II and so on.

the fact that their spiritual journeys and levels of spiritual maturity differ greatly.[10] He is not embarrassed to state that he wants to address those whose understanding of the Lord's Supper is only at the beginning stages. At the same time, there must have been moments in these 'familiar exercises' (his favored way of describing them[11]) when only the most seasoned believers would have followed him with ease—not that his vocabulary is abstruse, but he leads them into the deep things of God. Yet what is so impressive is the way in which his conviction that the whole counsel of God is for the blessing of the whole church of Christ comes to expression in his week-by-week pastoral preaching.

It seems to have been the standard view of the Independents that the Lord's Supper should be celebrated every week. Owen's view tends in that direction. In *A Brief Instruction in the Worship and Discipline of the Churches of the New Testament* (1667), which came to be known as *The Independents' Catechism* he wrote: 'How often is that ordinance [the Lord's Supper] to be administered' in broader terms: 'Every first day of the week, or at least as often as opportunity and conveniency may be obtained. —1 Cor. xi.26; Acts xx.7.'[12] The evidence seems to suggest however that, for whatever reason, weekly communion was not Owen's consistent practice.[13] On occasion his comments make clear that an interval of time has passed since he had previously addressed the congregation at the Lord's Table.

---

10. Cf. Owen, *Works*, 9:569–71, 615.

11. Owen, *Works*, 16:554. The adjective is perhaps more significant from a Latin thinker (as Owen was) than it might seem to us today: our word 'familiar' is derived from the same Latin root as 'family' For Owen, the Supper is the family meal of the children of God.

12. Owen, *Works*, 15:512, emphasis added.

13. Horton Davies states 'There is, however, complete unanimity amongst the English Independents in the weekly celebration.' It is however a question whether this is demonstrable, or indeed whether *The Apologetical Narration* which he cites, states it quite as baldly as this (infant baptism and the Supper are conjoined in its statement, and it is unlikely that *infant baptism* was administered *weekly* in these relatively smaller congregations). *The Worship of the English Puritans* (1948; repr., Morgan, PA: Soli Deo Gloria, 1997), pp. 206–207.

Another fascinating detail emerges from the fact that almost all Hartopp's transcriptions of Owen's sacramental discourses are specifically dated. In terms of substance the sermons divide into two categories: (i) A series of earlier sermons provides instruction on the doctrine of the Lord's Supper. (ii) Most of the later sermons serve to guide and enhance the experience of coming to the Supper. The original full title of the posthumous sermons suggests that these were all 'table sermons' and were therefore preceded by a longer sermon suited to the occasion. The brevity of the later ones also suggests this,[14] and in addition, on occasion Owen seems specifically to refer to something preached earlier in the service, whether by himself or another minister.[15]

However, two features of the sermons suggest that the wording of the original title (Delivered just before the administration …) was not applicable to all of them in the same way. The first is that Discourses II to VI in this collection are markedly longer than Discourses VII to XXV. Whereas the former must have extended to thirty to forty minutes, the latter were perhaps only ten minutes or so in length. In Owen's view, the Lord's Supper is designed to help us—whose minds are easily distracted—to 'fix' them on Jesus Christ by giving us an 'especial and peculiar communion with Christ in his body and blood.'[16] However, he believed this was poorly understood.

This may well explain a second feature of this collection. Discourses II to VI constitute a connected series of fortnightly

---

14. Thus, Owen can speak of 'a few words to prepare us for this ordinance.' Owen, *Works*, 16:560, 566, 592, 594.

15. See Owen, *Works*, 15:606: 'You have been minded of, and instructed in, the nature and benefit of our love to God.' Cf. *Works*, 16:609. The previous week a day of solemn fasting and prayer had been observed, and Owen had preached to the congregation on 2 Timothy 3:1, but it seems highly unlikely that it is to this sermon that he alludes when he says that they have already received 'so good and so seasonable a word unto the present occasion.… What you have heard may very well occasion us to think of that passage of the apostle … Ephesians iii.19,—'And to know the love of Christ which passeth knowledge'—since there seems to be no obvious connection between either the two texts or the two messages.

16. Owen, *Works*, 9:523.

addresses which Owen gave during an eight-week period between November 26, 1669 and January 21, 1670. In these five addresses he set out for his congregation a miniature eucharistic theology clearly designed to help them understand the doctrine of the Supper and to receive it with spiritual profit.

This five-part series was preached *prior to* the union in 1673 between Owen's congregation and that pastored by Joseph Caryl (1602–1673). Discourses VII to XXV were therefore delivered to a much larger congregation.[17] But, of greater interest, is something that (at least to the present writer's knowledge) seems to have gone unnoticed. *According to their dating these sacramental messages were not preached at communion services on the Lord's Day.* Each carries a mid-week date—and in every case, according to the Julian Calendar still in use in the United Kingdom during that period, the addresses were given on a Friday.[18] No internal explanation is given for this. But since all the messages in the series consistently carry a Friday date, it seems unlikely that the dates are in error. In addition, we know that Owen's congregation did gather on occasion on weekdays as well as on the Lord's Day.[19] This helps to explain why, consistently, these sermons are twice the length of the others. They are not 'Table Sermons.' This surmise seems to be confirmed by the fact that by the time the congregation was meeting in Bury Street, it had developed a tradition of gathering on the Friday prior to each celebration of the Lord's Supper, 'to spend an hour or two' for preaching and prayer.[20] So, what we have

17. At the time of the union, Owen's congregation had only thirty-five members plus himself; Caryl's congregation consisted of 136. See T. G. Crippen, 'Dr Watts's Church Book,' *Transactions of the Congregational Historical Society*, I (April 1901), 27–29. During Owen's ministry a further 111 people became members of the united congregation.

18. The transition from the Julian Calendar to the Gregorian Calendar did not take place in the United Kingdom until 1752.

19. A survey of the dates of the church meetings at which Owen handled various cases of conscience indicates that the congregation gathered on a variety of different days of the week. See *Works*, 9:358–405.

20. See 'From the Bury Street Church Records' in *Transactions of the Congregational Historical Society*, vol. vi (April 1915), 334-336. The Church Book

here, despite the original sub-title under which the sermons were published, are examples of instruction given on such preparatory occasions, while most of the other addresses were delivered immediately before the congregation received the bread and the wine at the Lord's Supper itself, and probably at the Table itself.

What then are, the salient points in Owen's pastoral theology of the Lord's Supper?

A Pastoral Theology of the Lord's Supper

The Supper was given to help 'fix' our faith on Jesus Christ. In view here (for Owen) is not the object of *fides generalis* (the veracity of God) or for that matter *fides specialis* as such (Christ as Savior of sinners), but specifically the humanity of Christ, particularly seen as His body and blood separated, the former bruised and the latter shed for the remission of sins.

Owen is here crafting lenses for the believer to penetrate to the heart of the gospel as Christ, understood according to Scripture, is portrayed visually and presents Himself to us. For example, now he pauses to say: 'Look at the violent death of Christ and consider its causes.'

The Death of Christ

Here Owen predictably employs Aristotelian categories. But these are only catalysts to aid understanding—they do not in any way affect the substance of his teaching. For, in essence he is saying:

See that the atoning death of Christ thus represented visually—

Is rooted in the love of God (moving cause);

Is necessary for our salvation because of our sin (procuring cause);

Reveals the righteousness of God (the efficient cause);

---

also records the use of the traditional Independent practice of praying before the distribution of the bread and then again before the distribution of the wine, 'which is done in a short prayer of eight to ten minutes.' *Tempora mutantur, nos et mutamur in illis!*

Expresses the condemnation of the law of God (the instrumental cause);

Displays the wickedness of men (the adjuvant cause).

Thus—

Faith grasps that the end of Christ's atoning death is the glory of God (final cause).[21]

In this way the covenant of grace is confirmed to us, and our faith is strengthened.

Just at this point Owen seems to press a pause button. What is the *existential importance* of this analysis of the *theology* of the Supper? He gives us an indication of exactly *how* it functions:

> We are not able to take this great mysterious fruit of God's love in gross, in the lump; and therefore he gives it out, I say, in parcels. We shall have the body broken to be considered; and the blood shed is likewise to be considered. This is the peculiar communion which we have with Christ in this ordinance; because there are peculiar objects for faith to act itself upon in this ordinance above others.[22]

Participation in the Supper

What then characterizes the congregation's participation in the Supper? It is a *commemoration*, for in it we call to mind the Savior's sacrifice; it involves a *proclamation* ('profession' is Owen's term) since in it we show forth the death of Christ. It is also a *benediction* (Owen's word is 'eucharistical') since in it we receive the cup of blessing and for it we give thanks; and it involves a covenant *consecration*, since at the Table God confirms or seals His covenant to us while we in turn seal our consecration to Him.

The effect of all this is to cause us to be thankful for the church of Christ and for the treasure He has given to her. Furthermore, since we have been commanded to observe the Supper, as we do so

---

21. Owen, *Works*, 9:525–26.
22. Owen, *Works*, 9:527.

we consciously yield to the authority of Christ. And as we regularly meditate on the significance of the Supper and frequently receive it we will discover that by and through it our faith becomes strong and stable.

On this basic outline, Owen builds in several ways. Having crafted lenses for us to see the significance of the Supper clearly, he now, as it were, provides us with a microscope through which to see greater detail.

The Supper helps us to 'fix' the gaze of faith on the person of Jesus Christ as Mediator of the new covenant. What are we to see and how is faith to act? What does it mean to 'remember His death' and to find in the Supper a 'representation of His love'?

Acting Faith

The exercise of faith at the Supper is first to 'call over' three things:

(i) *The faith of Jesus Christ in the face of His own death*. His goal was to deliver the elect from death, hell, Satan and sin; to do so He had to answer the accusations of the law, and undergo the curse of God to bring His children to glory—all this plus the implacable opposition He experienced. But, Owen asks, did Christ not experience despair on the cross and express it in His cry of dereliction? He answers: 'Give me leave to say, Jesus Christ saw more into the nature of the curse of God for sin than all the damned in hell are able to see; which caused a dreadful conflict in his human soul upon that prospect.'[23]

Here Owen stresses the reality of the humanity of Christ, and the extremity of the sufferings He endured—all under the hand of the Lord. In all this Jesus Christ exercised constant faith. It is on this that he wants us to focus, while at the same time notes 'I know little of what I say.'[24]

(ii) *The obedience of Christ in His death*. Here Christ's love for us is set on display. If that love was not conquered by death then nothing can withstand His determination to love us to the end.

---

23. Owen, *Works*, 9:533.
24. Owen, *Works*, 9:534.

And in this obedience to death there was complete willingness on Christ's part as well as perfect submission to the person and will of God, expressed in the perfect patience with which He endured the Cross.

(iii) *The death of Christ itself.* What did Christ do in order to save us? He became a bloody sacrifice; He experienced the shame and humiliation as well as the physical pain of crucifixion; He tasted the bitterness of a penal death.

All this needs to be seen when we hear the words 'Do this *in remembrance of me.*' Owen poignantly notes, 'These are the words we would use unto a friend, when we give him a token or pledge, "Remember me." What is the meaning of it? "Remember my love to you, my kindness for you; remember my person." There is a remembrance of love to be acted in this ordinance, as well as a remembrance of faith.'[25]

Thus, during the Supper, *acted faith* receives the benefits that flow from Christ; meanwhile *the believer's love* receives the Christ who brings with Him all the benefits.[26] The result is threefold. As recipients of the Supper we delight in Christ as one does in thinking of an absent friend—except the Lord Jesus is present! We find our hearts being filled with thanksgiving and thus 'bless' the cup of blessing. And as a result, our hearts are inclined to be obedient to the Lord's word—for those who love Him keep His commandments.[27] There is thus a mutual sealing of the new covenant in Christ.

Representing the Lord's Death

Along with this the Lord's Supper is a *representation* (or setting forth) of the Lord's death. It is set before us in a fivefold manner.

---

25. Owen, *Works*, 9:537. Despite his reputation for exhaustiveness in his treatment of a subject, Owen was well-schooled in the multi-dimensional nature of true rhetoric encapsulated by Aristotle in terms not only of *logos* and *ethos,* but also of the use of *pathos* as in the illustration he uses here.

26. Owen, *Works*, 9:537.

27. John 14:15, 21; 15:10.

He is set forth: by God (Rom. 3:25); in His passion; in terms of His promises; so that He may be received; and in terms of our incorporation into Christ.[28]It is also a *profession* of Christ. It involves a *consecration*, negatively to abstain from everything Christ has not appointed, and positively to observe all He has commanded us. The Christian accepts the shame of the gospel knowing that Christ's death brings life. Christians together show forth the Lord's death believing that all that can be charged against them has been charged against Him. Thus, the church testifies to Satan himself that he has been defeated.

Preparation for the Supper

Since this is the significance of the Supper, Owen held that preparation was an integral part of its celebration. This (as he makes clear) is true of all our spiritual duties,[29] and is shaped by (i) the fact that we are coming into the presence of a holy God through them, with His glory in view; (ii) that we need to recognize not only our distance from God as creatures but also our natural alienation from Him as sinners; and (iii) the particular ordinance in which we engage. Here we need to be convinced that God Himself has appointed it (lest we be guilty of false worship) and must also learn how to engage in it in a manner appropriate to it.

These, however, are simply general rules. How do they apply to the Lord's Supper?[30] Owen gives wise practical counsel about such matters as the most suitable time to engage in such preparation; but his chief focus is on answering the important 'How?' question.

---

28. In Hartopp's transcription here Owen appears to refer to the substance of his previous Friday exposition in this series in these words, 'This with all the concerns of it, I treated of *the last Lord's Day*, under the head of Recognition, or calling over the death of Christ … and so I shall not again insist upon it' (*Works*, 9:541, emphasis added). But the earlier extant exposition in which Owen discussed 'recognition' was given two weeks earlier on a Friday, not a Sunday. It is possible, therefore, that he had developed this during his preaching on the Lord's Day following.

29. Owen, *Works*, 9:544–53.

30. Owen, *Works*, 9:554–63.

Here he gives four practical pointers based on Zechariah 12:10, a text that epitomizes for him all that needs to be said: 'And I will pour on the house of David and on the inhabitants of Jerusalem the Spirit of grace and supplication; then they will look on Me whom they pierced. Yes, they will mourn for Him as one mourns for his only son, and grieve for Him as one grieves for a firstborn' (NKJV).

At the supper there is *meditation*—on the nature of our sin and the purity and holiness of God. In the light of these His infinite wisdom and love displayed at the cross shine brightly as we see them in Christ Jesus and experience the peace which is the goal God has in view for us. Owen is wise enough to caution that we could easily be overwhelmed by the riches of this text—use them 'singly in the duty' is his counsel. And focus on whatever aspect of the gospel is especially relevant to your present spiritual condition.[31]

There is also *self-examination*: Are we coming to the Table mourning for our sins? Are we conscious of specific sins? Have we grieved the Lord by forgetting the blessings we received last time we were at the Table? At the same time, is our faith real or hypocritical?

And then there needs to be both *supplication* 'which may inlay and digest all the rest in the soul,'[32] and a real *expectation* that God will meet with us in the ordinance He Himself has appointed.

All this could easily lead to an overwhelming sense of failure! If we are thus tempted, then, 'Let us admire the infinite patience of God, that hath borne with us all this while—that he hath not cast us out of his house.'[33]

With Owen at the Table

In these congregational fellowship meetings at which Owen expounded his eucharistic theology, and as we hear him give briefer communion addresses, we meet him as the pastor of a

---

31. Owen, *Works*, 9:560
32. Owen, *Works*, 9:562.
33. Owen, *Works*, 9:563.

congregation of perhaps two hundred members, with presumably children and visitors in attendance. In our mind's eye we can imagine ourselves seated in front of him as he stands behind a simple table, explaining the significance of the meal that has been prepared. His concern now is to help all sorts and conditions of Christians to experience that 'near, intimate communion with Christ, and participation of him' and that 'eating and drinking of the body and blood of Christ, with a spiritual incorporation thence ensuing'[34] which he believed was of the essence of the Supper.

To facilitate this, Owen leads us in a brief meditation on the person and work of Christ.[35] Preparation and self-examination both have their place. But they are preparatory; Christ Himself is the Supper. In the preaching of the gospel that preceded earlier in the service, the Father offered Christ to us. But now, at the Table, it is the Lord Jesus who offers Himself to us. Now the personal pronouns are first person singular: 'This is *my* body …. do this in remembrance of *me*.' The congregation has gathered to Christ. Since He is all-sufficient to save all who come to God through Him, the Doctor is now shining the spotlight of God's word on the fulness of Christ's grace. Thus (for example) he draws our attention to 1 Peter 3:18: Christ suffered for our sins, the just for the unjust, to bring us to God. A sense of awe and wonder falls on us as he says, his voice filled with deep *pathos*: 'He tells *you*, Is. liii.6, "all we like sheep have gone astray … the Lord hath made the iniquity of *us* all to meet on him." … "Be it so; all their iniquities be upon thee." "All the iniquities *of this congregation*," saith God, "be upon my Son Jesus Christ."'[36]

Again, we feel the same *pathos* as he comments on Isaiah 53:11 ('He shall see of the travail of his soul, and shall be satisfied').

It was a great work that Christ had to do. It is usually said 'We are not saved as the world was made, —*by a word*,' but there was *travail* in it: it is the word whereby the bringing forth of children

---

34. Owen, *Works*, 8:560.

35. What follows coalesces various comments to be found in the posthumous communion addresses.

36. Owen, *Works*, 9:567, emphasis added.

into the world is expressed, —the travail of a woman. And there are three things in that travail: —an *agony of mind, outcrying for help.* And *sense of pain*: all these things were in the travail of the soul of Christ. I will name the Scriptures, to call them to your remembrance:—

Now he mentions Christ's agony in Gethsemane (Luke 22:44), the strong crying with tears referred to in Hebrews (Heb. 5:7) and the pains of hell that took hold of Him (Ps. 116:3).

Yet again, he speaks about being conformed to Christ crucified and risen through union with Him (Phil. 3:10). This implies that we will suffer for Christ, in the strength of Christ, in imitation of Him, and for His glory. But it is also a call to mortify sin. Where can we find the motivation and enabling to do this? 'There is,' Dr Owen answers:

> no such sermon to teach *mortification of sin*, as the commemoration of the death of Christ. It is the greatest outward instruction unto this duty that God hath left unto his church. ... Do we see Christ evidently crucified before our eyes, his body broken, his blood shed for sin? And is it not of powerful instruction to us to go on to mortify sin? He that hath not learned this, never learned any thing aright from this ordinance, nor did he receive any benefit from it.[37]

Again and again he consistently points us to the Lord Jesus, to His sufferings for us, and especially to the way in which these were undergone out of unmerited love for us as sinners.

For this our Savior was willing to experience divine desertion. This was not the forsaking of His human nature by His divine nature or by the Spirit. But he only briefly guards us against heresy. Now he goes on to say:

> But the desertion was to *all influence of comfort* and *all evidence* of love from God the Father (who is the fountain of love and comfort), administered by the Holy Ghost. Hence some of our divines have not spared to say, that Christ did *despair* in that great cry, 'My God, my God,' etc. Now, *despair* signifies two things:—a

---

37. Owen, *Works*, 9:581–82.

total want of the evidence of faith as to acceptance with God; and *a resolution in the soul to seek no farther after it,* and not to wait for it from that fountain. In the first way Christ *did despair,* that is *penal only;* in the latter he *did not,* —that is *sinful also.* There was a total interception of love from God, but *not a ceasing* in him to wait upon God, for the manifestation of that love in his appointed time. Remember, Christ was thus forsaken that his people might never be forsaken.[38]

Thus we are brought to Christ.

Concluding Lessons

Owen handles other texts, and illumines other aspects of the work of Christ. Space forbids their exploration here. But we ought not to leave off eavesdropping on these services from almost three hundred and fifty years ago without asking if there are lessons we can learn from Owen for today. Several stand out clearly and are particularly relevant to those who have a special responsibility for the administration of the Lord's Supper. They can be enumerated briefly here:

1. Owen did not make the mistake of thinking that Christians have an intuitive understanding of the Lord's Supper. The truth is we may have an intuitive *misunderstanding* with everything else in the Christian life. We need to be given instruction from Scripture to help us to understand and enjoy the Supper. Assuming the accuracy of the specific dates on which Owen instructed his congregation, he had the pastoral wisdom to realize that much of this can and should be given outside of the immediate context of the actual administration of the Supper. In this way he, as it were, deposited resources into the account of his fellow believers on which they could draw as they remembered Christ in the actual event of participating in the Supper.

2. Owen was perfectly capable of engaging in polemics about the Supper (and did so engage). But his chief focus was not

---

38. Owen, *Works,* 9:587.

negative and polemical but positive and pastoral. God's sheep are not fed by their shepherd's ability to fight wolves, necessary although that may be, but by the way He leads them to pasture. In these addresses in preparation for, or given at, the Lord's Table, he is focused on Christ, on His character and His work as our Savior, and on His true presence with us as the Host who invites us to Himself.

3. Owen illustrates the way in which the ministry of the word and sacraments constitute one ministry because the preached word and the administered sacrament belong together to proclaim Christ crucified. The regular celebration of the Supper enabled him to help members of his congregation to focus their minds and allow their affections to linger on specific aspects of the person and work of Christ. Thus, their appreciation of His love would grow the more fully they came to reflect on the multi-dimensional and multi-valent character of His atoning work. In this way he makes it clear that the kind of frequent celebration of the Supper which he and his fellow Congregationalists commended (as did Knox and Calvin before them) did not render it commonplace. In fact, it created a greater appreciation of Christ *as crucified* and by its specific focus enabled a fuller and richer appreciation of His work of atonement (which is not the immediate theme of every passage of Scripture expounded during the services of the Lord's Day). This in turn aided believers to live in the consciousness of the love of the Christ who was crucified for them.

4. In a way far beyond any intention on his part—since he was addressing only his own congregation and had no plans to publish these sermons—Owen shows us how much can be taught about Christ little by little at the regular celebration of the Lord's Supper. It has been a great loss in the lives of many churches that enough time has not been given to the Table service; it is also a great loss when ministers do no more at the Table than read through the basic warrant for the Supper. Here above all places believers should have the opportunity to linger

long enough to be able to say, 'He brought me to the banqueting house, and his banner over me was love' (Song 2:4 NKJV).

5. Owen certainly believed in the importance of church discipline.[39] But his focus at the Table was not the exercise of discipline but the invitation in the Supper to receive, trust, know, to more fully understand and to reciprocate the love of Jesus Christ for His people. While he was never slow to speak of sin, his focus was not on the sin that might bar us from coming to, or receiving from, the Table, but on the One who died for and now welcomes sinners.

6. Whatever else a minister says about his own service, he *must* be able to tell his people that they are a congregation 'before whose eyes Jesus Christ was clearly portrayed among you as crucified' both in word and in sacrament.

In a sermon preached on Sunday July 6, 1673, a month after the union between the 'house church' he led and the more substantial Leadenhall Street fellowship, Owen very simply explained the mystery of the Lord's Supper. No doubt some of the members of this new united fellowship would often recall at other celebrations of the Lord's Supper the picture he painted that day. 'In this ordinance' he told them, there is a 'special exhibition or tender of Jesus Christ.'

> Here—
>> The Christ who presented Himself to God
>> on the Cross of Calvary as a sacrifice for our sins,
> and
>> Has presented Himself in heaven
>> to intercede for all for whom He atoned,
> now
>> presents Himself to us in the Supper,
>> as the One who has blotted out our sins.[40]

---

39. His two questions on the Lord's Supper in *A Brief Instruction in the Worship of God* are followed by fifteen pages on church discipline. See Owen, *Works*, 15:512–17.

40. Owen, *Works*, 16:529.

Thus, 'We say, we have in these things *experience of a peculiar communion* with Christ, in a way made proper in this ordinance, which is not to be found in any other ordinance.'[41]

Knowing this, the church of Jesus Christ continues to keep the feast. For Christ our Passover Lamb has been sacrificed for us, and now at the Table He gives Himself to us.

In dedicating these reflections to Joel Beeke I would also like to express my gratitude to God for his life and ministry, for his contributions to Owen scholarship, for his pastoral concern that the congregations he has served should enjoy the privilege of Christ's invitation to trust in Him and to feed on Him and drink from Him at the Lord's Table, and to acknowledge the privileges of the more than thirty years of friendship in Christ we have enjoyed.

---

41. Owen, *Works*, 16:622.

CHAPTER NINE

Principles and Practice for the Household: Thomas Gouge's Catechesis 'with Practical Applications' (1679)

RICHARD A. MULLER

O
NE of the most significant characteristics of seventeenth-century Reformed thought was its sense of the positive relationship between theological orthodoxy and practical piety, as evidenced in its consistent emphasis on the intimate relationship between faith and practice, doctrine and life. Thomas Gouge's *Principles of Christian Religion* (1679) illustrates this balance in its model of basic catechesis, doctrinal explanation, and practical application, in basic continuity with the Westminster catechisms, but adapted, in the decades following the Ejection of 1662, for use in the home under the direction of the head of the household.

Thomas Gouge (1605–1681), eldest son of the Puritan theologian William Gouge (1578–1653), was recognized in his own time as a highly significant author of works in Christian instruction and spirituality.[1] He was educated at Eton and at King's College,

---

1. See the accounts of his life in John Tillotson, *A Sermon Preached at the Funeral of the Reverend Mr Thomas Gouge, the 4th of Novemb. 1681 at S.*

Cambridge, beginning in 1626. He was elected a fellow of the college in 1628. Upon completion of his degrees, he served for close to three years in the parish of Coulsden in Surrey. Beginning in 1638, served as vicar of the parish of St Sepulchre in London, a position he held until the Act of Uniformity in 1662. Gouge's refusal to use the 1662 version of the Book of Common Prayer is also noted in the diary of Samuel Pepys.[2] Following his departure from St Sepulchre, he preached extensively in Wales, under license, as John Tillotson, then Dean of Canterbury, put it, 'from some of the Bishops.'[3]

His *Christian Directions, Shewing How to Walk with God All the Day Long*, first published in 1661, saw a second printing in the same year, a much expanded second edition in 1664, an abridgement in 1672, and further editions in 1674, 1675, 1679, 1680, 1684, 1690, 1729, 1730, 1734, 1742, 1752. A catechism entitled *The Principles of Christian Religion*, published anonymously but often attributed to Gouge, was published in 1645. Although the title is the same, Gouge's catechism of 1668 is an entirely different text. This latter work proved enormously popular, seeing further editions in 1670, 1672, 1673, 1674, 1675, 1679, 1680, 1684. Other works by Gouge, all related to issues in the spiritual life of Christians, are *Joshua's Resolution, or, the Private Christian's Duty in Times of Publick Corruption* (1663); *A Word to Sinners, and a Word to Saints* (1668, 1672, 1674, 1676, 1678, 1680, 1683, 1691, 1712,

---

Anne's Blackfriars with a brief account of his life (London: M.F. for Brabazon Aylmer, and William Rogers, 1682); Edmund Calamy, *an Abridgement of Mr Baxter's History of His Life and Times. With an account of the ministers, &c. who were ejected after the Restauration, of King Charles II*, 2nd ed., 2 vols. (London: for John Lawrence, et al., 1713), 1:8–11; also in idem, *the Nonconformist's Memorial: Being an Account of the Ministers, Who Were Ejected or Silenced after the Restoration, Particularly by the Act of Uniformity, Which Took Place on Bartholomew-Day, Aug. 24, 1662. Containing a Concise View of Their Lives and Characters, Their Principles, Sufferings, and Printed Works* (London: for J. Harris, 1777), 1:144–48.

2. Samuel Pepys, *Diary and Correspondence of Samuel Pepys, F. R. S. Secretary to the Admiralty in the Reigns of Charles II and James II.* Deciphered by J. Smith, with a life and noted by Richard Lord Braybrooke, 4 vols. (Philadelphia Lippincott, 1855), 1:310.

3. Tillotson, *Sermon*, p. 82.

1718), *The Young Man's Guide through the Wilderness of This World* (1670, 1672, 1676, 1680, 1696, 1713, 1719, 1734, 1752, 1792), *The Surest and Safest Way of Thriving* (1673, 1709, 1734), *God's Call to England for Thankfulness after Gracious Deliverances* (1680, 1720); *A Sermon on Good Works* (1734), and *The Christian Householder* (1787) a pamphlet abstracted from the 1679 edition of Gouge's *Principles*. A complete *Works* appeared in 1706 and again in 1815.[4]

Gouge's work reflects the strong catechetical interests of his times, both in its form and in its content, including the interest, after the Ejection of 1662, to maintain the Westminster catechetical tradition,[5] albeit in forms not overtly antagonistic to the authorities and in accord with his licensed task of preaching 'among the poor People, who were the more likely to regard his instructions, being recommended by his great charity.'[6] Again, Tillotson: rather than pressing the issue of conformity, Gouge 'thought he might doe as much or more good in another way which could give not offence.'[7]

Gouge's *Principles* was the product of a great era of catechetical instruction. In addition to the major catechisms used in the era, such as the Heidelberg Catechism and the two catechisms produced by the Westminster Assembly, there was a host of other catechetical exercises, often written by individual clergy for use in their own congregations or, particularly after 1662, by pastors and theologians for the sake of lay or household instruction, maintaining the instruction in doctrine and practice after the Ejection.[8] Many of these catechisms, moreover, were designed to move from a most basic Christian education to a somewhat more detailed level. Some,

---

4. *The Works of the Late Reverend and Pious Mr Tho. Gouge* (London: Tho. Braddyll, 1706). Also, *The Works of the Late Reverend and Pious Mr Thomas Gouge, in Six Parts* (Albany: George Lindsay, 1815).

5. Cf. Ian M. Green, *The Christian's ABC: Catechisms and Catechizing in England, c. 1530–1740* (Oxford: Clarendon Press, 1996), pp. 83 n169, 214–15.

6. Tillotson, *Sermon*, p. 83.

7. Tillotson, *Sermon*, p. 82.

8. See Green, *Christian's ABC*, pp. 187, 222, 227, et passim; also see Alexander F. Mitchell, *Catechisms of the Second Reformation ... with Historical Introduction and Biographical Notices* (London: James Nisbet, 1886).

as in the case of the pairs of catechisms written by John Owen (1616–1683) and John Flavel (1628–1691), by offering two distinct catechisms, one shorter for basic instruction and one longer and more elaborative, much after the model of the two Westminster catechisms. Flavel chose to use the Westminster Shorter Catechism as the basis for his elaboration, yielding a second level of instruction more detailed than the basic Westminster model but less than the Larger Catechism.[9] Others, as in the case of the catechisms written by Gisbertus Voetius (1589–1676), Joseph Alleine (1634–1668), and Thomas Vincent (1634–1678), the latter two also building on the Westminster Shorter Catechism, provide two levels of explanation in a single flow of catechetical instruction, employing the fairly simply model of adding subordinate questions and answers under each of the primary questions and answers.[10]

Like these contemporaries, Thomas Gouge saw the need to add further levels of instruction to a basic catechism and, like Voetius, he wrote the basic catechism himself.[11] Gouge, however,

---

9. Cf. John Owen, *The Principles of the Doctrine of Christ: Unfolded in Two Short Catechismes, Wherein Those Principles of Religion Are Explained, the Knowledge Whereof Is Required by the Late Ordinance of Parliament, Before Any Person Bee Admitted to the Sacrament of the Lords Supper* (London: R. Cotes, for Philemon Stephens, 1645); John Flavel, *An Exposition of the Assembly's Catechism, with Practical Inferences from Each Question* (London: for Tho. Cockerill, 1692).

10. Gisbertus Voetius, Catechesatie over den Heidelbergschen Catechismus, ed. Abraham Kuyper, from the 1662 edition of Poudroyen, 2 vols. (Rotterdam: Huge, 1891); Thomas Vincent, An Explicatory Catechism, of an Explanation of the Assemblies Shorter Catechism (London: George Calvert, 1673); Joseph Alleine [Allaine], A Most Familiar Explanation of the Assemblies Shorter Catechism (London: for Edward Brewster, 1674).

11. Thomas Gouge, *The Principles of Christian Religion Explained to the Capacity of the Meanest. With Practical Applications to Each Head* (London: Thomas James for Thomas Parkhurst, 1679). Note there are multiple paginations in the volume: prefatory materials are foliated in two main groups, the first indicated by an italicized *A* on the recto followed by a number; the second indicated by a Roman 'A' on the recto followed by a number; these are followed by three separately numbered paginations, herein noted as first, second, and third paginations in the footnotes by a bracketed number, e.g., [1], set prior to the page number.

proposed a somewhat different approach in his development of the catechesis, which was very much attuned to his work in Wales. There, as Tillotson commented, Gouge had 'two excellent designs. One, to have poor children brought up to reade and write, and to be carefully instructed in the principles of Religion: The other, to furnish persons of grown age, the poor especially, with the necessary helps and means of knowledge, as the Bible, and other Books of piety and devotion, in their own Language.'[12]

These goals are reflected in Gouge's catechetical work, the point of its three-fold structure being made clear in the title of the work itself. After his preface to families and heads of households, Gouge presents a basic catechism in eighty-five questions and answers, accommodated 'to the capacity of the meanest' or least-learned audience.[13] Following this basic catechism, he provides a foundational statement of six 'principles' drawn from the catechism on which the entire work rests. These principles, he indicates, are so simple and basic that even the 'grossly ignorant' or persons of 'weak memories' or the utterly illiterate can master them.[14] Following the six principles, Gouge offers a prayer to be taught to children and a lengthy instructional homily for the heads of households — all as preparation for the expanded catechism with its extended explanations of 'the principles of Christian Religion'.

The longer catechism with explanations and applications also follows a somewhat different form than other expanded catechisms of the era. Gouge also often varies his form in setting out his 'explications': sometimes they are couched as questions and answers, other times as expositions of principles and applications. He also follows a distinction between 'explication' and 'application', the former standing as a help to the head of household in dealing with doctrinal questions, the latter as the message for piety to be taught and applied in the life of the household. This distinction between the doctrine (whether positive or elenctic) and its practical

---

12. Tillotson, *Sermon*, p. 86.

13. Cf. Green, *Christian's ABC*, p. 251.

14. Gouge, *Principles of Christian Religion*, [1] p. 11.

or spiritual use is typical of Puritan sermons and is found also in more systematic Reformed theological works of the era, both among the British and among Dutch proponents of the Nadere Reformatie.[15]

Gouge's catechism needs also to be understood against the background of the debates of orthodoxy generally in the late seventeenth century and of the trials and tribulations of English Puritanism and Presbyterianism in the wake of the Restoration of 1660 and the Ejection of 1662. His catechism often reflects both the questions and the doctrinal content of the Westminster Shorter Catechism, in an era when the Thirty-Nine Articles, the Prayer Book, and the Anglican Catechism had, by law, become the official expression of English religion in all parish churches.[16] There were other attempts to do much the same thing: a method of catechizing specifically grounded in the Shorter Catechism was published in 1675 by the ejected minister, Thomas Lye.[17] Thomas Adams' *Main Principles of Christian Religion* (1675) simply takes the Shorter Catechism's questions, without explicit reference to their source, and then shows how they are in accord with the Thirty-Nine Articles and the Homilies prior to the presentation of a longer explanation of the doctrinal points.[18] In all three of these

---

15. Cf. e.g., Thomas Manton, *Christ's Eternal Existence, and the Dignity of his Person asserted and proved. In opposition to the doctrine of the Socinians. In several sermons on Col. i.17, 18, 19, 20, 21* (London: s.n., 1685); with the fairly consistent pattern in each *locus* in Thomas Watson, *A Body of Practical Divinity* (London: Thomas Parkhurst, 1692); and Wilhelmus à Brakel, *Logike Latreia, dat is Redelijke Godsdienst in welken de goddelijke Waarheded van het Genade-Verbond worden verklaard* (Dordrecht, 1700), trans. as *The Christian's Reasonable Service*, 4 vols., trans. Bartel Elshout, ed. Joel Beeke (Ligonier, PA: Soli Deo Gloria, 1992–1995).

16. A summary of the Presbyterian and Independent ministers' objections to the Articles, Prayer Book, and Anglican Catechism can be found in John Hunt, *Religious Thought in England from the Reformation to the End of the Last Century*, 3 vols. (London: Strahan, 1870–1873), 2:282–96.

17. Thomas Lye, *An Explanation of the Shorter Catechism* (London: A. M. for Thomas Parkhurst, 1675).

18. Thomas Adams, *The Main Principles of Christian Religion in an 107 short Articles or Aphorisms* (London: s.n., 1675).

documents, then, there is evidence of the several ways in which dissenting clergy maintained the Westminster tradition following the Ejection.

Catechization and the Religious Duties of the Household

Gouge's catechism rests on the foundational assumption that parents and heads of households are responsible for the religious instruction of all those in their care, whether children or servants.[19] If only in the sphere of Protestant instruction, this assumption can be traced as far back as the earliest catechisms of the Reformation, notably to the instructions to heads of households found at the end of Luther's *Small Catechism*. What Gouge supplied, however, in the extended version of his catechism published in 1679, was not merely the catechetical form and a basic instruction to heads of households, but an extended manual designed to explain the rationale and method of catechization in the home, including a full explanation of how the head of the household should train himself in a more detailed exposition of doctrine and practical application in order to be prepared for teaching the shorter forms of basic principles, questions, and answers to the young. Gouge's approach reflects a time when non-conformist families needed the full range of instruction and conforming families might well still desire a supplement to the official catechisms of the Anglican church following the loss of the Westminster Standards,[20] but it also reflects a more carefully designed pedagogical program than typically found in catechisms.

Proper catechization, in Gouge's view, would provide the young with a 'good and sure foundation' on which the build their lives. He notes that the gross ignorance of 'Fundamental Truths' even in older persons can be traced to the lack of early instruction in the 'Principles of Religion'. So instructed, the young will not fall prey 'to Atheists or Papists, or other Seducers' and will be more likely

---

19. Gouge, *Principles of Christian Religion*, fol. A3r; cf. Green, *Christian's ABC*, p. 71.
20. Cf. Green, Christian's ABC, p. 71.

to continue in the truths of God's Word.[21] Gouge admonishes parents not to avoid the work on grounds of its difficulty—for if catechization is not undertaken and knowledge of the true God and of Christ's work is absent from the home, there can be no clear expectation of divine blessing on a household, no expectation that children and servants will be inclined to serve God 'with honest and upright hearts'; no expectation of enlightened knowledge of God; no expectation of restraint of sin. It would be 'a dreadful thing,' he concludes, 'to be guilty of the blood of souls.'[22]

At the same time, if the task is undertaken willingly, God will bless the endeavor. What is more, Gouge indicates, use of the method embodied in his treatise will render the difficult work of catechizing 'as easie as reading anothers Sermon.'[23] The basic question should be 'propounded' and then the answer provided—initially by the parent but subsequently, from memory by one of the children or servants. Then each of the 'practical applications' should be set forth followed by a careful presentation of each 'Explication and Application.' One day in each week should be devoted to this exercise, at which time, 'It will be good and necessary that you appoint the several persons in your Families, to take their own times to learn an Answer or two weekly, so that they may be ready to rehearse it to you on the time you appoint for Catechising of them.'[24]

Gouge elaborates the theological foundation for the entire method in his sermon, 'The Christian Householder,' on Joshua 24:15: 'As for me, and my house, we will serve the Lord,' set after his introductory or foundational materials. There are four points or 'particulars' that are to be drawn from the verse: first, there is 'the person resolving,' namely Joshua, the head of the household; second, 'the Order of his Resolution,' that 'first *himself* will serve the Lord, and then his *House*'; third, 'the Extent of his

---

21. Gouge, *Principles of Christian Religion*, fol. A3r–v.

22. Gouge, *Principles of Christian Religion*, fol. A3v.

23. Gouge, *Principles of Christian Religion*, fol. A4r.

24. Gouge, *Principles of Christian Religion*, fol. A4r.

Resolution,' namely, 'his whole House'; and fourth, 'the Matter resolved on,' specifically, 'to serve God.' Taken together, these particulars indicate the scope of the passage, 'which is to press all Parents, Masters, and Governours of Families, to a constant and conscionable performance of Holy, and Religious duties, in and with their Families.'[25] Governors of families ought to govern—and governance does not consist merely in the righteous conduct of one's own life. It necessarily includes the supervision of others. The point made explicitly by Joshua can also be elicited from the lives of Abraham, Jacob, and David, as also from the command to Israelite fathers to teach the meaning of the Passover to their children. Nor does this commandment pass away with the proclamation of the gospel, as the Apostle Paul insists that Christian patents raise their children 'in the nurture and admonition of the Lord.'[26]

Once the point that parental care, specifically in matters of religion, is commanded by Scripture, as if the mere statement of the necessity were not enough, Gouge proceeds to a series of reasons in confirmation of the biblical argument. He has no qualms about putting the fear of God into the hearts of his readers. The first and foremost reason is God's own command to teach His laws diligently to children: the parental duty is commanded by God. Second, just as anyone would acknowledge that a minister of the gospel is in charge of his flock, so should all acknowledge that the parent or head of household ought to regard those with his house as his flock and be responsible for their souls. Gouge is pointed in his argument: 'If therefore your children and Servants live and die in their sins, through your negligence, their blood will be required at your hands.'[27] Third, diligent governance in spiritual matters is also required by 'Justice and Equity': on this issue, spiritual nourishment is no different than physical provision. Fourth, 'the curse of God hangs over those Families in which Religious duties are altogether

---

25. Gouge, *Principles of Christian Religion*, [2] p. 1.

26. Gouge, *Principles of Christian Religion*, [2] p. 2, citing Gen. 18:19; 35:2; Psalm 101:2; and Ephesians 6:4.

27. Gouge, *Principles of Christian Religion*, [2] p. 3.

neglected.'[28] By implication, failure of the head of the household to nourish all within his care may result not only in a curse upon him but upon all of the others in the house. Fifth, conversely, God's blessing will fall on the entire household if its religious duties are 'conscientiously performed.'[29] Such blessings may be evidenced directly or they may be evidenced in the comfort given to patents and masters by good children and servants. Sixth, 'manifold mischiefs' often follow on the 'neglect of family-duties'. Gouge gives examples: 'Domestic brawls and contentions' that divide the house against itself, husband against wife, wife against husband, masters and servants against each other, children in discord with parents. Where God is not served there can be no peace. Crimes are committed, large and small, and magistrates are called upon to enforce the law against members of the family—all of which could be prevented if only due service were rendered to God.[30]

The conclusion drawn by Gouge in a further series of recommendations is that not only the life of the home but also the life of the whole society begins with service to God in the household and that such service takes the form of daily prayer and reading of the Scriptures, keeping of the Sabbath, and the singing of Psalms, each of these forms being supported and nourished by proper catechization, specifically, in the basic teaching of 'the first Principles of Christian Religion' and their subsequent elaboration in ongoing weekly lessons.[31]

From Principle to Explication: Illustrations of Gouge's Doctrinal Expositions

The sheer size and detail of Gouge's catechism obviates the possibility of a full analysis of its contents. Several examples will have to suffice. Just as in his sermon to householders, Gouge often supplemented his arguments from Scripture with rational

---

28. Gouge, *Principles of Christian Religion*, [2] p. 4.
29. Gouge, *Principles of Christian Religion*, [2] p. 5.
30. Gouge, *Principles of Christian Religion*, [2] p. 6.
31. Gouge, *Principles of Christian Religion*, [2] pp. 14–20, 24–25.

arguments or 'reasons' buttressed with biblical citations and practical examples or applications, so also in his catechism proper does he include various rational arguments and applications, albeit not in such a way as to sever rational argumentation from a biblical foundation.

1. *Against Atheism: Arguing the Existence of God*

An example of Gouge's rational argumentation occurs in a lengthy section on the existence of God posed against various forms of atheism, found as a preface to answering the basic question (third in order in Gouge's catechism, paralleling the third question of the Westminster Shorter Catechism), 'Q. How do the Scriptures set forth God?'[32] The order and content of the questions preceding and following is significant to an understanding of what otherwise might be seen as a momentary exercise in natural theology. The first question and answer of Gouge's catechism, 'Q. What is every one most bound to know? Ans. God and himself,'[33] reflect a point fundamental to Reformed theology beginning with Zwingli's *Commentary on True and False Religion* (1525) and Calvin's *Institutes* (1536). The grounds given are entirely biblical and lead to the second

---

32. Gouge, *Principles of Christian Religion*, [3] p. 6; cf. *Shorter Catechism*, p. 154 [q. 3], in *The Confession of Faith and Catechisms, agreed upon by the assembly of divines at Westminster together with their humble advice concerning church government and ordination of ministers* (London: for Robert Bostock, 1649). Hereinafter, citations of the Westminster standards will follow this 1649 edition, with question numbers added in square brackets.

33. Gouge, *Principles of Christian Religion*, [3] p. 1, citing, with comment, Psalm 139:6; Exodus 18:10; John 17:3; Psalm 9:10; 1 Chronicles 28:9; Psalm 19:7; Revelation 3:19; Job 46:4; cf. Ulrich Zwingli, *De vera et falsa religione commentarius*, in *Opera completa editio prima*, ed. Melchior Schuler and Johann Schulthess, 8 vols. in 11 (Zürich: Schulthess and Höhr, 1828–1842), 3:155; cf. *Commentary on True and False Religion*, ed. Samuel Macauley Jackson and Clarence Nevin Heller (Philadelphia, 1929; reprint, Durham, N.C.: Labyrinth Press, 1981), p. 58; and John Calvin, *Christianae religionis institutio* (Basel: s.n., 1536), i (p. 42); idem, the sentence slightly expanded, *Institutio christianae religionis* (Strasbourg: Wendelin Rihel, 1539), i (p. 1); and idem, retaining the same wording, *Institutio christianae religionis* (Geneva: Robert Stephanus, 1559), I.i.1.

question and answer, 'Q. Where is this knowledge to be had? Ans. In the Word of God contained in the Scriptures of the Old and New Testament.'[34] Only after describing the canonical Scriptures and indicating, by way of application, that they are 'the Rule by which you must be governed and guided,' does Gouge come to his third question, 'Q. How do the Scriptures set forth God?' The third question itself, moreover, is answered by way of biblical citations: 'Ans. In his Nature; Exod. 3:14; John 4:24. 2. In his Persons; Matth. 28:19. 3. In his Properties; Exod 34:6. 4. In his Works; Rom. 1:20.'[35]

The order of the answer is also significant: Gouge moves from the nature of God as 'a Spirit of infinite Perfection' to the doctrine of the Trinity and only then to the discussion of divine properties or attributes. This is not what one would expect given the caricature of the older orthodoxy as arguing a rationalistic doctrine of essence and attributes and giving the Trinity second place.[36] The rational argumentation for God's existence and the application of the argument appear, then, following not only on a statement of the biblical foundation of Christian teaching but also on the statement of Gouge's third question and his identification of the four parts of his discussion of God—nature, Persons, properties, and works—as to be grounded in Scripture.

After propounding his third question and its answer and prior to his exposition of the doctrine of God in question and answer four,[37] following the standard and traditional rhetorical and scholastic order of questions, he indicates that:

---

34. Gouge, *Principles of Christian Religion*, [3] p. 2.

35. Gouge, *Principles of Christian Religion*, [3] p. 6.

36. Cf. the conclusions in Richard A. Muller, 'Unity and Distinction: The Essence of God in the Theology of Lucas Trelcatius, Jr.,' in *Reformation & Renaissance Review: Journal of the Society for Reformation Studies*, 10, no. 3 (2008 [published, 2010]), pp. 315–41; with the discussion in idem, *Post-Reformation Reformed Dogmatics: The Rise and Development of Reformed Orthodoxy, ca. 1520 to ca. 1725*, 4 vols. (Grand Rapids: Baker, 2003), 4:145–50.

37. Note that question four, 'What is God?' and its answer, 'God is a Spirit of infinite Perfection,' directly reflects question four of the *Shorter Catechism*, p. 158 [q. 4].

Being to speak largely of God, it will be expedient, first to prove the Being of God. We must understand, That there is a God, before we inquire What God is. ... That there is a God, is evident, from the glorious Fabrick of Heaven and Earth, with all the glorious Creatures therein; which glorious Building could never have been, if it had not an omnipotent Builder. And from the Powerful, wise, Harmonious Government of the World; which evidently points us to a Divine over-ruling Providence; and from the general sense and conscience of all Nations.[38]

Gouge offers no further elaboration of the proofs—he only presents rational grounds for belief, one cosmological and related to the doctrine of providence, the other rhetorical form the consent of all nations. The Reformed roots of these arguments go back as far as the Reformation; the former is found in Melanchthon, the latter in Calvin.[39]

Gouge's purpose in noting so briefly these rational grounds for belief in God becomes immediately evident in his extended applications, the initial series of which is intended for the reproof of the several kinds of atheists. His approach, moreover, is not to launch into a rational apologetic but rather to warn Christians against falling way from their trust in God and to call down divine warnings on the unfaithful—nor, indeed, does the use of rational argument and general human understandings at this point indicate any interest in natural theology. What we have in Gouge's proofs, as in the proofs found in the Reformed orthodox theologies of the era, is an exercise in rational and rhetorical argumentation illustrative of an apologetic purpose common to both so-called supernatural and natural theologies,[40] but specifically directed

---

38. Gouge, *Principles of Christian Religion*, [3] p. 6.

39. See Muller, *Post-Reformation Reformed Dogmatics*, 3:170–93. Note also that this mingling of a form of *a posteriori* cosmological argument with the rhetorical argument *e consensu gentium* is a characteristic pattern in the older Reformed orthodoxy. A detailed analysis of the proofs in Reformed orthodox theology can be found in John Platt, *Reformed Thought and Scholasticism: The Arguments for the Existence of God in Dutch Theology, 1575–1650* (Leiden: Brill, 1982).

40. Cf. Muller, *Post-Reformation Reformed Dogmatics*, 3:167–170, 192–193;

toward laity not aware of detailed controversies. Gouge explained his approach in his introductory epistle:

> Though in clearing the Truths, I had often occasion given of confuting very many Errors both of Papists, Socinians, and others, yet I purposely avoided it, because this Treatise was drawn up only for the benefit of the younger and weaker sort of Christians, especially those in Wales; who being destitute of these many helps of knowledge we in these parts enjoy, did earnestly desire me to publish in both Languages a Treatise that should contain all the Fundamental Principles of Religion, and that in a plain Stile and Method.[41]

Thus, in his exposition of the proofs, whether rational or rhetorical, Gouge reflects the standard patterns of argument in the Puritan and Reformed theologies of his time, adapting the doctrinal argumentation to a spiritual or pious use—evidencing Gouge's work among the poor rather than engaging in the more academic or intellectual polemics against rationalistic impiety that were also characteristic of the era.[42]

There are, Gouge indicates, three kinds of atheists standing in need of reproof: there are atheists 'in Opinion and Judgment, concluding … that there is no God'; atheists 'in wish and desire' who refrain from stating their disbelief but who hope that there is no God 'to take vengeance on their iniquity'; and atheists 'in practice' who acknowledge God's existence and deny Him in their

---

with idem, 'The Dogmatic Function of St. Thomas' Proofs: a Protestant Appreciation,' in *Fides et Historia*, vol. 24 (1992), pp. 15–29.

41. Gouge, *Principles of Christian Religion*, fol. A4r-v.

42. Cf., e.g., Richard Baxter, *The Reasons of the Christian Religion. The First Part, of Godliness: Proving by Natural Evidence the Being of God, the Necessity of Holiness, and a Future Life of Retribution. … the Second Part, of Christianity: Proving by Evidence Supernatural and Natural, the Certain Truth of Christian Belief* (London: R. White, 1667); William Bates, *Considerations of the Existence of God and of the Immortality of the Soul, with the Recompences of the Future State: for the Cure of Infidelity, the Hectick Evil of the Times* (London: J. D. For Brabazon Aylmer, 1676).

lives.[43] All such persons incline toward wickedness, but it is the third kind, the practical atheist, the person whose conduct implies atheism, who receives the most attention from Gouge, as it did from other Puritan writers of the era.[44] He presses the point that the secret atheist needs beware the omniscience of God who knows the inmost thoughts of the heart—just as the secretive sinner who hides his faults needs be reminded that God is everywhere present and sees all things.[45]

2. God's Providence—Exposition and Application

Whereas the Westminster catechisms arrive at the doctrine of providence[46] by way of the divine decrees, Gouge's catechism rests its argument on the standard distinction between the doctrine of God and the doctrine of God's works.[47] After, therefore, discussing the divine nature, the trinity of persons, and various attributes, Gouge indicates that he is taking up the second member of

---

43. Gouge, *Principles of Christian Religion*, [3] p. 7.

44. Cf. Stephen Charnock, *A Discourse upon Practical Atheism*, in *Several Discourses upon the Existence and Attributes of God* (London: for D. Newman, et al., 1682), pp. 1–46.

45. Gouge, *Principles of Christian Religion*, [3] p. 7, citing Ps. 139:2, 13; Jer. 23:23; Prov. 15:3.

46. The Puritan and later Reformed understanding of providence has been examined in Alexandra Walsham, *Providence in Early Modern England* (Oxford: Oxford University Press, 1999); Joel Beeke and Mark Jones, 'The Puritans on Providence,' in *A Puritan Theology: Doctrine for Life* (Grand Rapids: Reformation Heritage Books, 2012), pp. 163–79; and also Ronald J. VanderMolen, 'Providence as Mystery, Providence as Revelation: Puritan and Anglican Modifications of John Calvin's Doctrine of Providence,' in *Church History*, vol. 47 (March 1978), pp. 27–47; Barbara Donagan, 'Providence, Chance and Explanation: Some Paradoxical Aspects of Puritan Views of Causation,' *Journal of Religious History*, vol. 11, no. 3 (1981), pp. 385–403; idem, 'Godly Choice: Puritan Decision-Making in 17th Century England,' *Harvard Theological Review*, vol. 76 (July 1983), pp. 307–34; and Margo Todd, 'Providence, Chance, and the New Science in Early Stuart Cambridge,' in *The Historical Journal*, vol. 29, no. 3 (1986), pp. 697–711.

47. Cf. Gouge, *Principles of Christian Religion*, [3] p. 33; with *Larger Catechism*, pp. 72–72 [qq. 12, 14]; *Shorter Catechism*, p. 154–155 [qq. 7–8].

the bifurcation, the works of God, which itself divides into the discussions of creation and providence.[48] Gouge's discussion of providence, which follows on the doctrine of creation, begins with the simple definition: 'The Providence of God consisteth, as in preserving the Creatures which he made, so in his wise and powerful ordering of them.'[49] The phrase 'wise and powerful' echoes the Westminster catechisms.[50]

The explanation of providence following on Gouge's definition consists in four parts—three doctrinal sections, indicating in order, 'that there is a Providence,' 'the acts of Providence,' and 'the Properties of Gods Providence,' followed by an extended fourth section concerning the 'application' of the doctrine. Despite the polemical issues raised by Arminian, Socinian, and early modern Epicurean approaches to the doctrine, Gouge does not offer any of the extended proofs for the existence of providence such as can be found in standard works of the Reformed orthodox and Puritan writers,[51] again reflecting the use of the catechism not in more erudite circles but specifically among poorer households.

Accordingly, Gouge's interest in proof offers no evidence of a rationalistic tendency or of an interest in natural theology either on his part or as an aspect of polemic against a perceived problem. He merely notes a few of the 'multitude' of examples found in the world order and then correlates them with Psalm 104:20–21. As the Psalm indicates, God has made the darkness in which the 'beasts of the forest creep forth' (v. 20)—how providential it

---

48. Gouge, *Principles of Christian Religion*, [3] p. 33.

49. Gouge, *Principles of Christian Religion*, [3] p. 37.

50. Cf. *Larger Catechism*, p. 74 [q. 18]; *Shorter Catechism*, p. 155 [q. 11].

51. Cf., e.g., Zacharias Ursinus, *Explicationum catecheticarum, editio altera* (Cambridge: Thomas Thomasius, 1587), pp. 318–24; Edward Leigh, *A Systeme or Body of Divinity: consisting in ten books wherein the fundamentals of religion are opened; the contrary errours refuted; most of the controversies between us, the Papists, Arminians, and Socinians discussed and handled; several Scriptures explained, and vindicated from corrupt glosses*, 2nd ed. (London: A. M. For William Lee, 1662), III.ix (pp. 369–70; Franz Burman, *Synopsis theologiae et speciatim oeconomiae foederum Dei*, 2 parts (Geneva: Ioannes Pictet, 1678), VI.xliii.1–10 (pp. 318–20).

is, Gouge remarks, that the beasts 'go abroad to seek their prey, when men lie down to rest' but 'lie in their Dens all the day long, when men go abroad to work.' Even so, wild beasts are not as 'fruitful' as domesticated animals and, similarly, despite the vast numbers of wicked people in the world, the world is not overrun with destruction. 'These things, and many the like,' he concludes, 'as also the Universal care of all Creatures, and of his Church in special, do plainly argue a Divine Providence.'[52]

3. The Sabbath and Its Observation

Gouge's exposition of the fourth commandment engages a series of questions and issues that serve well to exemplify both the relationships of doctrine, argumentation, apologetics, and piety in his thought and the carefully-argued sabbatarian piety of early modern Puritan and Reformed thought.[53] He begins with a concise statement of the argumentative structure of the first table of the law: 'As the First Commandment shewed us the true and proper Object of Divine Worship. The Second, the Means of Worship: The Third, the Manner. So this Fourth, the special Time for Divine Worship.'[54]

As in the case of his doctrines of God and providence, Gouge offers an introductory rational argument—perhaps reflecting the growing apologetic interest in natural religion characteristic of the late seventeenth century and serving, as is the case with his previous ventures into more rational argumentation, perceived needs of heads of household faced with questions concerning the relationship of Christian thought and practice to natural religion

---

52. Gouge, *Principles of Christian Religion*, [3] p. 38.

53. Cf., e.g., Richard Baxter, *The Divine Appointment of the Lords day proved as a separated day for holy worship, especially in the church assemblies, and consequently the cessation of the seventh day Sabbath* (London: for Nevil Simmons, 1671). On the Sabbath debates, see Keith L. Sprunger, 'English and Dutch Sabbatarianism and the Development of Puritan Social Theology (1600–1660),' in *Church History*, vol. 51, no. 1 (1982), pp. 24–38; also note Beeke and Jones, 'John Owen on the Christian Sabbath and Worship,' in *Puritan Theology*, pp. 635–61.

54. Gouge, *Principles of Christian Religion*, [3] p. 206.

and the religious beliefs of non-Christian nations. Gouge's approach reflects the Reformed orthodoxy of the era, with its view of the availability and insufficiency of natural revelation and natural religion.[55] Even 'Heathens,' he indicates, with only the 'light of Nature' to guide them, recognize from the natural light that 'some time is to be set apart' for the worship of God and have often identified particular days: the Turks keep Friday as their Sabbath. The argument is of interest from a late seventeenth-century perspective. When Gouge was writing, the Turks were still advancing into Europe and were, in fact, drawing close to the gates of Vienna: they were perhaps the most despised and certainly the most dangerous pagans of the era. And even they, he notes, recognize the necessity of worship on a particular day. By implication, how much more ought Christians who have 'the light of Gods Word to direct them' to respect the consecration of a day to God.[56]

According to Gouge, the direction given by God's Word, in much the same language as the Westminster catechisms, respects the distinction of the testaments and the administrations of the covenant of grace: one day to be set aside is commanded by God, under the Old Testament, from 'the beginning of the World ... to the resurrection of Christ' it is the seventh day of the week, respecting the order of creation; but under the New Testament, from 'the resurrection of Christ ... to the end of the World,' it is the first day of the week, respecting the day of resurrection and the apostolic observation of 'the Lord's Day.'[57]

55. Cf. William Bates, *The Divinity of the Christian Religion, Proved by the Evidence of Reason* (London: J. D. For Brabazon Aylmer, 1677), pp. 1–3, 8–9; Matthew Hale, *Of the Nature of True Religion, the Causes of its Corruption, and the Churches Calamity, by Mens Additions and Violences: With the Desired Cure. In Three Discourses* (London: for B. Simmons, 1684), 1:1–3; Burman, *Synopsis theologiae*, I.ii.6–8 (p. 4); Campegius Vitringa, *Epitome theologiae naturalis: theses theologicae: et duae disputationes academicae de notione Spiritus S. Restricta ad Filium, & de progressu causarum secundarium in infinitum* (Leovarden: Tobias van Dessel, 1735), 3:98–124.

56. Gouge, *Principles of Christian Religion*, [3] p. 206.

57. Gouge, *Principles of Christian Religion*, [3] p. 207; cf. *Larger Catechism,*

Gouge entertains a significant level of detail here—more than one might expect in a catechetical instruction, but suited to the kind of questions that a head of household might need to answer, given the level of debate over the day of the Sabbath engendered by writers like Theophilus Brabourne and James Ockford.[58] He identifies the day of rest in paradise (Gen. 2:2–3) and the corresponding Sabbath commandment (Exod. 20:10–11), noting specifically the grounding of the commandment in the seventh day of creation. He then offers an extended discussion of the Christian shift of the Sabbath to the first day of the week, grounded in the resurrection, as identified by the Apostles.

Here, in contrast to other exposition in the catechism, Gouge cites the 'Learned' Beza's *Annotations* to the effect that an ancient copy of 1 Corinthians 16:2, where Christians are exhorted to gather

---

p. 112 [q. 116]; *Shorter Catechism*, pp. 165–66 [q. 59]; also note John Owen, *Exercitations concerning the name, original, nature, use, and continuance of a day of sacred rest wherein the original of the Sabbath from the foundation of the world, the morality of the Fourth commandment with the change of the Seventh day are enquired into: together with an assertion of the divine institution of the Lord's Day, and practical directions for its due observation* (London: R.W. for Nath. Ponder, 1671), pp. 430–36.

58. Theophilus Brabourne, *A discourse vpon the Sabbath day Wherin are handled these particulares ensuinge. 1. That the Lords day is not Sabbath day, by divine iustification. 2. An exposition of the 4. commandement, so farr fort has may give light vnto the ensueinge discourse: and particularly, here it is showne, at what time the Sabbath day should begine and end; for the satisfaction of those who are doubtfull in this point. 3. That the seaventh day Sabbath is not abolished. 4. That the seaventh day Sabbath is now still in force. 5. The authors exhortation and reasones, that neverthelesse there be no rente from our Church as touching practise* (S.l.: s.n., 1628); James Ockford, *The doctrine of the Fourth Commandement, deformed by popery, reformed & restored to its primitive purity objections answered, and the truth cleared* (London: G. Dawson, 1650); idem, *The tryal of the truth or rather, the law is the truth: Psalm CXIX, CXLII, wherein are presented to the upright in heart, certain theoretical queries … which queries particularly and especially tend to make way for the finding out whether it be our duty to keep holy the seventh day Sabbath* (Amsterdam: for the Author, 1656); and see Oscar Burdick, 'Sleuthing the origins of English Seventh Day Baptists in the 1650's: a Bibliography,' in *American Theological Library Association Summary of Proceedings*, vol. 38 (1984), pp. 134-45.

collections on the first day of the week, has added 'Lord's Day' to the text. Even so, that Apostles met on the first day of the week 'to Preach and Administer the Sacrament of the Lords supper.' This practice, Gouge adds, was 'ordained in Churches' by the Apostles on the basis of the authority that they had received from Christ.[59] Furthermore, 'the testimony of Ignatius, Justin Martyr, and divers of the ancient Fathers,' confirms that celebration of the Sabbath on the first day of the week was the Apostolic practice and the practice of the ancient church.[60]

The reason for the change of day is simple: it is the will of God that the Sabbath, as rightly observed should be 'a continual Commemoration of the glorious Resurrection of Christ, and of the great Work of Redemption accomplished by him.' There is, moreover, a significant parallel between the two holy days: after the work of creation, God rested and sanctified the seventh day— and just so, after the work of redemption, Christ 'rested and sanctified the Day of his Resurrection.'[61]

Once the day has been established, Gouge passes on—at considerable length—to his primary issue, namely, how the Sabbath 'is to be sanctified,' in terms both of the positive works and duties to be performed and of the things that are forbidden in order to preserve the sanctity of the day. First, Christians ought to rest from all 'worldly businesses and imployments.'[62] Gouge points to the works of a person's particular calling, by way of example, farming during harvest time: even if there have been days of rain prior to the Sabbath, such works as turning hay and gathering corn are not absolutely necessary. They should not be performed on the Sabbath. Similarly to be avoided are, 'shooting, bowling, wrestling, ringing, dancing; as also too liberal eating and drinking,

---

59. Gouge, *Principles of Christian Religion*, [3] pp. 207–208, citing Acts 1:2–3; 2:1; 20:7; and John 20:19, 26.

60. Gouge, *Principles of Christian Religion*, [3] p. 208.

61. Gouge, *Principles of Christian Religion*, [3] p. 208; cf. Baxter, *Divine Appointment*, pp. 182–83; and Owen, *Exercitations*, pp. 434–36.

62. Gouge, *Principles of Christian Religion*, [3] p. 209.

especially Wine or strong Drink, at least so much as may make us either drowse, or unapt to serve God with out hearts and minds', as stated in Isaiah, God requires that his people 'turn away their feet from doing their own pleasure on his holy-day.'[63] When not in attendance at formal services of worship, there should be 'private Duties' involving family worship.

Again reflecting the context of his work, Gouge notes several possible objections, notably pleas on behalf of servants who might require recreation and refreshment after a week of labor. Those who may be weary from hard work surely deserve rest, he comments, and 'if they be spiritually minded,' they should engage in 'holy and religious Exercises'; while those who would engage in 'bodily recreations' should do so on another day rather than 'steal away' a part of what is due to God.[64]

The Sabbath, then, is to be observed as a time of 'holy rest'. Beyond refraining from worldly pursuits, the Christian, as instructed by the head of household, should consecrate the day by engaging in 'spiritual duties.' Not only should Christians refrain from their own personal works and duties, they should also engage in 'the works of God,' specifically, in the 'duties of his Worship and Service.' These duties can be distinguished into three classes, public, private, and secret.[65] The public duty of worship, as argued by other Puritans, takes priority. There God is most highly honored and just as honor redounds to God, so is 'the greatest spiritual advantage,' namely, the gift of 'spiritual and heavenly' blessings, bestowed on God's people through right worship.[66] Through private duties, such as prayer, reading the Scriptures or other 'good books,' catechizing, repeating sermons, singing psalms, and engaging in 'holy conference,' render believers more

---

63. Gouge, *Principles of Christian Religion*, [3] p. 209, citing Isa. 58:13.

64. Gouge, *Principles of Christian Religion*, [3] p. 210.

65. Gouge, *Principles of Christian Religion*, [3] p. 210.

66. Cf. David Clarkson, *Publick Worship to be Prefer'd before Private*, in *Sermons and Discourses on Several Divine Subjects* (London: for Thomas Parkhurst, 1696), pp. 1021–1038; so also John Owen, *Exercitations*, pp. 448–49.

suited to their public duties. Heads of households are particularly encouraged to inculcate these private duties for the sake of all the souls in their charge. The 'secret' duties include personal reading, prayer, meditation, and self-examination—duties that reflect the close relationship between the individual soul and God.[67]

Beyond these duties of personal piety, there are also two kinds of works or duties that may be performed on the Lord's day, specifically, 'works of necessity' and 'works of mercy'. As to the first, Gouge does not enumerate. He simply warns that believers ought to attend to their business and 'worldly affairs' carefully so that apparent necessities do not arise out of 'negligence, or careless oversight.' Such seeming necessities are in fact sinful disruptions of the Sabbath. Works of mercy, such as gifts of charity, visiting the sick, 'instructing the ignorant, comforting the afflicted, resolving the doubtful, [and] reproving such as do amiss, especially such as live loosely and scandalously' are all commendable Sabbath exercises.[68]

Conclusions

Gouge's extended catechesis in his *Principles of Christian Religion* offers evidence of the adaptation of English Puritanism and specifically of the teachings of the Westminster catechisms to the conditions of dissent following the Ejection of 1662. It was designed not for parish use but for catechization by heads of households and embodied a program of education that was viewed positively by some of the Anglican clergy—notably in this case, John Tillotson. The doctrinal content and practical piety of Gouge's work point toward the broad relationship between Puritan or, more precisely, early modern English Reformed theology and various forms of continental Reformed orthodox theology, perhaps most notably the Nadere Reformatie project of communicating theology understood as a practical piety to laity in the vernacular. The doctrinal definitions found in the catechism quite consistently reflect the definitions and lengthier expositions found in the orthodox doctrinal systems of

---

67. Gouge, *Principles of Christian Religion*, [3] pp. 210–11.
68. Gouge, *Principles of Christian Religion*, [3] p. 212.

the era—but, with equal consistency, reflect the genre of catechesis with its emphasis on foundational or basic learning and on practical application. This practical application directed toward the unlearned is also evident in the way in which Gouge addressed controversies of his time, not elaborating at length against the learned infidelity of the era and introducing detail primarily in such places as would affect personal piety, daily Christian conduct, and Sabbath observance. Arguably, Gouge's expanded form, with its embedded educational program of addressing several levels of understanding as well as different age groups marks a major development in catechesis, well adapted to the needs of Nonconformity and Dissent in the late seventeenth century.

Part 3: Individual Snapshots of Puritan Piety

CHAPTER TEN

Daniel Dyke and The Mystery of Self-Deceiving

RANDALL J. PEDERSON

THE Puritan Reformation was primarily one of reform of the Christian life.[1] In fact, of all the Puritan treatises that were published in the late sixteenth and seventeenth centuries, the vast majority were manuals aimed at teaching readers how to go to heaven and live a godly life.[2] Here one thinks of Arthur Dent's *The Plain Man's Pathway to Heaven* (1601), a wildly successful book that inspired Bunyan's *Pilgrim's Progress*; and Lewis Bayly's *The Practice of Piety* (1611), a rigorous but equally successful text. Both books have received much attention in the scholarly world for their literary popularity and influence on the form.[3]

---

1. Literature on Puritanism and the Puritan Reformation is immense. For an introduction to Puritans and Puritanism, see Francis J. Bremer, *Puritanism: A Very Short Introduction* (New York: Oxford University Press, 2009); John Coffey and Paul C.H. Lim, ed., *The Cambridge Companion to Puritanism* (Cambridge: Cambridge University Press, 2008); and Joel R. Beeke and Randall J. Pederson, *Meet the Puritans: A Guide to Modern Reprints* (Grand Rapids: Reformation Heritage Books, 2006).

2. This Puritan emphasis was so prevalent that it earned Puritans the reputation of being 'the godly.' See, for instance, Patrick Collinson, *Godly People: Essays on English Protestantism and Puritanism* (London: The Hambledon Press, 1983).

3. See, for instance, Christopher Haigh, *The Plain Man's Pathways to Heaven: Kinds*

In comparison, however, little focus has been given to Daniel Dyke's (c. 1580–1614). *The Mystery of Self-Deceiving* (1614), an early modern national bestseller that moved the historian F. Ernest Stoeffler to opine on the work that 'Protestantism has produced no other treatise in which the psychology of sin was more exhaustively treated.'[4] Thus, in this essay, I will briefly discuss Dyke's life and work, and then move on to an analysis of *The Mystery of Self-Deceiving*.

The Life and Work of Daniel Dyke

Overall, little is known about Daniel Dyke and his brief career. He was born to William Dyke, a zealous Puritan minister, around 1580, matriculated at St John's College, Cambridge, c. 1593, and graduated BA in 1595/6, and MA in 1599 from Sidney Sussex College, where he became a fellow in 1606, when he earned his BD. While not much is known about his clerical career, other than that he seems to have met with some measure of popularity, what is known is that he died in 1614.[5]

Dyke is said to have kept a private diary and catalog of his sins, upon which he would reflect every evening and morning and cry out for mercy; and he was known to have been a vigilant Sabbatarian, preparing long in advance for the Lord's Day.[6]

---

of Christianity in Post-Reformation England (New York: Oxford University Press, 2007), pp. 1–16; and Charles E. Hambrick-Stowe, *The Practice of Piety: Puritan Devotional Disciplines in Seventeenth-Century New England* (Chapel Hill: The University of North Carolina Press, 1982), where Puritan devotional manuals are discussed as primarily intending to foster heart religion.

4. F. Ernest Stoeffler, *The Rise of Evangelical Pietism* (Leiden: Brill, 1965), p. 75.

5. Patrick Collinson, 'Dyke, Daniel (d. 1614),' in *Puritans and Puritanism in Europe and America*, ed. Francis J. Bremer and Tom Webster, 2 vols. (Santa Barbara, CA: ABC-CLIO, 2006), 1:81; 'Dyke, Daniel,' in *Oxford Dictionary of National Biography* (Oxford: Oxford University Press, 2004). Henceforth cited as *ODNB*. In some of the older literature, such as Benjamin Brook's *Lives of the Puritans*, there seems to be some confusion between Dyke's clerical career and that of his father, about whom much more is known. See, for instance, Patrick Collinson, 'Dyke, William,' *ODNB*.

6. Daniel Dyke, *The Mystery of Self-Deceiving; Or, A Discourse and Discovery of the Deceitfulness of Man's Heart* (London, 1642), 'The Epistle Dedicatorie.' Here Dyke is said to have 'Every Sabbath morning, or night before, to review

He is known primarily through his writings, all of which were 'perfected' and published posthumously by his lesser known but no less prolific brother, Jeremiah Dyke (1584–1639), vicar of Epping.[7] Upon reading his brother's diary, Jeremiah remarked: 'surely we will never begin to know divinity or religion till we come to know ourselves.'[8]

Daniel Dyke published several treatises, none of which received the wide fame and circulation of *The Mystery of Self-Deceiving*. In 1616, a small book of sermons on Psalm 124 was published called *Certain Comfortable Sermons*. The collection seems to have been preached much earlier, around the time of the Gunpowder Plot. *Two Treatises* was also issued from the press in 1616 and contains an elaborate discussion on repentance and Christ's temptations, the latter of which has been published more recently as *Michael and the Dragon*. In 1617, *Six Evangelical Histories* presented a collection of brief commentaries on various events depicted in the Gospels. In 1633, another collection of Dyke's treatises was published, which was followed by a collected *Works* in 1635, as well as various impressions of earlier works.

The Mystery of Self-Deceiving

We will now turn to a discussion of *The Mystery of Self-Deceiving* and see what it reveals about the Puritan practice of self-analysis.[9]

---

the faults of the whole week; and at the end of every month survey the whole month's transgression. This did he daily, weekly, and monthly, thereby the better to humble himself for his sins, and renew his practice of repentance.' He further kept set hours of study and would devote himself to reading, prayer, meditation, and repetition, by which he 'became wiser than his ancients and teachers.'

7. Dyke, *The Mystery of Self-Deceiving*. For further study on Jeremiah Dyke, see 'Dyke, Jeremiah,' *ODNB*; and Patrick Collinson, 'Dyke, Jeremiah (1584–1639),' in *Puritans and Puritanism in America*, 1:81–82.

8. Cited in Robert Warren Daniel, "'Have a little book in thy conscience, and write therein': Writing the Puritan Conscience, 1600–1650,' in *Sin and Salvation in Reformation England*, ed. Jonathan Wills (New York: Routledge, 2015), p. 258.

9. For a broader picture of early modern Protestant religious practice, see Alec Ryrie, *Being Protestant in Reformation Britain* (New York: Oxford University Press, 2013).

A Culture of Despair?

Certain books within the Protestant tradition, and specifically within Puritanism, have had a reputation for fostering a 'culture of despair'.[10] Two books that are often mentioned in this regard are Thomas Shepard's *The Parables of the Ten Virgins*, a collection of widely influential sermon series preached from 1636 to 1640 on false converts, and Daniel Dyke's *The Mystery of Self-Deceiving*.[11] Dyke's work has been criticized for typifying the problems that some have seen to be so characteristic of Puritanism, that is, a supposed inability to ever come to a full state of assurance and self-acceptance.[12] Scholars often cite as an example the inner turmoil of Nehemiah Wallington, a London woodturner who recorded his life's struggles in copious detail, or that of Joan Drake, a Puritan woman who was convinced she had committed the unpardonable sin.[13]

---

10. See Ryrie, *Being Protestant in Reformation Britain*, ch. 2; Jürgen Schlaeger, 'Self-Exploration in Early Modern English Diaries,' in *Marginal Voices, Marginal Forms: Diaries in European Literature and History*, ed. Rachel Langford and Russell West (Amsterdam: Rodopi, 1999), pp. 29-32.

11. See Alan Heimert and Andrew Delbanco, ed., *The Puritans in America: A Narrative Anthology* (Cambridge, Mass.: Harvard University Press, 1985), pp. 171ff; and for Shepard's troubled spirituality, Michael McGiffert, ed., *God's Plot: Puritan Spirituality in Thomas Shepard's Cambridge* (Amherst: University of Massachusetts Press, 1994).

12. Frederic Regard, ed., *Mapping the Self: Space, Identity, Discourse in British Autobiography* (Université de Saint-Etienne, 2003), p. 43. For a corrective to issues on Puritan assurance, see Joel R. Beeke, *Assurance of Faith: Calvin, English Puritanism, and the Dutch Second Reformation* (New York: Peter Lang, 1991).

13. For a detailed life of Wallington and his struggles, see Paul S. Seaver, *Wallington's World: A Puritan Artisan in Seventeenth-Century London* (Stanford: Stanford University Press, 1985), especially chapter 1, 'The Examined Life.' Wallington wrote extensive diaries and was said to have attempted suicide no less than a dozen times in his youth. On Drake and her despair, see Baird Tipson, *Hartford Puritanism: Thomas Hooker, Samuel Stone, and Their Terrifying God* (New York: Oxford University Press, 2015), pp. 294ff; Ryrie, *Being Protestant*, p. 27. It is also noteworthy that Shepard himself had been on occasion suicidal prior to finding relief. Elizabeth Reis, *Damned Women: Sinners and Witches in Puritan New England* (Ithaca: Cornell University Press, 1997), p. 54. Finally, see Kate

But, as we shall see, this is not entirely an accurate depiction of the Puritan's spiritual pilgrimage. While there were critics of Puritan introspection in the seventeenth century and afterwards, they generally failed to recognize how Puritan introspective books were used or for whom they were intended. Such books as *The Mystery of Self-Deceiving* were targeted toward the complacent professor of religion or temporary believer. They were not intended to discourage the godly in their Christian life, or to overwhelm them with the possibility that they too might be lost; and while most Puritans believed that the elect were few in number, they were cognizant that some members of their society were of a weak temperament, and they produced literature to help them.[14] By stripping bare all the false pretenses that plague the unconverted, the aim of discriminative literature was to encourage the godly in their path toward heaven and to convict the unbeliever of the folly of their sin that they too might be saved. The desired effect was to produce a 'sincere convert' more than it was to shatter or diminish assurance.[15]

A Bestselling Quarto

Published in quarto, *The Mystery of Self-Deceiving* contains thirty-one chapters that unveil the deep and tangling intricacies of human self-deception. It was a national bestseller and went through numerous printings in the seventeenth century. It was popular in America, and was translated into Danish, Dutch,

---

Narveson, 'Resting Assured in Puritan Piety: The Lay Experience,' in *Puritanism and Emotion in the Early Modern World*, ed. Alec Ryrie and Tom Schwanda (New York: Palgrave Macmillan, 2016), pp. 166-92.

14. See, as an example of this palliative genre, Joseph Symonds, *The Case and Cure of a Deserted Soul* (Edinburgh: Robert Bryson, 1642); Christopher Love, *The Dejected Soul's Cure* (London: John Rothwell, 1657); and William Bridge, *A Lifting Up for the Downcast* (1649).

15. As an example of this sort of discriminatory preaching, see Thomas Shepard, *The Sincere Convert: Discovering the Small Number of True Believers and the Great Difficulty of Saving Conversion* (London, 1641), and his subsequent *The Sound Believer* (London, 1649). See also Dyke, *The Mystery of Self-Deceiving*, ch. 30.

French, German, and Hungarian.[16] It was the thoroughness of
the work and its appeal for advancing 'heart religion' that earned
Dyke the international reputation of being the 'profundissimus
scrutator' of hypocrisy.[17]

Sources

Throughout the text, Dyke's chief authority, other than the Bible,
is Augustine, whose meditations on the divided self has been a
paradigm for Christian reflection since the fourth century.[18] Other
sources include Aristotle, Chrysostom, Bernard of Clairvaux, John
Foxe, Plato, Jerome, Seneca, Junius, Aelius Donatus, Pliny, and

16. See Michael P. Winship, *Godly Republicanism: Puritans, Pilgrims, and a
City on a Hill* (Cambridge: Harvard University Press, 2012), p. 141; Gina
Dahl, *Books in Early Modern Norway* (Leiden: Brill, 2011), p. 85; Brook,
Lives of the Puritans, 237; Keith L. Sprunger, *Dutch Puritanism: A History
of the English and Scottish Churches of the Netherlands in the Sixteenth
and Seventeenth Centuries* (Leiden: Brill, 1982), p. 359; Peter Damrau,
The Reception of English Puritan Literature in Germany (London: Maney
Publishing, 2006), pp. 97-100; *Mapping the Self*, 43; and J.R. Tanis, *Dutch
Calvinistic Pietism in the Middle Colonies: A Study in the Life and Theology
of Theodorus Jacobus Frelinghuysen* (Martinus Nijhoff, 1967), p. 22; Willem
op' t Hof, 'Puritan Emotions in Seventeenth-Century Dutch Piety,' in
Puritanism and Emotion in the Early Modern World, ed. Alec Ryrie and
Thom Schwanda (New York: Palgrave Macmillan, 2016), p. 235.

17. Gisbertus Voetius, *De theologia practica, in Selectarum disputationum
theologicarum* ... (Utrecht, 1648-1669), III, 4, 11, and *De simplicitate et
hypocrisi*, II, 483. Cited in Theodore D. Bozeman, *The Precisianist Strain:
Disciplinary Religion and Antinomian Backlash in Puritanism to 1638*
(Chapel Hill: University of North Carolina Press, 2004), p. 90. More recently,
Constance M. Furey has called Dyke 'the great Puritan depth psychologist.'
Furey, *Poetic Relations: Intimacy and Faith in English Reformation* (Chicago:
University of Chicago Press, 2017), p. 132.

18. See Augustine, *Confessions*. Numerous editions of the *Confessions* exist,
including the Latin. A widely used and readable translation by Henry
Chadwick was published by Oxford University Press in 1991. On the issue
of the divided self, see David C. Steinmetz, 'Calvin and the Divided Self
in Romans 7,' in *Augustine, the Harvest, and Theology (1300-1650): Essays
Dedicated to Heiko Augustus Oberman in Honor of his Sixtieth Birthday*,
ed. Kenneth Hagen (Leiden: Brill, 1990), pp. 300-13. Calvin preferred the
'older Augustine, who argued that grace places the believing self in conflict
with itself ...'

others. Dyke was, as was to be expected of a university-trained pastor, well versed in antiquity, the histories, and the learned languages of Latin, Greek, and Hebrew.[19]

Synopsis

Any reading of Dyke's *The Mystery of Self-Deceiving* is aided by Jeremiah Dyke's preface to the work in which he speaks of his brother's overall aim in writing the text. Dedicated to Lucy Russell, Countess of Bedford (d. 1627), a significant patron of the Puritan cause,[20] Jeremiah writes that his brother's work 'contains the right ... art of knowing [oneself and] discovers unto us the intricate windings and turnings of the dark labyrinths of [the] heart.' Further, the diligent reader will discover 'that dangerous art of self-sophistry displayed, by which millions of souls are enwrapped in the snares of Satan ...'[21]

The book itself can be divided into two main parts, the first being an explanation of the doctrine of the heart's deceitfulness (chapters 1-28), and the second being exhortations to make use of such a doctrine through practical means (chapters 29–31). Rather than give a chapter-by-chapter account of Dyke's arguments and exhortations, I will here only provide a synopsis of significant themes, arguments, and admonishments.

The Labyrinth of Self-Deception

For the doctrine of self-deceit, Dyke expounds Jeremiah 17:9-10: 'The heart is deceitful above all things, and evil, who can know it? I the Lord search the heart and try the reins, that I may give

---

19. For the rigors of a classical Puritan education in Dyke's time, see Sarah Bendall, et al, *A History of Emmanuel College, Cambridge* (Woodbridge: Boydell Press, 1999); John Morgan, *Godly Learning: Puritan Attitudes towards Reason, Learning, and Education, 1560-1640* (Cambridge: Cambridge University Press, 1986); and Alan P.F. Sell, *The Theological Education of the Ministry: Soundings in the British Reformed and Dissenting Traditions* (Eugene: Pickwick, 2013).

20. See Marion O'Connor, 'Godly Patronage: Lucy Harrington Russell, Countess of Bedford,' in *The Intellectual Culture of Puritan Women, 1558-1680* (New York: Palgrave Macmillan, 2010), pp. 71-83.

21. Dyke, *Mystery of Self-Deceiving*, Sig. A4.

to every one according to his ways, according to the works.'[22] In minute detail, Dyke outlines the intricacies of the deceitful human heart, and how such deception is prevalent not only within society, but in the 'whole soul ... the understanding, the will, [and] the affections.'[23] This deceit plagues every child of Adam and Eve, and the only person who was 'without guile' was Christ. In fact, even when grace comes into and transforms the heart of a believer, there is still enough of the 'old man' remaining that the heart of even the best might still be said to be 'deceitful.'[24] It is the tenor of one's life that distinguishes the regenerate from the unregenerate. The former delves into occasional sins, whereas the deceitfulness of the latter affects 'the whole course of their lives.'[25]

This self-deceit has its origins in original sin, when Adam and Eve, and by virtue of their parentage, all humanity were complicit in the 'willful conspiring with the devil' in the Garden of Eden. The darkness and despair into which humanity was cast is, says Dyke, aptly described by Augustine in his *Confessions*.[26] Here Dyke quotes Augustine's inner dialogue questioning his ability to trust himself, being susceptible to self-deception because of sin.[27] This inner corruption is so prevalent that it is like Hercules's monster: when one head is cut off another rises in its stead.[28]

---

22. Dyke, *Mystery of Self-Deceiving*, p. 1.

23. Dyke, *Mystery of Self-Deceiving*, p. 3.

24. Dyke, *Mystery of Self-Deceiving*, p. 4.

25. Dyke, *Mystery of Self-Deceiving*, pp. 4-5.

26. Dyke, *Mystery of Self-Deceiving*, pp. 6-7.

27. In fact, as other historians have observed, it is possible to see Dyke's *Mystery* as a Puritan reflection on Augustine's concept of the divided self. See Augustine, *Confessions*, trans. Henry Chadwick (New York: Oxford University Press, 1991); John D. Cox, *Shakespeare and the Dramaturgy of Power* (Princeton: Princeton University Press, 1989), pp. 75-6; and John D. Cox, *Seeming Knowledge: Shakespeare and Skeptical Faith* (Waco: Baylor University Press, 2007), p. 13. Cox writes, 'Dyke's chief authority is Augustine, whose meditations on the divided self in *The Confessions* are the *locus classicus* for the psychology of moral self-reflection.'

28. Dyke, *Mystery of Self-Deceiving*, p. 7.

There is only one way to uncover the heart's deception, and that is through the illumination of God's Spirit through His Word. The Word is that 'light which shineth in this darkness'; it is 'a glass, wherein we may behold the smallest wrinkle of deceit whatsoever.'[29] God's Word is such that it is an 'anatomizing knife' that cuts through the 'monster' of deceitfulness. Dyke writes that while it is impossible to fully discover the 'infinite number of the veins of deceitfulness,' it is possible to categorize deceitfulness generally into two sorts: the deceitfulness whereby we deceive others only and that whereby we deceive ourselves.[30]

For the first, Dyke details two species of deceit, that whereby one conceals what is and the other where something is counterfeited. Here Dyke, as an example of the first kind, describes the deception carried out by the Church of Rome and quotes John Foxe on how it exercised power and rule 'under the pretense of Peter's chair.'[31] For the second, which is the main issue for which Dyke wrote the treatise, 'self-deceit' is that deception which affects the mind and affections and permeates the whole course of one's actions.[32]

In typical Ramist fashion, Dyke further delineates self-deceit into various subtypes. One such subtype is the deception of believing that one is not as bad as he in truth is. It is his 'self-love' and 'self-deceit' that leads him astray, just as the Pharisee who 'crackles and cracks in the Gospel that he is not unjust, nor an extortioner.'[33] In this class of self-deception, one does not feel his inner corruption, and acts or

---

29. Dyke, *Mystery of Self-Deceiving*, pp. 8-11.

30. Dyke, *Mystery of Self-Deceiving*, pp. 12.

31. Dyke, *Mystery of Self-Deceiving*, 16-17. See John Foxe, *Acts and Monuments* (London, 1570). For Foxe's influence on the English Reformation, see John N. King, *Foxe's 'Book of Martyrs' and Early Modern Print Culture* (Cambridge: Cambridge University Press, 2006); D.M. Loades, *John Foxe and the English Reformation* (Aldershot: Ashgate Publishing, 1997); and Elizabeth Evenden and Thomas S. Freeman, *Religion and the Book in Early Modern England: The Making of Foxes' 'Book of Martyrs'* (Cambridge: Cambridge University Press, 2011).

32. Dyke, *Mystery of Self-Deceiving*, pp. 38.

33. Dyke, *Mystery of Self-Deceiving*, pp. 38-9.

behaves as though he were a moral person. But Dyke clarifies that such restrained behavior is not owed to one's moral nature but to the restraining grace and power of God that 'moderates' and 'bridles' their corruption. Thus, even in the unregenerate, it is because of God that one is not given over to 'pride, lust, [and] cruelty'; however, self-deception is such that the unregenerate imagine themselves to be 'framed of some pure mold, and ... of a better nature and disposition.' Their moral behavior, however, flows not from faith but from self-love. Dyke thus admonishes his readers 'diligently to examine whether the rest and silence of our corruption be from the restraining, or the renewing spirit ...'[34] The former evinces a graceless soul, the latter a renewed nature.[35]

Another related subtype of self-deception is to believe that one cannot fall into certain vices or temptations merely because they have hitherto in life been avoided. Here Dyke cites the story of Peter in the Gospel, 'who had so opened his ears to the voice of his own deceitful and lying heart that he could not believe Christ himself, the God of truth, forewarning him of his threefold denial.'[36] This disposition to sin, even among 'the best of us,' is due to original sin, in which we are 'bred and born,' and thus inherit a 'corrupt and rotten nature' prone to 'the vilest and most loathsome sins.'[37] Though there may be some sins that we are not as tempted toward as others, as Luther who said he never felt himself inclined to covetousness, there is no sin to which we cannot fall were God to withdraw his 'underpropping hand.'[38] To Plato's dictum, 'Have I done any such like thing?' upon hearing of another person's faults, Dyke adds, 'May I not do the like or worse?'[39]

---

34. Dyke, *Mystery of Self-Deceiving*, pp. 41-2.

35. The Puritan practice of self-examination, in which one probes deeper into the recesses of the heart to try to discern the work of God is the cornerstone of Puritan piety, especially in the pilgrim motif. See, for instance, Kathleen M. Swaim, *Pilgrim's Progress, Puritan Progress: Discourses and Contexts* (Urbana and Chicago: University of Illinois Press, 1993), chs. 5, 8.

36. Dyke, *Mystery of Self-Deceiving*, pp. 43-4

37. Dyke, *Mystery of Self-Deceiving*, p. 44.

38. Dyke, *Mystery of Self-Deceiving*, p. 45.

39. Dyke, *Mystery of Self-Deceiving*, p. 46.

Yet another subtype, which Dyke further breaks down into three classes, is when a person believes they are in a 'good and happy' estate with God when, in truth, they are without God and in a miserable condition.[40] The first class of person here are the 'rich worldlings' who believe they are the 'special darlings of God' because of their material prosperity. Dyke counters that if such is true, then why is heaven void of worldly treasure? Indeed, 'if silver and gold be our happiness, then it is in the earth, and so, which is strange, it is nearer hell ... than heaven ... let me have heaven's misery, take thou hell's happiness.'[41] Dyke does acknowledge, as did most Protestants, that earthly riches can be an instrument of virtue, and do much good in the world, as, for instance, the case of Job who blessed others with his wealth, but they are only ever an instrument, much in the same way that 'a good pen is the instrument of writing.'[42] Dyke admonishes that the bestowment of wealth is often given in judgment, with a view to damnation, and it is the duty of the reader to discern the source of his or her wealth.[43] Dyke sees wealth as a vehicle for good for those upon whom it is bestowed by God 'in love' and for the good of others. But for the rich worldling, Dyke has scathing words:

---

40. Dyke, *Mystery of Self-Deceiving*, p. 49.

41. Dyke, *Mystery of Self-Deceiving*, pp. 51-2.

42. Dyke, *Mystery of Self-Deceiving*, p. 53.

43. Dyke, *Mystery of Self-Deceiving*, 54. A common misunderstanding of the Puritan view of wealth is that God's favor is to be equated with one's material worth and possessions. In this paradigm, those who are poor are the object of God's wrath and disfavor. Dyke rejects this view of wealth and argues the opposite. For a further corrective to the notion, see Margo Todd, *Christian Humanism and the Puritan Social Order* (Cambridge: Cambridge University Press, 1987), pp. 118ff. Another error is Max Weber's idea that 'with heaven and hell heavily on their minds and spirits and suspecting the deep human potential for self-deception in assessing one's spiritual estate, Puritans supposedly searched for some outward empirical sign, a tangible proof, of divine hope and favor that would confirm their hope of salvation. That came ... in work and wealth—by getting rich in the emerging marketplace of capitalism.' Roy M. Anker, *Self-Help and Popular Religion and Early American Culture: An Interpretive Guide* (Westport: Greenwood Press, 1999), pp. 46-7.

The Lord turns his back upon him, even then when his hand reaches forth these outward things under him. In his anger he gives supposed felicities to the wicked, which in his mercy he denies to the godly. He puts them into the fatter pastures because he means to kill them, and causes these to feed on the bare commons ... If the stalled ox had reason, would he be so senseless as to think his master loved him better than his fellows, because of his more liberal food? Know it then thou rich worldling, God only fattens you for the slaughter.[44]

The second class of self-deception is those who live outwardly respectable lives and who believe that heaven is certain because of such right living. Dyke calls them the 'civil judiciary' because they judge themselves to be a moral and civil person in the world. But such a life is no different than that of a Pharisee. The reader must discern whether he or she falls into this class; Christ must 'wash and wipe his disciples feet; his blood must be both water and towel too. Renounce then thine own righteousness, even spiritual, much more civil, and trust only to his.'[45] The third class is that of the 'loose libertine' or 'carnal Gospeler.' They are those who 'turn the grace of God into wantonness' and believe they are 'in a good case before God,' but in truth live lives that are 'most vile and vicious.'[46]

Dyke spends considerable time discussing the self-deceit of 'temporary believers' and various other self-deceptions before he closes his work with various 'uses' of the doctrine.[47] The uniqueness of *The Mystery of Self-Deceiving*, at least in its genre of literature, is the thoroughness to which Dyke goes to uncover every possible area of self-deception. Stoeffler's opinion that no other Protestant work came close to uncovering the psychology of sin is probably correct. Harry Clark wrote that 'Dyke constructs a

---

44. Dyke, *Mystery of Self-Deceiving*, p. 55.

45. Dyke, *Mystery of Self-Deceiving*, p. 60.

46. Dyke, *Mystery of Self-Deceiving*, pp. 60-5.

47. See Dyke, *Mystery of Self-Deceiving*, 65-124; 137-357. Dyke does devote a chapter near the middle of the work on the 'use' of the doctrine to that point (See pp. 126-36).

labyrinth of conceptual contrivances, liberally mingling elements of accusation, exhortation, and especially psychological analysis.' In short, 'he strives for nothing less than a comprehensive typology of deception and self-deception.'[48] But as thorough the problem is, the remedy, cure, or 'use' of the doctrine, while not as detailed or intense, it is no less compelling.

The 'Uses' of the Doctrine

In the penultimate and ante-penultimate chapters, Dyke outlines several practical uses of the doctrine of self-deception. While he did include periodic uses throughout the book as a whole, here he presents ways that readers can apply the text to their life and so overcome their inclination to self-deceit. He does this in two ways. First, he proposes five uses of the doctrine; and second, he presents 'sincerity' as the highest and noblest perfection attainable in this life.

The five uses are first 'for watchfulness.' Given the severity and 'cunning tricks' of the deceitful heart, we should 'always be suspicious, and jealous over our hearts in all places, and upon all occasions in our solitariness, in our company, in our business with men, in our dealings with God, in hearing, praying, meditating; in our dealings also with Satan, in wrestling with his temptations.'[49] The second use is to bind oneself to God through personal covenanting, and with solemn vows, oaths, and resolutions to fight against the deceitfulness of the heart. While not every Puritan freely endorsed the use of such covenanting, for the main, personal covenanting had been engaged in for several generations. The earlier diaries of Richard Rogers and Samuel Ward, for instance, evince such practice, as do the later works of Cotton Mather and Jonathan Edwards.[50] John Walter has called

---

48. Henry C. Clark, *La Rochefoucauld and the Language of Unmasking in Seventeenth-Century France* (Genève: Librarie Droz, 1994), pp. 76-7.

49. Dyke, *Mystery of Self-Deceiving*, p. 357.

50. David George Mullan, *Scottish Puritanism, 1590-1638* (New York: Oxford University Press, 2000), p. 200; M.M. Knappen, ed., *Two Elizabethan Puritan*

Puritans 'covenanting citizens' for their use of public and private protestation and oaths.[51] Dyke recommends that one 'register and record ... in accounts-book' one's covenant and recall it when temptation rises.[52]

The third use is 'for wisdom to apprehend all good opportunities.' When one's heart is prepared and in a good frame, then 'is the time ... to fall to prayer, to confession of ... sins, to reading, to all the good exercises of repentance and invocation ...'[53] The fourth use is for 'strait examination of our hearts.' Here, says Dyke, one ought to 'keep an audit in our conscience, ever and anon calling them to their accounts.' Even further, Dyke advises, 'let us chastise our selves every morning, examine ourselves every evening, even in the silence of the night, as we lie waking on our beds.' Indeed, there should be 'daily, yea, hourly reckonings kept with our hearts ...'[54]

The fifth use is 'for exhortation to sincerity,' which is the antithesis of hypocrisy and deceit. Here one should pray with the prophet, 'renew a right spirit in me' (Ps. 51). Wherever the Bible speaks of perfection is 'to be understood of sincerity in the feeling of imperfection, and in an earnest desiring, and aspiring after perfection.'[55] Wherever sincerity is, God 'covers and cures all other infirmities.'[56]

The Puritan emphasis on sincerity and a sincere conversion has been noted by various scholars.[57] While one cannot attain moral

---

Diaries by Richard Rogers and Samuel Ward (Gloucester: Peter Smith, 1966), pp. 64, 80, 83; Cotton Mather, *Diary*; Jonathan Edwards, *Resolutions*.

51. See John Walter, *Covenanting Citizens: The Protestation Oath and Popular Political Culture in the English Revolution* (New York: Oxford University Press, 2017).

52. Dyke, *Mystery of Self-Deceiving*, pp. 361-3.

53. Dyke, *Mystery of Self-Deceiving*, p. 364.

54. Dyke, *Mystery of Self-Deceiving*, p. 368.

55. Dyke, *Mystery of Self-Deceiving*, pp. 374-5.

56. Dyke, *Mystery of Self-Deceiving*, p. 375.

57. See, for instance, Abram C. Van Engan's seminal work, *Sympathetic Puritans: Calvinist Fellow Feeling in Early New England* (New York: Oxford University Press, 2015), where the author argues that Puritan conversion

perfection in this life, he can strive after a virtuous disposition. As Karen Halttunen wrote:

> When the Puritan asked himself, 'Am I saved?' he implicitly questioned whether or not he was sincere. According to John Howe, a post-Restoration Puritan leader, 'Sincerity is a most God-like excellency; an imitation of his truth, as grounded in his all-sufficiency; which sets him above the necessity or possibility of any advantage by collusion or deceit; and corresponds to his omnisciency and heart-searching eye.'[58]

Similarly, Dyke wrote: 'Sincerity is the girdle whereby all other graces are tied close unto us.' It is the 'highest perfection' one can attain to in this life, and envelopes the whole of a person's conduct.[59] Where sincerity is, 'God both covers and cures all other infirmities'; it 'adds to the glory of our good actions' and mirrors God's own hatred against deceitfulness; within trials and temptations, sincerity makes us 'valiant' and 'courageous' and creates 'in us a true, manly, generous, and heroical spirits.'[60]

Dyke's stress on sincerity was a common Puritan motif as seen in other writers of the Puritan Reformation. For instance, John Preston wrote, 'in the performance of all the Duties of Sanctification, *Sincerity* is all in all.'[61] But the demand for sincerity went beyond simple truth-telling: Puritans insisted on a genuine and godly disposition, not only for life, in how one dealt with others or oneself, but before God with a sincere conversion. The notion of a 'sincere convert' was as common within Puritanism as Sabbath keeping, and it was understood that such was a gift

---

could be authenticated by the display of a tender heart and the emotional and sincere embrace of one's brokenness.

58. Karen Halttunen, *Confidence Men and Painted Women: A Study of Middle-Class Culture in America, 1830-1870* (New Haven: Yale University Press, 1982), p. 53.

59. Dyke, *Mystery of Self-Deceiving*, p. 369.

60. Dyke, *Mystery of Self-Deceiving*, pp. 371, 377, 383.

61. John Preston, *The New Covenant, or the Saint's Portion* (London, 1629), p. 1.

of grace that one could not invent.[62] But how does one actually come to possess sincerity? First, one should always 'possess his heart with the apprehension of God's presence, and so keep it in his fear continually, to walk, as Enoch did with God, as being in his eye; and with Moses, seeing him that is invisible … it is impossible for a man to speak as in God's presence, and not to speak sincerely.'[63] Secondly, we ought 'diligently to review all our works of obedience, as once God did his of creation, and so observe the peace and comfort of conscience which we find, when we do good things with good hearts, as on the contrary the trouble and disquiet of mind when we do otherwise.'[64] Third, we must pursue 'humiliation of spirit'; for the heart to be whole, 'it must first be rent and broken.'[65] Finally, the faith that sees the sincerity of God's love in Christ's death to us, and sees how 'Christ gave his heart to be pierced for us, cannot but make us return the like sincerity of heart and affection to God.'[66]

Conclusion

When one reads *The Mystery of Self-Deceiving* it is possible to come away with the impression that the book overwhelmingly focuses on the nuances of self-deceit and either minimizes or betrays adequate remedies for a troubled conscience. Such a perception comes from the fact that most of the book is devoted to 'Hercules's Monster,' and contains only a few chapters on remedies against deceitfulness. But such a reading would be misguided. For one, though Dyke does wait until the end to outline his paradigm of achieving sincerity, he is constantly asking his readers to engage in self-examination along the way; he does not merely state the problem, but asks his reader to actively engage in assessing oneself.

---

62. George McKenna, *The Puritan Origins of American Patriotism* (New Haven: Yale University Press, 2007), pp. 27-8; and Van Engen, *Sympathetic Puritans*.

63. Dyke, *Mystery of Self-Deceiving*, pp. 380-1.

64. Dyke, *Mystery of Self-Deceiving*, p. 381.

65. Dyke, *Mystery of Self-Deceiving*, pp. 382-3.

66. Dyke, *Mystery of Self-Deceiving*, p. 383.

Additionally, the ultimate goal of *The Mystery of Self-Deceiving* was to foster a culture of sincerity in life and thought. Were one to abandon all forms of self-pretense and deception, and lay all bare before God, one could come to a true, sincere, and abiding faith. Not only can such a person anticipate the future blessedness of heaven, he can also find joy and assurance in the here and now.

CHAPTER ELEVEN

Milton's Sonnet on His Blindness and the Puritan Soul

LELAND RYKEN

WHEN I was required to memorize John Milton's (1608–1674) sonnet on his blindness as a high school sophomore, I sensed that the poem was something momentous, but I understood little of what made it great. The door to a fuller understanding was opened when I came to specialize in Milton in graduate school, and for nearly half a century this poem has ranked second only to Psalm 23 as my favorite short poem.

My goal in this essay is to explore the poem as an expression of the Puritan soul. Before I answer the question of what things make the poem Puritan, I need to briefly explicate the poem itself.

The Poem

Here is the text of the poem:

> When I consider how my light is spent
> E're half my days in this dark world and wide,
> And that one talent which is death to hide
> Lodg'd with me useless, though my soul more bent
> To serve therewith my Maker, and present
> My true account, lest he returning chide,

'Doth God exact day-labor, light denied?'
I fondly ask. But Patience, to prevent
That murmur, soon replies: 'God doth not need
Either man's work or his own gifts; who best
Bear his mild yoke, they serve him best. His state
Is kingly; thousands at his bidding speed
And post o'er land and ocean without rest:
They also serve who only stand and wait.[1]

In its external format, this poem is an Italian sonnet—a fourteen-line poem with an intricate rhyme scheme. More specifically, the rhyming words fall into the prescribed pattern of abba abba cde cde. The content of an Italian sonnet is packaged as an octave (eight-line unit) that asks a question, raises a doubt, or poses a problem, and a sestet (six-line unit) that answers the question, resolves the doubt, or solves the problem. Milton's poem is built on this problem-solution format.

The topic of Milton's poem is acceptable service to God. Using the resources of high art, Milton implicitly asks, What does it take to please God? The answer is that God demands service from all His people, appropriate to the type of service that a person is capable of performing. The key verb *serve* appears three times in Milton's poem and is the linchpin on which the poem rests.

The poem contrasts two types of service. The assumption of the octave is that God requires active service in the world. But this premise, thoroughly Puritan in nature, produces a growing anxiety for the speaker because he has recently gone blind and cannot perform active service (or so the newly blind Milton thought). As the poet's meditation winds its way toward a resolution, an alternate type of service is found and declared to be equally acceptable to God.

The poem arises from a specific occasion in the poet's life, namely, Milton's becoming totally blind at the age of forty-four. The sentiments expressed in the poem are appropriate to that

---

1. John Milton, Sonnet 16, in *Poems, Etc. upon Several Occasions* (London: Tho. Dring, 1673), p. 59.

moment in the life of Milton, who could not have foreseen that he would continue to have an active public and literary life, and that he would write his three major works, including *Paradise Lost*, in his blindness. I will note in passing that the title by which the poem has come to be known—'On His Blindness'—was supplied by an editor a century after the poem's composition.

Lyric poems are usually structured on the principle of contrast, and Milton's sonnet runs true to form. The poem contrasts two types of acceptable service to God. The speaker's disordered way of thinking in the octave is mirrored in the piling up of subordinate clauses until the convoluted syntax collapses under its own weight. By contrast, the reply of Patience marches clearly in simple syntax. Despite the unwieldy syntax of the octave, the poem as a whole turns on a simple principle: I ask—Patience replies. The poem's change of focus from self to God is deftly imaged in the shift in pronouns between the octave (I, my, my, me, my, my, my, I) and sestet (his, his, him, his, his). All of the foregoing contrasts embody a conflict between despair in the octave and a mixture of relief, consolation, and triumph in the sestet.

The poem has a double argument. On the one hand, it is one of the most famous poems of resignation in the English language. But a proper interpretation of the poem's conclusion shows that it is just as thoroughly a poem of vindication or justification for the speaker: 'they also serve' who cannot perform active work in the world.

Despite all of the biographical particulars that make up the texture of the poem, we must always cling to the principle that literature also presents universal human experience. Milton's poem deals with such universal experiences as irremedial loss of something seemingly essential to life, physical handicap, and enforced inactivity. Yet the poem is not about a physical crisis. In keeping with the Puritan principle of the primacy of the spiritual, the poet wrestles with a spiritual crisis of soul, not the physical trials of being blind.

That, in brief, is the poem. My further purpose is to place the poem into its seventeenth-century Puritan context. I will provide a series of answers to the question, What makes this poem an expression of the Puritan soul?

The Poet

The first thing that is Puritan about Milton's famous sonnet is its author. John Milton was born in 1608 into a Puritan family living within sight of St Paul's Cathedral in London. Something of the Puritan makeup of the family can be gleaned from the fact that Milton's father had been permanently exiled from his childhood home at the age of twenty when his Roman Catholic father found him reading an English Bible in his room. John Milton the poet received a classical Christian education such as Puritan theory endorsed, and we might note that Milton's own educational treatise *Of Education* is unsurpassed as a summary of Puritan educational ideals. After receiving his elementary education at the famed St Paul's School in his own London neighborhood, Milton earned degrees from Christ's College of Cambridge University, next to Emmanuel College the most Puritan of the Cambridge colleges in the seventeenth century.

Like most Cambridge students of the time, Milton was theoretically headed for the ministry, but his Puritan convictions disqualified him from serving in the Church of England. Milton himself spoke of have been 'church-outed by the prelates.'[2] Milton scholars have debated about when Milton decided against the ministry as his vocation, but a more accurate conclusion is that he never did decide against the ministry; he simply shifted from the pulpit to the pen as the venue of ministry.[3] Milton's mention of his 'one talent' in the sonnet on his blindness may be a reference to his having felt called to be a poet from early years and throughout his life.

When the Puritan Revolution took root in England in the seventeenth century, Milton's superior intellectual and linguistic

---

2. John Milton, *The Reason of Church Government*, in *John Milton: Complete Poems and Major Prose*, ed. Merritt Y. Hughes (New York: Odyssey Press, 1957), p. 671. Henceforth cited as *Complete Poems*.

3. This is the thesis of Jameela Lares, *Milton and the Preaching Arts* (Pittsburgh: Duquesne University Press, 2001).

abilities made him a much-desired contributor to the Puritan cause, so he laid aside his poetic ambitions for twenty years to become a public spokesman for the Puritan movement. He wrote volumes of polemical prose on the standard Puritan topics of political freedom, ecclesiastical nonconformity, and the authority of the Bible to determine faith and practice. A strong Puritan sense of duty underlay Milton's diversion from his poetic calling, as enshrined in his own explanation: 'I perceived that if I ever wished to be of use, I ought at least not to be wanting to my country, to the Church, and to so many of my fellow Christians, in a crisis of so much danger; I therefore determined to relinquish the other pursuits in which I was engaged, and to transfer the whole force of my talents and my industry to this one important object.'[4] Milton became foreign secretary (technically 'Secretary of Tongues' and later Latin Secretary) to Oliver Cromwell and was one of the most prominent political figures on the international scene.

The significance of Milton's public years is not only that they were a twenty-year break from writing poetry but also that midway through this time (1652) he became totally blind. His blindness was hastened by the energy with which he threw himself into writing for the Puritan cause. When the monarchy was restored in 1660, Milton lived in hiding for a time and was temporarily imprisoned. His anti-royalist Puritan books were publicly burned. Milton lived his final days in a house near the nonconformist cemetery Bunhill Fields. When he died in 1608, he was buried (as his father had been) inside the parish church of St Giles Cripplegate in central London. Something of the nonconformist history of the church is suggested by the fact that today the church contains, in addition to a life-size bronze statue of Milton, busts of John Bunyan and Oliver Cromwell. Martyrologist John Foxe lies buried inside the church.

While my interest in this essay is the poem that Milton wrote, his Puritan life is relevant to that subject. If we are informed about how thoroughly Milton embodied the principles of Puritanism,

---

4. Milton, *Second Defense of the English People*, in *Complete Poems*, p. 830.

we can be predisposed to see the Puritan nuances in his sonnet, and we can have confidence in claiming them. Furthermore, sentiments expressed in a lyric poem often acquire depth of field when we know their real-life context. The earnestness of Puritan belief in Milton's sonnet on his blindness is not mere lip service. In modern parlance, Milton walked the walk. The resignation in the face of adversity to which the poem gives expression was present in Milton's life as well. Milton said regarding his blindness: 'I may oftener think on what [God] has bestowed than on what he has withheld.'[5]

The real-life context of Milton's sonnet gives his poem the quality of a personal testimony offered to the public. It is one of two sonnets in which Milton expresses his thoughts and feelings about his blindness. These poems have the public force of a Facebook statement posted by a well-known person today.

'When I Consider': The Puritan
Genre of Self-Examination

Placing Milton's sonnets into a Puritan context has been my specialized scholarly project for the past quarter of a century. One interesting fact that has emerged is that Milton regularly creates a work of high art out of a genre that was ordinarily expository and non-literary. For example, he wrote a sonnet 'on the religious memory of Mrs. Catherine Thomason my Christian friend deceased' that follows all the conventions of Puritan funeral sermons for women.[6] Similarly, a sonnet addressed to a virtuous young girl of Milton's acquaintance is a poetic version of a note of spiritual encouragement from a confidant. And so forth.

Milton's sonnet on his blindness follows this paradigm. The Puritans were enthusiasts for multiple types of meditation, one of which was introspective self-examination. The purpose of such

---

5. *Second Defense*, in *Complete Poems*, p. 826.

6. As I have shown in my essay '"Milton's Sonnet 14" and Puritan Funeral Sermons for Women', in *Milton's Legacy*, ed. Kristin A. Pruitt and Charles W. Durham (Selinsgrove, PA: Susquehanna University Press, 2005), pp. 136–48.

self-examination was to take stock of one's spiritual state, either to determine assurance of salvation or to spur one's progress in sanctification. Puritan self-examination was a form of accountability before God. New England Puritan John Higginson (1616–1708) defined self-examination as 'an enquiry into the inward Acts of our Souls, trying by the Word of God, whether we have the truth of Saving Grace in us ..., judging our spiritual Estates before God.'[7] That description fits Milton's sonnet perfectly: it is an inquiry into the author's spiritual state before God, and the inquiry is rooted from start to finish in the Bible.

Charles E. Hambrick-Stowe has explored the schedule by which the Puritans conducted their personal self-examination.[8] Self-examination could be as regular as a daily accounting or a weekly preparation for Sunday observance or the Lord's Supper. Or it might be governed by the yearly cycle, with the turning of the year being particularly highlighted. Other occasions mentioned by Puritan preachers were one's birthday and times of spiritual crisis. Milton's sonnet written on his twenty-fourth birthday ('How Soon Hath Time') exemplifies the first category. The sonnet I am considering was an exercise in spiritual self-examination on the occasion of the spiritual crisis engendered by Milton's becoming totally blind.

What is Puritan about Milton's sonnet on his blindness? The genre is, a fact that we might overlook if we were not thinking in terms of the Puritan tradition of spiritual self-examination. The poem begins with a formula that names the meditative stance in its pure form: 'When I consider ...' After that, the poet assembles his meditation right before us, step-by-step. In a sermon on 'Exact Walking', John Preston (1587–1628) engages in an extended discussion of the need to 'consider' as part of self-examination,

---

7. John Higginson, 'Some Help in Self-Examination', in *Our Dying Saviour's Legacy of Peace* (Boston: by Samuel Green for John Usher, 1686), pp. 117–88.

8. Charles E. Hambrick-Stowe, *The Practice of Piety: Puritans Devotional Disciplines in Seventeenth-Century New England* (Chapel Hill: University of North Carolina Press, 1982), pp. 169–74.

governed by the prayer, 'Let us beseech God to open our eyes to enable us to consider.'[9] In his sonnet, Milton heeds the Puritan dictum to 'consider', in this case his altered service to God now that he is blind. The content of Milton's consideration is tailored to the occasion of his crisis: it is not an accounting of the events of the day but a wrestling with the problem of how to render acceptable service to God. The quest to stand approved before God is the ultimate goal of Puritan self-examination, and Milton's sonnet fits the paradigm.

'A Perfect Rule of Faith': The Biblical Presence in Milton's Sonnet

Charles Spurgeon (1834–1892) famously said of John Bunyan (1628–1688) that 'the very essence of the Bible flows from him. He cannot speak without quoting a text, for his soul is full of the Word of God.'[10] The same is true of Milton and indeed of most Puritans. Both the argument and poetic texture of Milton's sonnet come largely from the Bible.

Familiarity with the Bible sprang from how the Puritans viewed the Bible. To begin, the Bible was regarded as the only final authority for religious belief. Thomas Shepard (1605–1649) called the Bible 'a perfect rule of Faith and Holiness, according to which all doctrines are to be tried, and all controversies decided'.[11] William Perkins (1558–1602) similarly called the Bible 'our rule and square, whereby we are to frame and fashion all our actions'.[12]

Flowing from its divine authority, the Bible was regarded as an infallible guide to daily living. Richard Sibbes (1577–1635)

---

9. John Preston, *Sermons Preached before His Majestie, and upon other special occasions* (London: John Beale for James Boler and Joane Greene, 1631), p. 99.

10. Charles Spurgeon, *C. H. Spurgeon's Autobiography* (Edinburgh: Banner of Truth, 1973), 2:159.

11. Thomas Shepard, *A Short Catechism Familiarly teaching The Knowledge of God, and of our Selves* (Cambridge, MA: Samuel Green, 1654), p. 14.

12. William Perkins, *A Treatise of the Vocations, or Callings of Men*, in *The Workes of that Famous and Worthy Minister of Christ in the Universitie of Cambridge, Mr William Perkins* (London: John Legatt, 1626), 1:767.

wrote that 'there is not any thing or any condition that befalls a Christian in this life but there is a general rule in Scripture for it.'[13] By rooting his sonnet so thoroughly in the Bible, Milton shows that he views it as his guide for solving the problem with which he wrestles in the poem.

There is a literary as well as religious dimension to the biblical presence in Milton's poetry. The Miltonist who directed my dissertation made the excellent point in his published explication of Milton's sonnet on the Piedmontese massacre ('Avenge, O Lord, Thy Slaughtered Saints') that in Milton's day 'biblical language [itself] appealed strongly to the imagination.'[14] It could not have been otherwise in view of how the Bible encompassed a Puritan's life in personal reading, at mealtime, in family devotions, in conversation, and in sermons. We can see, then, that Milton and Bunyan made a literary as well as religious move when they made their works a mosaic of biblical references. They were appealing to their readers' imagination as well as soul.

Milton's sonnet validates all that I have said about the Puritan devotion to Scripture. The poem's line of thought in the octave, and much of its language and imagery as well, are derived from two parables of Jesus in the Gospel of Matthew. One is the parable of the workers in the vineyard (Matt. 20:1–16), which supplies the images of day labor and night as cessation from work. It is also the basis for the ideas of God as the one who calls His creatures to work and who judges their effort, along with the creature's obligation is to serve God actively. Supplementing this is the parable of the talents (Matt. 25:14–30), which supplies the references to the slothful servant who hides his one talent, and the master who returns from a long journey and casts the slothful servant into outer darkness. This parable, too, teaches that God calls people to work for Him, with divine judgment based on a person's action or lack of it.

---

13. Richard Sibbes, *The Complete Works of Richard Sibbes*, ed. Alexander Balloch Grosart (Edinburgh: James Nichol, 1862), 7:204.

14. Kester Svendsen, 'Milton's Sonnet on the Massacre in Piedmont', *Shakespeare Association Bulletin*, vol. 20 (1945), p. 148.

With those two parables serving as a frame, Milton weaves other key biblical verses into his tapestry. One is the statement of Jesus regarding the man born blind that neither he nor his parents sinned 'but that the works of God should be made manifest in him,' supplemented by the statement that he 'must work the works of him that sent me, while it is day: the night cometh, when no man can work' (John 9:1–4, KJV [which was Milton's preferred English Bible]). In the sestet, the master biblical image comes in the last line, with its picture of waiting on God, a Christian virtue that the Bible commends in many passages.

Other biblical allusions and echoes also permeate the poem, but I have said enough to validate my claim that one thing that makes Milton's sonnet on his blindness an index to the Puritan soul is the way in which Milton bases the poem's argument on biblical doctrine and draws upon the Bible for much of his poetic texture. For the rest of this essay I will explore the Puritan doctrinal matrix out of which the poem arose.

'Doth God Exact Day-Labor?': The Puritan View of Work

The octave of Milton's sonnet is a progressively worsening anxiety-attack, and it is rooted in Puritan views of work and vocation. No Christian group thought and wrote more helpfully on the subject of work than the Puritans, and that thinking informs the first eight lines of Milton's sonnet. To keep the discussion brief, I will explore three Puritan tenets that lie behind Milton's thinking and feeling in the octave of his sonnet.

First, the Puritans believed that God calls all people to their work in the world. This is the famous Puritan concept of vocation. Perkins asserted in his classic *Treatise of the Vocations or Callings of Men* that 'every person ... without exception must have some personal and particular calling to walk in.'[15] The parable of the talents readily entered Puritan discussions of the need to work, just as it enters Milton's sonnet. Richard Steele (1629–1692) wrote that 'he that hath lent you talents hath also said, Occupy till

---

15. Perkins, *Vocations*, in *Workes*, 1:755.

I come.'[16] Richard Baxter (1615–1691) similarly directed, 'Acquaint yourselves with all the talents which you receive from God, and ... keep a just account of your receivings.'[17] In Puritan thinking, everyone has a vocation with attendant duties.

A second and related cornerstone of Puritan thinking about vocation is that God is the one who calls people to their tasks and the judge to whom people are accountable. Perkins wrote that 'God himself is the author and beginning of callings.'[18] That being the case, those who work in their callings must do so in an awareness that they are accountable to God as the judge of their efforts. Baxter advised that Christians must do their work 'as in [God's] sight, passing to his judgment,' while Cotton Mather (1663–1728) enjoined, 'Let every Christian ... act in his occupation with an eye to God, act as under the eye of God.'[19] In the complete works of Thomas Manton (1620–1677), two whole volumes are taken up with sermons on the parable of the talents, and one of Manton's main points is that God will conduct 'an exact account' of how we have exercised the talents He has given.[20] In a Puritan context, much is at stake in whether and how people pursue their callings in the world.

Thirdly, to make matters even more problematical for Milton in his state of recent blindness, the drift of Puritan thinking was to give priority to the active life and to disparage idleness and inactivity. Theoretically the Puritans found a place for rest and

---

16. Richard Steele, *The Tradesman's Calling* (London: Samuel Spring, 1684), p. 23.

17. Richard Baxter, *A Christian Directory*, in *The Practical Works of Richard Baxter* (Ligonier, PA: Soli Deo Gloria, 1990), 1:112. We might say that keeping a just account of his receivings in regard to his talents is exactly what Milton does in his sonnet.

18. Perkins, *Vocations*, in *Workes*, 1:750.

19. Baxter, *Christian Directory*, in *Works*, 1:97; Cotton Mather, *A Christian at His Calling*, in *Puritanism and the American Experience*, ed. Michael McGiffert (Reading, MA: Addison-Wesley, 1969), p. 127.

20. Thomas Manton, *The Works of Thomas Manton* (London: James Nisbet and Company, 1872), 9:450.

recreation in their lives, but in practice they gave precedence to work.[21] Not surprisingly, Baxter was a particular exponent of elevating work and action: 'Naturally action is the end of all our powers. ... It is for action that God maintaineth us and our abilities: work is the moral as well as the natural end of power. ... It is action that God is more served and honoured by.'[22] 'God doth allow none to live idly,' wrote Arthur Dent (1553–1607), while Robert Bolton (1572–1631) called idleness 'the very rust and canker of the soul.'[23] An early signpost to Protestant thinking on the elevation of the active life and demotion of non-work was Martin Luther's commentary on Genesis 2:15: 'Man was created not for leisure but for work.'[24]

The complex of ideas that I have covered—that everyone has a calling, that God is the one who calls and will judge on the basis of diligence exerted, and that the active life is what pleases God preeminently—are well known features of Puritanism. If we ask how this Puritan thinking informs Milton's sonnet, the answer is that the octave of the poem does not exist apart from it. Milton's anxiety (perhaps even a panic attack) is rooted in Puritan thought, and his anxiety about being unable to perform active service in the world is an important part of the Puritan soul that is my subject in this essay. We can trace two main motifs in the octave, both stemming from the framework I have sketched. They are the nature of the speaker's fear and the extremity of it.

The poet's fear centers in his inability to perform active work in the world, at the very time that he was one of the most prominent figures on the international European scene. The opening reference to light being spent is a double comment. It denotes Milton's

---

21. As I have shown in *Redeeming the Time: A Christian Approach to Work and Leisure* (Grand Rapids: Baker, 1995).

22. Baxter, *Christian Directory*, in *Practical Works*, 1:376.

23. Arthur Dent, The Plain Man's Path-way to Heaven (London: Robert Dexter,1601), p. 192; Robert Bolton, General Directions for a Comfortable Walking with God (Ligonier, PA: Soli Deo Gloria, 1991), p. 77.

24. Martin Luther, *Luther's Works*, ed. Jaroslav Pelikan (St. Louis: Concordia, 1958), 1:103.

blindness and also signals his inactivity from labor, along the lines of the parable of the workers in the vineyard (who were day laborers, hired by the day) and Jesus' comment about working 'the works of him that sent me, while it is day: the night cometh, when no man can work.' The fear about being inactive is not merely physical but also spiritual. With Puritan warnings about the need to give a good account to God, Milton ponders his inability to 'present a true [adequate] account' when his Maker returns after a long journey, with threat of chiding or judgment for inactivity. The parable of the master and stewards is the biblical subtext for this part of the sonnet, and the final judgment is the doctrinal framework.

The extremity of the speaker's fear is subtly conveyed. The most telling detail is Milton's linking himself by way of allusion with the one-talent, slothful steward of Jesus' parable. What was the fate of that steward? He was cast into outer darkness, hence Milton's reference to the talent being 'death to hide'. Other touches amplify the speaker's terror. The word 'spent' in the opening line is a financial image, signaling that the speaker begins his meditation in the position of a bankrupt. The word 'useless' in line four is evocative in itself, given the Puritan preoccupation with being useful to God, and it, too, is a financial term that can be linked with the unprofitable steward who hides the money entrusted to him and thereby does not earn interest or usury on his master's money. Finally, the overloaded syntax of the octave, with its superabundance of subordinate clauses heaped one upon another, embodies the distraught state of the speaker's thinking.

That, in brief, is a Puritan's anxiety over not serving God actively in the world, and as we move away from this anxiety vision we need to note that the speaker himself sees the futility of his disordered meditation. He 'fondly' asks the question of whether God will judge him for inactivity. 'Fondly' in Renaissance usage meant 'foolishly'. As the speaker comes to his senses, he realizes that no one works in the vineyard after nightfall. God does not expect work from someone who cannot perform it. The poet further stigmatizes his disordered meditation as being a 'murmur', with a weight of biblical references informing the word.

'Patience Soon Replies': The Puritan Virtue of Patience in Adversity

The second main movement of Milton's sonnet, following anxiety over inaction, is the silencing of the speaker's fear by a personified Patience. Patience in adversity was a prime Puritan virtue and a leading theme in the Puritans' writing and preaching. The starting point for their thinking was that 'it is the part of a Christian to suffer.'[25] George Swinnock (c. 1627–1673) wrote that 'saints in this life must look to suffer. Affliction is their portion. ... God hath decreed the saints to distress.'[26]

Starting from that premise, the Puritans developed an extensive body of writing on patient endurance and triumphant suffering as an ideal. As I develop the correspondence between that writing and Milton's sonnet, it will be evident that the vocabulary of Milton's sonnet (and the same thing is true of other sonnets by him) regularly uses the same words as Puritan religious writing on the same themes. As I quote from Puritan sources in the following paragraph, three key terms found in Milton's sonnet also appear in Puritan sources. They are the words patience (or its oppose impatience), murmur, and wait.

The keynote in Puritan writing about patience in adversity is that Christians have the spiritual resources to submit to divine providence without murmuring. Richard Bernard (1568–1620), for example, wrote: 'And therefore we may learn patience in affliction, and not be impatient ... nor murmur, lest God punish us.'[27] John Cotton (1584–1652) was of the opinion that 'you will stand in need of no small patience to wait long; you must be content to wait long upon God. ... You must bear all things patiently.'[28] And George Eves (c. 1613–1667) enjoined his congregation to 'wait upon [God],'

25. Thomas Adams, *The Works of Thomas Adams* (Edinburgh: James Nichol, 1861–1862), 3:24.

26. George Swinnock, *The Works of George Swinnock* (Edinburgh: James Nichol, 1858), 2:402.

27. Richard Bernard, *Ruths Recompense* (London: Simon Waterson, 1628), pp. 37–38.

28. John Cotton, *The Way of Life* (London: L. Fawne and S. Gellibrand, 1641), p. 121.

adding that 'it is the duty and the practice of God's people to bear the evils which he lays upon them with meekness and patience, … and not to murmur.'[29]

Milton's sonnet carries over these words and thoughts. For Milton, too, patience prevents his murmur against God's providence. For him, too, waiting on God is a spiritual virtue that he attains with confidence.

'They Also Serve Who Only Stand and Wait'

A superficial and incorrect reading of Milton's sonnet is that it repudiates the Puritan bias in favor of active service that informs the octave of the poem. But the alternate service that the poet discovers at the end of the poem is just that—an alternate service. The poet finds an avenue of service different from active work, but he does not disparage active service itself.

It is easy to see how the octave of the poem is rooted in Puritan thought and feeling. It is harder to prove that the alternate service celebrated at the end of the poem is equally Puritan. I am ready to make that case.

The first thing we need to determine is what the conclusion of the poem claims. What does it mean to 'only stand and wait'? Over the years I have struggled to find the right terminology for this. To call it passive service does not quite hit the target. If we start with Milton's physical situation now that he is blind, certainly we can say that he is thinking of a service of private retirement, in contrast to being in the public eye of the nation and continental Europe. I remember explicating the poem for an audience of retirees who found it easy to see their own experience in the poem—the experience of living in private retirement instead of public service, as forms of active work and the physical abilities that enabled them are increasingly taken away.

But more profound meanings are also present at the poem's close. Commentators on the poem regularly note that an adequate

---

29. George Eves, *The Churches Patience and Faith in Afflictions* (London: G. Bedell and T. Collins, 1661), p. 5.

solution to the poet's opening problem is attained in lines 9–11, with the declaration that 'who best bear his mild yoke, they serve him best.' A commentator correctly notes that the last three lines are 'extraneous in the apparent unity of an argument on justification', adding, 'What more remains to say? But no; now God is glorified.'[30] Someone else notes in the same vein that 'Patience has given an adequate answer by line eleven .... To discern what is superadded is to understand why the ending of the sonnet is triumphant rather than resigned.'[31]

So what is going on in the last three lines, and in what ways are these lines cut from the very same cloth as Puritan writings? The ending of Milton's sonnet draws upon the angelology (study of angels) in the Middle Ages and Renaissance. It was a commonplace that there were two orders of angels—the active ones who traversed the earth doing God's work, and the contemplative ones who remained always in God's heavenly court, worshiping and praising God. This medieval distinction lived on in Milton's Protestant milieu. While the Puritans did not accept the medieval hierarchy of angels, they did recognize in Scripture a twofold office exercised by angels: divine worship and earthly service (Ps. 103:20; Heb. 1:6, 14).[32]

The argument of the last three lines of Milton's sonnet rests on this distinction of angelic duties. The 'they' of the famous aphorism that makes up the last line of the poem are both people, who lack the powers of flight ascribed to the active angels in lines 12–13, and contemplative angels in God's presence. The image of standing and waiting is an image of monarchy, depicting courtiers who stand in waiting for service at a court. This is supplemented by

---

30. Paul Goodman, *The Structure of Literature* (Chicago: University of Chicago Press, 1954), p. 2.

31. Alan Rudrum, *A Critical Commentary on Milton's Comus and Shorter Poems* (London: Macmillan, 1967), p. 101.

32. William Ames, *The Marrow of Theology*, trans. and ed. John D. Eusden (repr., Grand Rapids: Baker, 1997), 103 (1.8.39). See Joel R. Beeke and Mark Jones, *A Puritan Theology: Doctrine for Life* (Grand Rapids: Reformation Heritage Books, 2012), 185–86.

the evocative associations of the word *wait*. Tracing the meanings of waiting on God through the Bible yields a many-sided and evocative collection of favorite verses.

Instead of tracing the image of waiting on God through the Bible, my purpose is to show the Puritan context of Milton's final consolation. As I quote selected passages from Puritan writings, I would ask my readers to be looking for two things. At the lexical level, we can discern the very words that Milton employs in his sonnet, especially the words patient (or a variant), yoke, murmuring, serve (or a variant), and waiting (or a variant). At the ideational level, it is important to note that the sentiments expressed in the sestet of Milton's sonnet are no less Puritan than those we find in the octave.

For example, Milton's declaration that 'God doth not need either man's work or his own gifts' finds these parallels in Puritan writing: God 'needeth not us nor our service, either on earth or in heaven;' 'God need[s] none of our works.'[33] Supplementing these statements about how God's glory is not dependent on active work from His creatures are statements that the worship of God and submission to His providence, even in adversity, is an acceptable form of service. Here is William Bates (1625–1699) on that subject: 'As a servant that stands and waits upon his master's pleasure, as truly serves him, as he that is most industrious in his business; so by an humble patient waiting upon your heavenly Lord ... you as truly please and glorify him, as when your active powers were fresh and lively, and you went about doing good.'[34]

I will add just a few more choice Puritan quotations that confirm how both the vocabulary and sentiment of Milton's closing lines conform to his Puritan milieu. The following statement comes from John Flavel's (1628–1691) classic book on providence: 'It will turn to a double advantage to you to continue in a quiet

---

33. Samuel Rutherford, *Letters of Samuel Rutherford* (Edinburgh: Banner of Truth, 1984), p. 614; Baxter, Christian Directory, in Practical Works, 1:111.

34. William Bates, *The Whole Works of the Rev. W. Bates* (Harrisburg, VA: Sprinkle, 1990), 4:243.

submissive waiting upon God. For though you do not yet enjoy the good you wait for, yet all this while you are exercising your grace. ... All this time the Lord is training you up in the exercise of faith and patience.'[35] If submission to God's providence is one strand in the service portrayed at the poem's conclusion, surely worship, too, is intended in the picture of standing and waiting in God's heavenly court. Sibbes had this to say about worship as a form of service (and I remind my readers that the concept of how to serve God acceptably is the main subject of Milton's sonnet): 'We serve [God] with inward worship and service ... when we love God above all, and fear him above all, and delight in him above all, ... this is the immediate service of God in our hearts.'[36]

The element of contemplation also enters Milton's picture of the second category of angels, who were, after all, known as the contemplative angels. William Whately (1583–1639) said regarding meditation that 'this also is an excellent service of God,' while Bates wrote that in heaven the saints 'are all united in that most joyful work of worshiping, or glorifying, and praising God.'[37]

Conclusion: The Puritan Soul

As I conclude my essay, I will briefly address three topics: how Milton's Puritan milieu helps to explain the poem he wrote, what makes up the soul of a Puritan, and how these things apply to our lives today.

By placing Milton's sonnet into a Puritan context, I have answered five significant questions about the poem—how Milton came to write a piece of introspective self-examination, why the poetic texture is a mosaic of biblical references, why the prospect of an inactive life produced anxiety for the poet who had recently gone blind, why a personified Patience is what points the poet in

---

35. John Flavel, *The Mystery of Providence* (Edinburgh: Banner of Truth, 1963), p. 196.

36. Sibbes, *Works*, 6:504–505.

37. William Whately, *Prototypes* (London: George Edwards, 1640), 247; Bates, *Works*, 3:36.

the right direction, and how an alternate type of service was ready at hand for the Puritan poet.

Secondly, if we take the poem as an example of the Puritan soul, we learn important things about it. The Puritan soul wished above all to please God by rendering acceptable service. While the default bent of a Puritan soul was to serve God through active work in the world, that default mode was not the only one. For Puritans, the primacy of the spiritual was the foundation on which everything else rested. Accordingly, they valued the praise and worship of God, submission to His providence, and patience in adversity as forms of spiritual service on a par with work.

Finally, what is the takeaway value for our encounters with Puritan writing, in this case literary writing of the highest order? I can say regarding my experience of Milton's sonnet over half a century of teaching it and speaking and writing about it that the magic never ends. One Saturday afternoon I entered my office to find an email from a former student who has suffered from chronic fatigue syndrome her entire adult life, thanking me for introducing her to Milton's sonnet and 'his wonderful life'. On another occasion a former student placed a 'stickem' note on my office door informing me that Milton's sonnet had sustained him over twenty years of missionary service in Japan. I also remember an exchange about Milton's sonnet with a former student and Milton enthusiast when she underwent a prolonged bedridden pregnancy, and an email from a total stranger who is blind.

Milton took the comforting, biblical insights of the Puritans, whose writing was prolix and style utilitarian, and crafted them into succinct poetry that is the very touchstone of high art.

CHAPTER TWELVE

A String of Pearls (Psalm 119): The Biblical Piety of Thomas Manton[1]

J. STEPHEN YUILLE

MYSTICISM is rooted in the conviction that we can attain an immediate knowledge of God and His will through personal experience as we listen for His voice in our hearts—a voice we discern in 'gusts of emotion' and 'inner urgings'.[2] Regrettably, such mysticism is the presumptive position within large segments of evangelicalism today. Many believe they are able to sense the Holy Spirit working directly (apart from the Bible) within them, producing impulses and intuitions as a means of communicating His will to them. In so doing, they

---

1. *Author's note:* Since first meeting Dr Joel Beeke ten years ago, I have benefited greatly from his faithful example and ministry. I count it a privilege, therefore, to contribute a chapter to this festschrift composed in his honor.

2. J. I. Packer and Carolyn Nystrom, *Guard Us, Guide Us: Divine Leading in Life's Decisions* (Grand Rapids: Baker, 2008), p. 14. How are we to understand our 'inner urgings'? According to John Murray, we will experience feelings, impressions, convictions, etc, as we respond to the Holy Spirit's work of illumination 'through the Word of God.' However, this is not to be confused with the mystic's belief that the state of our consciousness (i.e., feelings) is the result of a 'direct intimation' of the Holy Spirit's will to us. See John Murray, 'The Guidance of the Holy Spirit', in Sinclair B. Ferguson, *From the Mouth of God: Trusting, Reading, and Applying the Bible* (Edinburgh: Banner of Truth, 2014), p. 185.

have made their relationship with God contingent upon nebulous feelings. Even more troubling is the fact that they have made an unwarranted cleavage between the Spirit of God and the Word of God, thereby divorcing the Holy Spirit from the only infallible and sufficient revelation that He has given us—namely, the Bible.

My goal in this chapter is to put forth an alternative model of biblical piety (or, spirituality) by turning to the example of Thomas Manton (1620–1677), and my prayer is that past wisdom will prove richly instructive for present church life.

Life and Ministry

Thomas Manton was born at Lydeard St Lawrence, Somerset, on March 31, 1620.[3] After completing grammar school, he enrolled at Wadham College, Oxford, and graduated four years later with a Bachelor of Arts. Since advanced degrees did not require his presence at Oxford, he would go on to complete the Bachelor of Divinity in 1654 and the Doctor of Divinity in 1660 while engaged in ministry.

---

3. The standard account of Manton's life is: William Harris, 'Some Memoirs of the Life and Character of the Reverend and Learned Thomas Manton, D. D.', in Thomas Manton, *The Complete Works of Thomas Manton*, 22 vols. (London: James Nisbet, 1870–1875; repr., Birmingham: Solid Ground Christian Books, 2008), 1:vii–xxxiii. Harris's biographical sketch is based upon two earlier accounts: (1) William Bates, 'A Funeral Sermon Preached upon the Death of the Reverend and Excellent Divine, Dr Thomas Manton', in Manton, *Works*, 22:123–47; and (2) Anthony Wood, *Athenae Oxonienses*, 2 vols. (London, 1691), 2:446–48. Additional summaries of Manton's life are found in: (1) Edmund Calamy, *The Nonconformist's Memorial: Being an account of the ministers, who were ejected or silenced after the Restoration, particularly by the Act of Uniformity, which took place on Bartholomew-day, Aug. 24, 1662* (London, 1775), 1:138–41; and (2) Joel R. Beeke and Randall J. Pederson, *Meet the Puritans: With a Guide to Modern Reprints* (Grand Rapids: Reformation Heritage Books, 2006), pp. 407–409. For a more thorough analysis of Manton in his historical context, see (1) Derek Cooper, 'The Ecumenical Exegete: Thomas Manton's Commentary on James in Relation to its Protestant Predecessors, Contemporaries and Successors' (PhD thesis, Lutheran Theological Seminary, 2008); and (2) Adam Richardson, 'Thomas Manton and the Presbyterians in Interregnum and Restoration England' (PhD thesis, University of Leicester, 2014).

Upon his ordination to the diaconate in 1639, Manton embarked on his first lectureship at the parish church of Culliton (Colyton), Devon. In order to avoid the growing political unrest in the region, he moved a short time later with his new bride, Mary Morgan, to London. In 1644, St Mary's Stoke Newington was sequestered, and the pastorate was offered to Manton. He held this position until becoming pastor of St Paul's Covent Garden a few years later.

These were eventful years for the nation, and Manton found himself in the midst of significant social and political upheaval. In 1641, Parliament passed the Grand Remonstrance, which eventually led to the Civil War between parliamentarians and royalists. After the former's victory in 1646, Charles I attempted to persuade Scotland to invade England under the promise that he would establish Presbyterianism. Disappointed by the Long Parliament's unwillingness to confront the king, General Pride (commander of the New Model Army) 'purged' it of close to two hundred members in 1648. The remaining members constituted the new Rump Parliament, which eventually tried and executed the king for treason. Manton played no role in this. While it is true that he served as one of the three clerks at the Westminster Assembly, penned the introduction to the documents of the Westminster Assembly, preached occasionally before Parliament, and prayed at various ceremonies related to Oliver Cromwell's Protectorship, Manton remained a committed royalist. He was one of fifty-seven divines who signed a protest against the Rump Parliament's plan to execute the king.

Despite his outspoken opposition to the regicide, Manton was a prominent figure during Oliver Cromwell's protectorate. He quickly became a leading voice in political and theological matters, serving on numerous commissions. After Richard Cromwell's protectorate failed in 1660, General Monck restored the Long Parliament by re-instating those members who had been excluded twelve years earlier. It immediately dissolved itself and convened the new Convention Parliament, composed mostly of Presbyterians favorable to the return of Charles II. Manton was very active in this endeavor. According to J. C. Ryle, 'If there was one name which more than another was incessantly before the public for several years about the period of the Restoration, that name was Manton's.'[4] He was one of the delegates who met with Charles II at Breda, in order to negotiate the terms of his return.

Upon his restoration, the king convened the new Cavalier Parliament, thereby sweeping away any hopes for compromise between Presbyterians and Episcopalians. It passed the Act of Uniformity in 1662, requiring all who had not received Episcopal ordination to be re-ordained by bishops; moreover, it required ministers to declare their consent to the entire Book of Common Prayer and their rejection of the Solemn League and Covenant. As a result, approximately two thousand ministers (including Manton) left the Church of England. While actively seeking accommodation for Presbyterians within the national church, Manton continued to preach privately. Because of his violation of the Five Mile Act, he was imprisoned for six months in 1670;[5] however, the political indulgence two years later allowed him to preach openly at his home in Covent Garden. Soon after, he became a lecturer at Pinner's Hall, and remained in this capacity until his death on October 18, 1677.

At Manton's funeral, William Bates preached on 1 Thessalonians 4:17, 'And so shall we ever be with the Lord.'[6] In the course of his sermon, he praised his close friend for 'the holiness of his person,' extoling in particular his 'constancy,' 'loyalty,' 'charity,' and 'humility.'[7] Bates also praised Manton for 'the quality of his office,' affirming that he possessed 'a clear judgment, rich fancy, strong memory, and happy elocution.'[8] These 'parts,' coupled with his extraordinary knowledge of Scripture, made him an

---

4. J. C. Ryle, 'An Estimate of Manton', in Manton, *Works*, 2:vii.

5. This Act prohibited ministers from coming within five miles of the parish church from which they had been ejected.

6. Bates, 'Funeral Sermon', in Manton, *Works*, 22:123–47. J. C. Ryle provides an insightful assessment of Manton as a 'man', 'writer', 'theologian', and 'expositor.' 'Estimate of Manton', in Manton, *Works*, 2:iii-xiii.

7. Bates, 'Funeral Sermon', in Manton, *Works*, 22:146.

8. Bates, 'Funeral Sermon', in Manton, *Works*, 22:143.

excellent minister of the gospel. According to Bates, the goal of Manton's preaching was to 'open' eyes so that people might see 'their wretched condition as sinners'; to cause them to flee 'from the wrath to come'; to make them 'humbly, thankfully, and entirely' receive Christ as their all-sufficient Savior; and to edify them 'in their most holy faith'.[9] The style of Manton's preaching was commensurate with his goal. 'His expression,' writes Bates, 'was natural and free, clear and eloquent, quick and powerful … this man of God was inflamed with a holy zeal, and from thence such ardent expressions broke forth as were capable to procure attention and consent in his hearers.'[10]

By all accounts, Bates's high estimation of Manton's preaching was fully warranted.[11] According to Edmund Calamy, Manton 'left behind him the general reputation of as excellent a preacher as this city or nation hath produced.'[12] He preached numerous miscellaneous sermons, plus extensive series on the Lord's Prayer, Christ's temptation, Christ's transfiguration, Isaiah 53, 2 Thessalonians 2, Matthew 25, John 17, Romans 6 and 8, 2 Corinthians 5, Hebrews 11, Psalm 119, James, and Jude.[13] Manton placed such importance

---

9. Bates, 'Funeral Sermon', in Manton, *Works*, 22:144. Manton was Calvinistic in soteriology. See *Works*, 3:328–31; 5:475–84; 12:295–96, 314–15; 20:326, 361. However, he modeled his preaching on Christ, particularly His free offer of the gospel. See *Works*, 13:293. For a brief discussion of the relationship between his soteriology and preaching, see Donald J. MacLean, 'Thomas Manton (1620–1677)', in *James Durham (1622–1658) and the Gospel Offer in its Seventeenth-Century Context* (Vandenhoeck & Ruprecht, 2015), p. 197–214.

10. Bates, 'Funeral Sermon', in Manton, *Works*, 22:144–45.

11. In the opinion of Archbishop James Ussher, Manton was one of the 'best preachers in England.' As cited by Harris, 'Some Memoirs', in Manton, *Works*, 1.xi.

12. Edmund Calamy, *An Abridgement of Mr Baxter's History of His Life and Times* (London, 1702), p. 210.

13. Manton's published works include close to 1,000 sermons gathered into twenty-two volumes. Interestingly, they do not contain a single polemical or doctrinal treatise. All of his writings, therefore, are expositional. In the opinion of Hughes Oliphant Old, Manton's published works 'probably give us the best sustained impression of Puritan preaching which is available.' *The Reading and Preaching of the Scriptures in the Worship of the Christian*

on preaching because he viewed it as a means of grace in which Christ was present.[14] To put it another way, he was convinced that preaching possesses 'a ministerial efficacy by which the authority and sovereign efficacy of the Spirit is conveyed'.[15] For this reason, he affirmed that we ought to listen to the Bible 'as if we had heard [God] utter and pronounce it with his own mouth, or had received it immediately by oracle from him.'[16]

This conviction is apparent throughout Manton's sermons, but nowhere more prevalent than in his 190 sermons on Psalm 119.[17]

Church, 7 vols. (Grand Rapids: Eerdmans, 2002), 4:301. For an analysis of Manton as a biblical interpreter, see Derek Cooper, *Thomas Manton: A Guided Tour of the Life and Thought of a Puritan Pastor* (Phillipsburg: P&R Publishing, 2011), pp. 79–142. Cooper's study focuses on Manton's sermons on the Book of James.

14. Manton champions the Reformed position of *fides ex auditu*. The implication is that if we absent ourselves from preaching, we isolate ourselves from God's grace. For more on the Puritans' emphasis on the life-giving power of the Bible, see J. I. Packer, *A Quest for Godliness: The Puritan Vision of the Christian Life* (Wheaton: Crossway Books, 1990), pp. 281–284.

15. Manton, *Works*, 4:132. He would agree wholeheartedly with John Calvin's assertion (based on Rom. 10:17) that 'when it pleases the Lord to work', preaching 'becomes the instrument of his power.' *Commentaries on the Epistle of the Apostle Paul to the Romans*, in *Calvin's Commentaries*, 22 vols. (Grand Rapids: Baker Books, 2003), 19:401. Arnold Hunt points to two sources for the Reformed method of preaching. The first is Paul's portrayal of the inseparable link between preaching, hearing, and believing, as articulated in Romans 10:17. The second is Aristotle's theory of perception, according to which hearing contributes most to 'the acquisition of knowledge.' *The Art of Hearing: English Preachers and Their Audiences, 1590–1640* (Cambridge: 2010), pp. 22–23. For more on the relationship between the Reformed method of preaching and the Reformed doctrine of Scripture, see Mary Morrissey, 'Scripture, Style, and Persuasion in Seventeenth Century English Theories of Preaching', *Journal of Ecclesiastical History*, vol. 53, no. 4 (October 2002).

16. Manton, *Works*, 7:261.

17. These sermons are found in *Works*, vols. 6–9. According to Bates, Manton preached them 'in his usual course of three times a week'. 'To the Reader', in Manton, *Works*, 6:2. In describing Manton's audience, Vincent Alsop writes, 'They can here with safety read what with great danger they formerly heard.' 'To the Reader', in Manton, *Works*, 6:4. This remark seems to imply that Manton preached this series of sermons under some duress—perhaps in the late 1660s, after the passing of the Five Mile Act.

He begins his series by affirming that this psalm is 'a choice piece of Scripture' because it provides a description of 'true blessedness'.[18] In Manton's opinion, blessedness is humanity's greatest longing; however, very few people find it because they mistake either its 'end' or 'means'.[19]

The End of Blessedness

Many people err in its 'end', meaning they seek it in the wrong place. Manton develops this assertion in his exposition of Psalm 119:12: 'Blessed art thou, O LORD.' Here, he puts forth six propositions concerning blessedness. First, 'God is over all, and above all, blessed enough in himself, and needs nothing from us to add to his happiness and perfection.'[20] Manton's point is that God is a perfect being.[21] By this, he means that 'there is such an absolute perfection in [God's] nature that nothing is wanting to it or defective in it, and nothing can be added to it to make it better.'[22] Because He is a perfect being, God is necessarily sufficient and satisfied in Himself; that is to say, 'his happiness lies in knowing himself, in loving himself, in delighting in himself.'[23] Do we have any effect upon this blessed God? 'He is above our benefits and injuries,' says Manton.[24]

Second, 'though God stands in no need of us, yet he is willing to communicate his blessedness, and to make us happy in the enjoyment

---

18. Manton, *Works*, 6:5. Manton sees little coherence in Psalm 119 as a whole, commenting, 'Many of the sentences have no other connection than pearls upon the same string.' *Works*, 7:95. Also see 8:134.

19. Manton, *Works*, 6:6.

20. Manton, *Works*, 6:111. This proposition is derived from Romans 9:5; Psalm 16:2; Proverbs 8:30–31.

21. For more on the Puritan understanding of God's perfect being, see J. Stephen Yuille, 'The Boundless and Blessed God: The Legacy of Amandus Polanus in the Theology of George Swinnock', in *Learning from the Past: Essays on Reception, Catholicity and Dialogue in Honor of Anthony N. S. Lane*, eds. Jon Balserak and Richard Snoddy (London: T&T Clark, 2015), pp. 147–62.

22. Manton, *Works*, 7:236.

23. Manton, *Works*, 6:109.

24. Manton, *Works*, 6:111.

of himself.'[25] God does this in two ways.[26] First, He communicates His blessedness to us 'mediately' in the present through secondary means. These include 'common mercies' such as life, light, warmth, and health, which He gives through the sun, rain, plants, and animals, and 'special mercies' such as grace, comfort, peace, and joy, which He gives through the Word and seals. Second, God communicates His blessedness to us 'immediately' in the future without the use of secondary means. This is the happiness of heaven, when our knowledge of Him will be full and perfect, constant and complete, resulting in hitherto unknown delight as we rest fully and finally in Him.

Third, 'the word of God, especially the gospel part, does only teach us the way how we may be blessed in the enjoyment of God.'[27] For Manton, it does so by informing us that in Christ we are freed from God's wrath and received into His favor; we are 'under the special care and conduct of God's providence'; we possess 'a sure covenant-right to everlasting glory'; and we enjoy 'sweet experiences of God's goodness' and 'a great deal of peace.'[28]

Fourth, 'if we would profit by the word of God, we must go to God, and desire the light and strength of his grace.'[29] We are entirely dependent upon God to lead us in the way of blessedness;[30] therefore, He must teach us 'outwardly' through the ministry of His Word and 'inwardly' through the work of His Spirit.[31] The Holy Spirit's work includes the illumination of the mind so that 'we come to apprehend the things of God in a spiritual manner,' as well as the inclination of the heart and will.[32] Manton summarizes as follows: 'When God

---

25. Manton, *Works*, 6:111. This proposition is derived from Psalm 8:3–4; 16:11; 1 Corinthians 15:28.

26. Manton, *Works*, 6:112.

27. Manton, *Works*, 6:112. This proposition is derived from 1 Timothy 1:11.

28. Manton, *Works*, 6:14–15. For more on the blessings of the gospel, see 9:106–107.

29. Manton, *Works*, 6:113. This proposition is derived from Psalm 16:7; John 6:44.

30. See verses 12, 26, 27, 29, 33, 34, 64, 66, 73, 108, 124, 125, 135, 144, 169.

31. Manton, *Works*, 6:115.

32. Manton, *Works*, 6:116.

teaches, truth comes upon us with more conviction and demonstration (1 Cor. 2:6), and so has a greater awe and sovereignty ... It does not only stay in the fancy, float in the brain, but affects the heart.'[33]

Fifth, 'the more we are brought to attend upon the word, and the more influence the word has upon us, the nearer the blessing.'[34] According to Manton, God's Word alone teaches us how 'to love [God] and enjoy him as our chief good, and to glorify him as our utmost end.'[35] In short, it tells us that we must be 'conformed' to His nature. This occurs when we 'we love what he loves, and hate what he hates.'[36] As we become more like Him, we naturally grow in our enjoyment of Him.

Sixth, 'it is not only an affront put upon God, but also a great wrong, to neglect the word of God, and the way he prescribes, and to seek blessedness in temporal things.'[37] Manton is adamant that 'temporal things' cannot provide us with true blessedness: they cannot fill the heart because they are finite in nature; they cannot reach the heart because they are material in nature; and they cannot satisfy the heart because they are temporal in nature. The soul can only find happiness in that which is suited to it. This means 'the infinite God' alone can satisfy us.

'Thou art good, and doest good,' declares the psalmist (v. 68). In his exposition of this verse, Manton declares that, because God is blessed in Himself, He is *summum bonum*—the chief good.'[38]

---

33. Manton, *Works*, 6:118.

34. Manton, *Works*, 6:113. This proposition is derived from Proverbs 8:34; Acts 8:36.

35. Manton, *Works*, 6:109.

36. Manton, *Works*, 6:110.

37. Manton, *Works*, 6:113. This proposition is derived from Psalm 16:11.

38. Manton, *Works*, 7:236. At times, the Bible compares God to that good which is *essential*: He is life, light, food, water, and rest (Pss. 36:9; 116:7; John 1:4, 9; 4:10; 6:51; James 1:17). At times, it compares Him to that good which is *beneficial*: He is home, health, peace, fire, and refuge (Pss. 42:11; 57:1; 90:9–10; Zech. 2:5; 2 Cor. 13:11). At times, it compares Him to that good which is *delightful*: He is wealth, honor, wine, joy, and pleasure (Job 22:24–25; Ps. 43:4; Isa. 25:6; 33:21; Zech. 2:5).

He is 'good of himself, good in himself, yea, good itself.'[39] He is 'originally' good because He is the fountain of all good. He is 'infinitely' good because His goodness is full and complete. He is 'eternally' good because His goodness is without 'addition' or 'subtraction.' That being the case, our blessedness necessarily lies in taking Him as our 'portion' (v. 57). As Manton explains, the term 'portion' comes from the distribution of the land of Canaan to the Israelites, and serves to convey the reality that God alone is our inheritance.[40] He is the sum and substance of all the promises: 'I will be their God, and they shall be my people' (Jer. 31:33). He is the very heaven of heavens: 'In thy presence is fullness of joy; At thy right hand there are pleasures forevermore' (Ps. 16:11). And He is what Christ purchased for us: 'For Christ also hath once suffered for sins, the just for the unjust, that he might bring us to God' (1 Pet. 3:18).

For Manton, therefore, true blessedness is not rooted in life's changing conditions and circumstances but in an unchanging God. We are made for eternity, and we are made for something greater than ourselves—something greater than anything this world has to offer. This *something* is God, of course. He created us in His image, so that we might find our rest and center in Him.[41] When we take Him as our portion, we find in Him all we could ever want: an eternal and spiritual good, suitable to our every need. For this reason, we must, in the words of Manton, 'fix [our]

---

39. Manton, *Works*, 7:236. Also see 7:107–109.

40. Manton, *Works*, 7:105.

41. The framework for this teleological view of the image of God is found in Aristotle, who writes, 'There is some end (τέλος) of the things we do, which we desire for its own sake.' This 'end' is 'the chief good' (happiness), which is 'always desirable in itself and never for the sake of something else.' On this point, see *Nicomachean Ethics*, in W. D. Ross (ed.), *The Works of Aristotle*, vol. 9 (Oxford: Oxford University Press, 1963), 1.2, 4, 7, 13. For Aristotle, the conclusion is primarily ethical; that is, the happy man is the virtuous man— virtue being the mean between two extremes. While embracing aspects of Aristotle's framework, Manton rejects his view of the virtuous man. For him, our 'chief end' is the blessed God.

end and scope, which is to be everlastingly happy in the enjoyment of God.[42]

The Means to Blessedness

In addition to mistaking the 'end' of blessedness, Manton affirms that many people err in its 'means'; that is to say, they pursue blessedness in the wrong way. As Manton makes clear in his sermons on the opening verses of Psalm 119, the only way to the blessed God is through the Word of God.

God's Word dictates, firstly, the 'course' of our 'life': 'Blessed are the undefiled in the way, who walk in the law of the LORD' (v. 1).[43] Here, the psalmist describes how the blessed walk (they are 'undefiled in the way') and where the blessed walk ('in the law of the LORD'). From this Manton concludes that the only way to true blessedness is found in 'sincere, constant, uniform obedience to God's law.'[44] Such obedience means endeavoring to 'approve' ourselves to God.[45] Manton is careful to note that there is a two-fold obedience in Scripture: 'legal,' which is perfect conformity to God's will; and 'gospel' (or, 'evangelical'), which is sincerity in seeking to obey God's will.[46] 'This sincere obedience,' says Manton, 'is known by our endeavors after perfection, and our repentance for defects.' He adds, 'Where there is a general purpose to please God, and a hearty sorrow when we offend him, this is the sincerity which the gospel accepteth of.'[47]

God's Word dictates, secondly, the 'frame' of our 'heart': 'Blessed are they that keep his testimonies, and that seek him with the whole heart' (v. 2).[48] Manton sees two features of the blessed man in this verse. The first is what he keeps: God's 'testimonies'. This keeping

---

42. Manton, *Works*, 2:137. This citation is from a sermon on Luke 9:57–62.

43. Manton, *Works*, 6:15, 38.

44. Manton, *Works*, 6:9.

45. Manton, *Works*, 6:11.

46. Manton, *Works*, 6:20. Also see 6:357; 7:96; 9:223.

47. Manton, *Works*, 6:97.

48. Manton, *Works*, 6:15, 38.

of God's Word is possible because God 'enlightens' our minds to understand His will and 'frames' our affections to obey His will. Manton concludes: 'So long as we bewail sin, seek remission of sin, strive after perfection, endeavor to keep close and be tender of a command, though a naughty heart will carry us aside sometimes, we keep the testimony of the Lord in a gospel sense.'[49]

The second feature of the blessed man is what he seeks: God 'with the whole heart'. According to Manton, the 'whole heart' denotes 'extension of parts' (the mind, affections, and will), and 'intension of degrees' (the highest elevation of our hearts).[50] We are not to understand this pursuit of God in 'the legal sense with respect to absolute perfection,' but in a gospel sense, meaning we are to use 'all good means to cleave to God,' repent of 'our defects … with kindly remorse,' and seek 'pardon and peace in Christ's name.'[51] Manton's point is that the blessed man no longer sins by way of course. 'We might fall into the dirt,' says he, 'but we do not wallow in it like swine in the mire.'[52]

God's Word dictates, thirdly, the 'integrity' of our 'obedience': 'They also do no iniquity: they walk in his ways' (v. 3).[53] Having considered 'holiness' in terms of its 'subject' ('the life of man') (v. 1) and 'object' ('the heart of man') (v. 2), Manton now turns to its expression, which consists of two parts. The first is 'negative': there is 'an eschewing of sin,' in that the blessed 'do no iniquity.'[54] How is this possible? For Manton, the answer is that those who 'do no iniquity' are those to whom God 'imputeth no sin to condemnation' because they 'are renewed by grace, and reconciled to God by Christ Jesus.'[55] Because of their new identity in Christ, they make it their business to avoid sin: they do not sin with the

---

49. Manton, *Works*, 6:20.
50. Manton, *Works*, 6:26–27.
51. Manton, *Works*, 6:27–29.
52. Manton, *Works*, 6:34.
53. Manton, *Works*, 6:38.
54. Manton, *Works*, 6:29.
55. Manton, *Works*, 6:30.

whole heart, but with the 'dislike and reluctance of the new nature'; they do not sin by way of course, meaning it is not 'easy,' 'constant,' or 'frequent' to them; they do not rest in sin, in that 'they do not lie and wallow there like swine in the mire'; finally, they struggle against sin, groaning under its 'relics.'[56] The second expression of holiness is 'positive': there is 'a studying to please God,' in that the blessed 'walk in his ways.' Simply put, their desire is not only to 'avoid evil' but to 'do good.'[57]

In sum, for Manton, the means to true blessedness is a life conformed to God's Word and a heart committed to God's Word. He believes this is clearly evident in how Psalm 119 portrays the centrality of God's Word in the blessed man's prayers and pursuits.

The Psalmist's Prayer

'Thou hast commanded us to keep thy precepts diligently. O that my ways were directed to keep thy statutes' (vv. 4–5). For Manton, the expression, 'O that,' reveals the psalmist's serious desire, arising from his disappointment with anything less than a life conformed to God's Word. It articulates his realization that he cannot walk in God's way without God's help.[58] For this reason, he looks to God in complete dependence: 'Make me to go in the path of thy commandments' (v. 35). Because we are ignorant (in mind) and impotent (in will), we need 'a double assistance from God' whereby He enlightens our mind and inclines our will.[59] This emphasis on divine instruction is a central motif in Psalm 119.[60] The psalmist is convinced that only the 'entrance' of God's Word 'giveth light' (v. 130).[61]

---

56. Manton, Works, 6:33–34.

57. Manton, Works, 6:37.

58. Manton, Works, 6:113. Also see 9:37–51.

59. Manton, Works, 6:360–61. Also see 6:370–71; 8:41–42; 9:247–52. Manton repeatedly differentiates between 'practical' knowledge and 'speculative' knowledge (i.e., 'a bare notion of things'). See Works, 6:51–52, 65–67, 256–58, 341–42; 7:271–73; 9:32–33.

60. This is evident in the frequency of his requests: 'Teach me' (vv. 12, 26, 33, 64, 66, 68, 108, 124, 135); and 'Give me understanding' (vv. 27, 34, 73, 144, 169).

61. Manton, Works, 8:352–53.

First, God's Word is a manifesting light (*lux manifestans*). 'Open thou mine eyes that I may behold wondrous things out of thy law,' cries the psalmist (v. 18).[62] Manton explains that when God opens our eyes, He does not grant 'new revelations' but the ability to see 'wonders' in His Word; that is, He gives us 'a clear sight of what is already revealed.'[63] This involves a 'double work.' The first work is negative, whereby God removes 'the veil' of carnal knowledge, carnal affection, and carnal sense.[64] Because of our spiritual blindness, 'the eyes of the understanding must be opened by the spirit of wisdom and revelation (Eph. 1:17–18). Though truths be plainly revealed by the Spirit of God in Scripture, yet there must be a removal of that natural darkness and blindness that is upon our understandings.'[65] The second work is positive, whereby God infuses light. Manton is careful to distinguish this illumination from 'simple nescience' (a mere ignorance of the truth), 'grammatical knowledge' (a mere repetition of the truth), and 'dogmatical knowledge' (a mere articulation of the truth). Illumination entails 'experimental knowledge', which is 'applicative', in that it makes us wise; 'affective', in that it moves us; 'transformative', in that it changes us; and, finally, 'prevailing', in that it enables us 'to bridle lusts and purify the conscience.'[66]

Second, God's Word is a directing light (*lux dirigens*). 'Thy word is a lamp unto my feet, and a light unto my path' (v. 105). It is a light by reason of 'direction', as it shows us 'the right way to our desired end.'[67] It is also a light by reason of 'conviction', as it shows us our 'errors and mistakes ... in judgment and practice.'[68] 'Wherewithal shall a young man cleanse his way?' asks the psalmist (v. 9). The answer is by 'taking heed' to God's Word. Commenting on this

---

62. Also see verses 105, 130.
63. Manton, *Works*, 6:164.
64. Manton, *Works*, 6:164.
65. Manton, Works, 6:342.
66. Manton, *Works*, 6:166–67.
67. Manton, *Works*, 8:65.
68. Manton, *Works*, 8:66.

verse, Manton declares that the Bible serves, firstly, as the 'rule' of holiness.[69] This means it reveals the only way of 'reconciliation with God' (how to be cleansed from the guilt of sin) and the only way of 'subjection to God' (how to be cleansed from the filth of sin). The Bible serves, secondly, as the 'instrument' of holiness. That is to say, God uses it to cleanse our hearts. 'It is,' says Manton, 'the glass that discovers sin, and the water that washes it away.'[70]

Third, God's Word is a quickening light (*lux vivificans*). 'I will never forget thy precepts: for with them thou hast quickened me' (v. 93).[71] According to Manton, there are two 'quickenings' in the believer's experience.[72] The first is regeneration, which he describes as 'the first infusion of the life of grace'.[73] By virtue of this 'infusion', God causes us 'to love what we naturally hate, and to hate what we naturally love'; moreover, He turns us 'from the creature to [Him]', 'from self to Christ', and 'from sin to holiness'.[74] The second quickening is renewal 'when from cold, sad, and heavy, we are made lively, and so not only have life, but enjoy it more abundantly.'[75] When God renews us, He breathes 'upon his own work.'[76] We need Him to do this when, in the midst of duty, we are overcome by 'deadness of spirit' arising from our 'negligence' and 'carnal liberty.' At such times, God excites 'the operative graces such as faith, love, hope, and fear.'[77] We also need Him to quicken

---

69. Manton, *Works*, 6:84.

70. Manton, *Works*, 6:85.

71. Also see verses 19, 25, 37, 40, 50, 93, 107, 149, 154, 156.

72. Manton, *Works*, 7:429. Also see 6:395–96, 435–38; 8:102–4; 9:84–89.

73. Manton, *Works*, 8:103.

74. Manton, *Works*, 7:439.

75. Manton, *Works*, 7:429.

76. Manton, *Works*, 8:103. 'By this first work of grace we have three advantages': (1) 'an inclination and tendency towards what is good'; (2) 'a preparation of heart for holy actions'; and (3) 'a power and an ability to do good works.' God gives 'his quickening, actuating, assisting grace, for the improving of these principles infused, that their operations may be carried forth with more success.' *Works*, 6:362–63.

77. Manton, *Works*, 8:103.

us in affliction, when we are overwhelmed by 'vehement sorrow and brokenness of heart.'[78] He does so by reviving 'our suffering graces, as our hope of eternal life and eternal glory, patience and faith, and so puts life into us again, that we may go on cheerfully in our service.'[79]

Fourth, God's Word is a comforting light (*lux exhilarans*). 'Let, I pray thee, thy merciful kindness be for my comfort, according to thy word unto thy servant' (v. 76).[80] For Manton, God's Word strengthens in the midst of trouble.[81] This 'strengthening' occurs when 'faith is confirmed, love is increased, or hope is enlivened.'[82] This is 'the business and design of Scripture,' in that it brings us 'to believe in God, and to wait upon him for our salvation; to hope either for eternal life, which is the great benefit offered in the Scriptures, or those intervening blessings which are necessary by the way.'[83] In this manner, it is a 'strong' comfort. All other comforts are weak because they are susceptible to affliction, death, and judgment. In addition, it is a 'full' comfort. It speaks to every conceivable trouble: 'no strait can be so great, no pressure so grievous, but we have full consolation offered us in the promises against them all.' Finally, it is a 'reviving' comfort, in that 'faith penetrates into the inwards of a man, does us good to the heart; and the soul revives by waiting upon God, and gets life and strength.'[84]

Our constant prayer, therefore, is for God to teach us His Word. It is the chosen means by which He 'delights to work' in us.[85] It contains truths that are able to stir our affections. It speaks,

---

78. Manton, *Works*, 6:265.

79. Manton, *Works*, 6:240.

80. Also see verses 26, 50, 52.

81. Manton, *Works*, 8:353. Also see 6:221–24, 271–73; 7:29–38, 301–04, 331–35, 423–27; 9:23–24.

82. Manton, *Works*, 7:47.

83. Manton, *Works*, 7:28. It comforts by way of its doctrines, examples, and promises. *Works*, 7:32–34.

84. Manton, *Works*, 7:29.

85. Manton, *Works*, 7:433.

for example, of God's authority, 'charging and commanding us'. It tells of God's 'great love to us in Christ, whom he has given to die for us.' And it promises 'no less than eternal and complete blessedness both for our bodies and souls.' When God teaches us, these truths come alive to us.

The Psalmist's Pursuit

Given the fact that the Spirit of God only works through the Word of God, Manton is convinced that we should 'busy ourselves' with it.[86] The psalmist declares: 'I will meditate in thy precepts, and have respect unto thy ways. I will delight myself in thy statutes: I will not forget thy word' (vv. 15–16). In his sermons on these verses, Manton highlights three steps to pursuing God's Word.

The first is meditation: 'I will meditate in thy precepts.'[87] In Manton's estimation, meditation is 'not a thing of arbitrary concernment … but of absolute use, without which all graces wither.'[88] It is of such value because it fastens truths upon 'the mind and memory'; shows 'the beauty' of divine truths; prevents 'vain thoughts'; and nurtures 'knowledge and godliness.'[89] When we meditate upon God's Word, we digest it; that is, we bring its truths to remembrance so that we might ponder them until they are impressed 'upon the heart.'[90] Specifically, 'we meditate of God that we may love him and fear him; of sin, that we may abhor it; of hell,

---

86. Manton, *Works*, 7:433.

87. For the psalmist's meditation on God's Word, see verses 23, 27, 48, 78, 97, 99, 148.

88. Manton, *Works*, 6:141. The subject of meditation appears repeatedly throughout Manton's collected works. His most extensive treatment is found in his ten sermons on Genesis 24:63, 'And Isaac went out to meditate.' See *Works*, 17:263–350.

89. Manton, *Works*, 6:143. Also see 7:19, 479–82; 8:12–13.

90. Manton, *Works*, 6:138. For more on Puritan meditation, see J. Stephen Yuille, 'Conversing with God's Word: Scripture Meditation in the Piety of George Swinnock', *Journal of Spiritual Formation and Soul Care*, vol. 5 (2012), pp. 35–55. The goal of meditation is to apply Scripture successively to the faculties of understanding, affections, and will.

that we may avoid it; of heaven, that we may pursue it.'[91] Without this kind of focus, Manton warns that we quickly 'muse' on 'trifles' and 'that which is evil.'[92]

The second step in our pursuit of God's Word is delight: 'I will delight myself in thy statutes.'[93] We delight in God's Word because of its 'excellency'.[94] It is a 'clear' Word because it fully reveals God to us. It is a 'good' Word because it satisfies all of our needs. It is a 'pure' Word because it reflects God's holiness. It is a 'sublime' Word because it contains 'excellent truths and glorious mysteries'. It is a 'sure' Word because its promises never fail. Our 'sweet sense' of its goodness means we 'delight and rejoice in it above all things.'[95] Such delight is of great value because it 'draws us off from carnal vanities', and removes 'the tediousness of religious exercises'.[96]

The third step in our pursuit of God's Word is remembrance: 'I will not forget thy word.'[97] 'To forget is to neglect', says Manton.[98] We forget 'notionally' when we no longer remember things formerly known, and we forget 'affectively' when we are no longer moved by things we know.[99] In marked contrast, 'to remember is

---

91. Manton, *Works*, 6:144.

92. Manton, *Works*, 6:144–45. For some insight into Manton's emphasis on solitude, see Crawford Gribben, 'Thomas Manton and the Spirituality of Solitude', *Eusebeia: The Bulletin of the Jonathan Edwards Centre for Reformed Spirituality* 6 (Spring 2007): 21–23.

93. For the psalmist's delight in God's Word, see verses 14, 16, 20, 24, 35, 38, 40, 47, 48, 70, 72, 77, 92, 97, 103, 113, 119, 127, 129, 131, 143, 159, 162, 163, 167, 174.

94. Manton, *Works*, 9:202–4. Also see 6:149–50; 7:463–64; 9:21–22. God's Word is 'good' (v. 39), 'right' (v. 75), 'faithful' (v. 86), and 'true' (v. 160). It 'endureth forever' (v. 160). It is the psalmist's 'song' (v. 54), and 'better than thousands of gold and silver' (v. 72).

95. Manton, *Works*, 6:129.

96. Manton, *Works*, 6:150.

97. For the psalmist's remembrance of God's Word, see verses 22, 30, 44, 51, 55, 56, 59, 60, 61, 67, 69, 83, 87, 88, 93, 94, 100, 101, 102, 104, 109, 110, 115, 117, 129, 141, 153, 157, 161, 166, 168, 173, 176.

98. Manton, *Works*, 7:428.

99. Manton, *Works*, 6:153. Also see 7:76–77; 8:115.

to esteem.'[100] The fruit of 'esteem' is obedience. Hence the psalmist declares: 'Thy word have I hid in mine heart, that I might not sin against thee' (v. 11). Preaching on this verse, Manton notes, firstly, the psalmist's 'practice': he hides God's Word in his heart. This is done when we 'cherish' it by giving 'a constant respect to it, that we may not transgress it as it is a rule, nor lose it as it is a treasure.'[101] Manton notes, secondly, the psalmist's 'aim': that he might not sin against God. In short, our 'knowledge of' and 'delight in' God's Word always leads to 'practice.'[102] 'They that love God will love his word,' says Manton, 'and if they love it they will live by it, and square their actions accordingly.'[103]

Conclusion

In sum, 'meditation breedeth delight, and delight helpeth memory and practice.'[104] This three-fold emphasis is how Manton understands the blessed man's pursuit in Psalm 119, and it is this emphasis that invariably shapes Manton's biblical piety. At the foundation stands the conviction that as we love and obey God's Word, the blessed God communes with us by His Spirit, conveying sweet influences upon our soul through His Word. Thus, we expect God to speak to us—not subjectively through inner urgings, but through His Word.[105] The Bible is God's voice—that which 'goeth forth' out of God's 'mouth' (Isa. 55:11). It bridges the expanse between heaven and earth, infinite and finite, Creator and creature. It is as powerful as the 'rain' and 'snow' that 'cometh

---

100. Manton, *Works*, 7:428.

101. Manton, *Works*, 6:99–100.

102. Manton, *Works*, 6:107. Elsewhere, he states, 'Love cannot be hidden, but it will break forth into action.' *Works*, 9:205.

103. Manton, *Works*, 7:118.

104. Manton, *Works*, 6:146.

105. This emphasis is not confined to Manton's exposition of Psalm 119, but occupies a significance place throughout his collected sermons. See *Works*, 1:93–97, 272–73; 3:64; 4:114–78; 5:481–82, 487–500; 9:335–36, 345–46, 10:110, 201, 221, 227–40; 11:21–23; 12:293, 319–21; 15:154–74, 385–87; 16:294; 17:126–35, 353–63; 18:16, 20, 25–26.

down from heaven, and returneth not thither, but watereth the earth, and maketh it bring forth and bud, that it may give seed to the sower, and bread to the eater' (Isa. 55:10). For this reason, we listen to the Bible as if we heard God speaking to us from heaven, rejoicing like those who find 'great spoil' (v. 162).

Part 4: Later Heirs of Puritan Piety

CHAPTER THIRTEEN

J. C. Philpot and Experimental Calvinism

ROBERT W. OLIVER

I AM glad to be able to take this opportunity to express my gratitude to Dr Joel Beeke for his ministry and teaching and for his personal encouragement. The publication of this Festschrift is surely an opportunity to acknowledge his role in the recent recovery of Reformed experimental theology. My personal contact began with his publication of the English translation of Wilhelmus a Brakel's *The Christian's Reasonable Service*. As our friendship developed we realized that life and ministry of J. C. Philpot (1802–1869) had played an important part in the pilgrimage of us both. There are aspects of Philpot's teaching that we can no longer accept but we appreciate the importance of much of what he stood for. It seemed appropriate therefore to explore this theme in this essay.

I grew up under a ministry that was in the Philpot tradition while Dr Beeke in quite a different denomination on another continent regularly heard the sermons of J. C. Philpot read when no preacher was available. We now both differ from his understanding of some teachings of Scripture particularly on gospel invitations and also the relation of the Christian to the moral law. To question aspects of a man's teaching should not lead to over-reaction and total dismissal. It is important to acknowledge the profit received from the life and ministry of J.C. Philpot. My aim is therefore to review aspects of his teaching which are of permanent value. We have at times discussed these issues together, but I must make it clear that Dr Beeke cannot be held responsible for my views which may be nuanced in ways different from his own.

Education

Joseph Charles Philpot was born on 13 September 1802, the third son of Charles and Maria Philpot. Charles was Rector of Ripple, a small coastal parish in East Kent. At that time of Joseph's birth and throughout much of his childhood Britain was locked into a gruelling war with Revolutionary and then Napoleonic France. Living near the Kent coast, where the English Channel is at its narrowest, the family was in the most vulnerable part of the Kingdom. Many years later in the last year of his life, Philpot made an interesting reflection on the state of the country at the time of his birth:

> It would require a volume (and a most interesting volume it would be, if a writer should ever arise, sufficiently gifted to unfold the state of England at this critical period) fully to explain all this. Suffice it to say, that never at any period since the Revolution has England been in greater peril from intestine strife, weak ministries, corruption in every part of the State, and a gigantic army on the other side of the Channel ready to invade our shores with an overwhelming force.[1]

While precautions against invasion must have been evident in the surrounding area, life in Ripple Rectory seems to have continued peacefully although sadly of the eight children that Maria Philpot bore only four survived childhood. The scholarly rector soon realized that Joseph was the brightest of his sons and took his education in hand at an early age so that he had made considerable progress in Latin and Greek before he was sent to Merchant Taylors

---

1. J. C. Philpot, 'Recollections of the Late William Huntington by William Stevens', *Reviews* (London: Frederick Kirby, 1901), 2:631. Philpot's reference to the Revolution refers to the Revolution of 1688 in Britain.

School, London at the age of nine. Advance seemed assured until bronchial illness struck and in his own physician son's words Joseph was sent home to 'be cured or die'.

He survived and after a lengthy convalescence, during which he read widely, he was sent back to London, this time to St Paul's School, from there he was awarded an open scholarship to Worcester College Oxford. There he emerged as one of a group of very able students drawn to Oxford in those years. Despite another bout of serious illness, he proved himself academically, gaining first class honours in classics in 1824. This success could open the way to an academic career in the university with a secure future, but by now his father had died. Charles Philpot had been able to lay the foundations of an excellent education, but sadly he appears to have lacked a real understanding of the gospel. Joseph's widowed mother appears to have been in the same state, but that was to change. By the time of his graduation from Oxford she had left the Rectory and moved to the nearby town of Walmer, where she was cared for by her elder daughter Frances Maria. Joseph felt obliged to provide partial support for the family. This family responsibility was a major factor in the events that led him to accept the offer of a generously paid post as a tutor to the two sons of Edward Pennefather, a wealthy Irish lawyer, and his wife Susannah. In spite of the fact that prospects at Oxford would suffer, early in 1826 he crossed the Irish Sea to begin his work at Delgany, County Wicklow.[2]

Conversion

Ireland proved to be the scene of Philpot's conversion. On his own testimony when he arrived, 'though highly moral as far as regards man and having a great respect for religion, the grace of God had

---

2. In my *History of the English Calvinistic Baptists,* I accepted Dr J. H. Philpot's statement in *The Seceders* that JCP went to Rathsallagh. It has been pointed out to me that Pennefather did not move to Rathsallagh from Delgany until 1834. In addition Rathsallagh is twenty-five miles from the coast across the Wicklow Mountains, whereas Delgany is only one mile. This would explain JCP's statement that after he was separated from his beloved he galloped his horse along the beach in deep distress.

not then touched my heart'.[3] For over a year all went well and then he fell in love with Anne the eldest daughter of the family. Anne's parents could see that marriage to an impecunious and fragile don would be impracticable and so the young lady was sent away to stay with relations, while Philpot worked out the remaining three months of his contract. In a sermon many years later he referred to this experience as 'a very great trial and affliction, which I cannot name, but it was one of the greatest sorrows I have ever passed through in my life, and it was in and under that affliction that the Lord was pleased, I have every reason to believe, to begin his work of grace upon my soul…. [T]hough not without a hope in God's mercy, I was not favoured until some years after with any special manifestation of Christ.'[4] It was at this time that Philpot met John Nelson Darby. Darby was then a curate in the Church of Ireland, but like Philpot was later to secede, becoming a leader among the 'Brethren'.

Stadhampton and Chiselhampton

In the Autumn of 1827 he resumed life at Oxford as a fellow of Worcester College also to prepare for ordination in the Church of England. This took place in the cathedral at Oxford in June 1828. He returned to his college as an earnest young Evangelical whose views and tastes were no longer those of many of his colleagues. He soon incurred the hostility of the Provost and realized that his future lay outside of the university. He therefore accepted the curacy of the two adjoining parishes of Stadhampton and Chiselhampton seven miles south of Oxford, although at first remaining resident in College. His two parishes had been the childhood home of the Puritan divine, John Owen (1616–1683), whose father had been rector there in the early seventeenth century. Philpot threw himself into the work, quickly learning to adapt his teaching to the understanding of a congregation largely

---

3. *Letters by the Late Joseph Charles Philpot… with a Brief Memoir of His Life and Labors*, ed. W. Clayton Clayton (London: J. Gadsby, 1871), p. 14.

4. Philpot, *Letters*, pp. 14–15.

composed of agricultural workers but without compromising his own convictions. Reflecting later he wrote:

> Cold, dry learning is not wanted in the pulpit. What is wanted there is experience in the heart, life and feeling in the soul, and such a measure of divine power resting upon the spirit as shall clothe the ideas that spring up with clear simple suitable language within the comprehension of the most uneducated hearer. A ministry of this kind will be fresh, original stamped with a peculiar impress, and carry with it a weight and power which manifests its divine Author.[5]

His ministry soon filled the churches of Stadhampton and Chiselhampton, drawing hearers from neighboring parishes. The workload inevitably increased and he took lodgings in the village. While there he made the acquaintance of William Tiptaft (1803–1864), vicar of the nearby parish of Sutton Courtenay. Tiptaft was to become a lifelong friend and shortly a friend in need, when Philpot's health broke down in the spring of 1830. This seemed to have been brought about by nervous exhaustion and the damp climate of his parish. He had become depressed by the rigid formality of the Anglican services together with the ungodliness of many of his parishioners including the parish clerk at one extreme and the squire and his wife at the other. In this depressed condition described by his son as a nervous breakdown he was also struggling with the doctrine of sanctification and a growing awareness of the power of indwelling sin. Tiptaft rescued him and took him off to his own home from where he went later to stay with his mother and sisters at Walmer in Kent.

It was the end of 1831 before Philpot was fit enough to return to his parishes, by which time Tiptaft, no longer able to endure the restraints and worldliness of the Church of England, had resigned his charge at Sutton Courtenay and was in process of building a

---

5. J. C. Philpot, 'The Use of Commentaries,' in *Contemplations and Reflections of J. C. Philpot from His Reviews*, e-book, Bible Truth Forum, p. 163, accessed November 20, 2017, http://grace-ebooks.com/library/J.%20C.%20Philpot/ JCP%20Contemplations%20and%20Reflections.pdf.

Dissenting Chapel at Abingdon. Not surprisingly Tiptaft's actions incurred the wrath of the Bishop of Salisbury and the disgust of the local Anglican clergy and gentry. Philpot shared his friend's convictions and his continued association with him must have complicated his own associations with the church hierarchy. It proved increasingly difficult to continue his own ministry in the Church of England, but his decision was not easy as he found an increasing spiritual response to his ministry. Eventually however, the pressure proved overwhelming and at last in March 1835 he followed his friend, resigning not only his parishes but also his college fellowship, the tenure of which was conditional upon his being a communicant member of the Church of England.

Secession

Philpot explained his reasons for secession from the Church of England in a lengthy letter to the Provost of Worcester College, soon published as a separate a tract which sold widely. It becomes clear that, although Philpot had become a convinced credobaptist it was an inability to endure the sheer worldliness that pervaded the life of the established Church of England that forced him to the breaking point. He was also burdened by the fact that he was by law required to use a liturgy that assumed that all worshippers were regenerate.

> I confess that only but very lately the sin of remaining in her [the Established Church] has been forcibly laid upon my conscience. I have felt of late that, by continuing one of her ministers I was upholding what in the sight of the holy JEHOVAH is hateful and loathsome. I have felt that by standing up in her pulpit, I was sanctioning a system in principle and practice, in root and branches corrupt before God.

He continued:

> Can a man, for instance, who has known the work of regeneration in his own soul, and whose conscience is made tender by the blessed Spirit, go on to lie unto God by thanking him for regenerating infants? Can he who has been sprinkled with the

blood of Christ, and has been fed with his flesh, continue long to give the elements of his body and blood to the unbeliever, the self-righteous, and the ungodly?

The inevitable conclusion followed: 'From this unholy and worldly system I now secede'.[6]

Philpot, now without income, had only slender resources upon which to fall back. He was however wonderfully provided with friends and support.

As events unfolded in the providence of God, Philpot did not need to keep a school, although he would have proved a good teacher. The Wiltshire farmer, Joseph Parry, who had befriended him had high hopes that he could be retained as pastor of the little Baptist chapel at Allington, a hamlet near Devizes. He spent an extended period at Parry's farm and was baptized as a believer in Allington Chapel by John Warburton of Trowbridge in September 1835.

Although he was usually to spend a month each summer at Allington where some of his closest friends lived, he was drawn to the East Midlands, the home district of William Tiptaft whose sister, Deborah was married to William Keal, a physician in Oakham the county town of Rutland, England's smallest county. In Oakham and in Stamford, Lincolnshire some twelve miles distant, congregations of Dissenters had been gathered in part through the preaching of Tiptaft. To each of these congregations Philpot preached to increasing assemblies until it became clear that these were to be the spheres of his life's work. In addition, Philpot was drawn to the Keal's eldest daughter, Sarah Louisa, whom he married in 1838. From 1840 until 1849 he was co-editor of the Gospel Standard magazine with John M'Kenzie of Preston, Lancashire until the latter's death in 1849. Thereafter he edited the magazine alone until his death at the end of 1869. The reading public for this magazine had originally been drawn from the congregations visited by William Gadsby on his preaching tours up and down the land. It promoted a strong experimental

---

6. 'J. C. Philpot to the Provost of Worcester College, Oxford, 28th March 1835', *The Seceders*, ed. J. H. Philpot (London: Farncombe, 1931), 1:276–88.

or experiental emphasis, which was ably expounded by Philpot's clear prose.

An Experimental Ministry

Philpot was publishing sermons in response to popular demand before he began to write for the Gospel Standard. Some of his early sermons may appear to be unduly severe in their criticisms of an inadequate religion. His criticisms may be just but he tended to denounce rather indiscriminately. His younger son was to comment on one of the early sermons, 'he has not yet learned to temper valiancy [sic.] with discretion nor to speak comfortably to the weaker brethren'.[7] Later he admitted that he had been rash in some of his pronouncements. But convinced that true religion was the work of the Holy Spirit in the soul of man he dared not allow his hearers to deceive themselves by resting in anything short of a clear heart-felt knowledge of Christ and of His saving work. The deadness that pervaded so much of the Anglicanism of the day was also to be found among Dissenters. It was also a time of increasing doctrinal weakness. The old Calvinism had in many places hardened into a rigid Hyper-Calvinism.

Philpot was probably aware of this problem before his secession, but was certainly soon to experience it more directly. There seems to have been a great deal of theoretical Calvinism in English Evangelicalism. He describes a visit to Plymouth in June 1837:

> The religion of this place seems to be chiefly Bible religion, of which there is a vast abundance of every kind and in every direction. I heard last Lord's Day evening, John Hawker, a son of the Doctor. If the father were like the son, I would not give a shilling a year for a seat under him. Abundance of Scripture, a copious supply of dry doctrine, a tolerable quantity of pride, and enough presumption to stock half a dozen pulpits seemed to me to make up the sermon.

Plymouth was a city which had been regarded as a stronghold of evangelical Calvinism both in the Established Church as well as in Nonconformity. Over against what he perceived as dead orthodoxy,

---

7. *The Seceders*, 1:355.

Philpot longed for a ministry that would speak to the heart and under the blessing of God would transform the life. In the same part of the country he came upon a situation where another minister was: 'one of your dead Calvinists, and had a great knowledge of the word, and a great aptitude at quoting it. But texts and chapters are a poor bulwark against sin…. A small portion of godly fear will do more against sin than a concordance, or even Bagster's family Bible with a million of marginal references. A paper religion is a poor affair.' In the same letter to his friend Joseph Parry he concludes: 'Let me whisper this in your ear, that a sound creed, and a profession of experimental religion, too, cannot open a man's eyes to see, nor his heart to love, the secret track of a living soul. Therefore, friend Parry, marvel not if Particular Baptists' churches and ministers hate you as bad as Wesleyans and Independents.'[8]

Philpot's experiences in both church and chapel were convincing him that there was much doctrinally sound Christianity that never reached the heart and seemed not to touch men's lives. He was hungry for a living experience of Christ.

Before his own conversion Philpot had bought a copy of the *Hymns of Joseph Hart* (1712–1768), perhaps to relieve the tedium of a long coach journey. This little book included a remarkable account of Hart's conversion, backsliding and spiritual recovery. After his own call by grace *Hart's Hymns* had a new and powerful impact upon Philpot who frequently recommended it to others. He took very seriously its warnings against inadequate or indeed empty professions of faith. Hart wrote:

> A form of words, though e'er so sound,
> Can never save a soul;
> The Holy Ghost must give the wound,
> And make the wounded whole.[9]

Its remarkable descriptions of the person and sufferings as well as the triumph of Christ provided abundant fuel for meditation.

---

8. 'JCP to Joseph Parry, June 3, 1837', in *The Seceders*, 1:318–19.

9. Joseph Hart, *Hymns* (London: 1911), p. 122.

The problem of false conversions was not new. The Puritans had had to deal with it in the aftermath of the Reformation when many had made a profession of Reformed Christianity without a change of heart. These people were often described in the seventeenth century as gospel hypocrites. Richard Sibbes (1577–1635), referred to such characters in a sermon:

> What is the reason that a simple man, a weak man, he lives Christianly, and dies in the faith he lived by, whereas a great man, in conceit, in knowledge, he lives wickedly, and dies worse? Because the one hath not his knowledge of the Spirit. The Spirit of God never opened his eyes: the Spirit of God never persuaded him. He hath it in books, in education and the like. There are none that hold out but those that have the Spirit of God to be their teacher and persuader. We must see things in their proper light. The Spirit of God hath to deal with the heart. God only hath power of that.[10]

Philpot began his ministry in the aftermath of the eighteenth-century Evangelical Revival which had been marked by a recovery from dead Christianity. Many who had been recovered from a dead profession were blessed with remarkable experiences of assurance. But by the 1830s there is evidence that assurance was often too lightly assumed, sometimes conviction of sin was automatically assumed to indicate faith in Christ. Whereas Philpot's method of dealing with this issue usually was to describe and analyze the spiritual conditions of his hearers, the Puritan method was to begin with the relevant doctrine and then apply it to experience. With prayer Philpot thought long and hard about the distinction between true and false religion.

At this period of his life some of Philpot's best friends were concerned that there was a lack of balance in his preaching. Reviewing one of his most widely known early sermons, 'The Heir of Heaven', William Gadsby said that 'a little more expression of the glory of Christ; of what God in His rich grace has made His

---

10. *The Complete Works of Richard Sibbes* (Edinburgh: James Nichol, 1864), 7:438.

people in Christ, and what they desire from Christ, and of the way in which the Holy Spirit draws them from self to Christ would have been an additional glory to the discourse.'[11]

There is a great deal of description in Philpot's preaching and certainly in his early ministry very little exhortation. This seems to have arisen from his teaching on inability. Scripture teaches clearly that 'there is none that doeth good, no not one' (Rom. 3:12). Mainstream Puritan teaching, found in the 1646 Westminster Confession of Faith (16.3) and the 1677/1689 Baptist Confession of Faith (16.3), said of believers:

> Their ability to do good works is not at all of themselves, but wholly from the Spirit of Christ. And that they may be enabled thereunto, besides the graces they have already received, there is required an actual influence of the same Holy Spirit, to work in them to will, and to do, of His good pleasure: yet are they not hereupon to grow negligent, as if they were not bound to perform any duty unless upon a special motion of the Spirit; but they ought to be diligent in stirring up the grace of God that is in them.[12]

Philpot, however, applied the doctrine of inability to the point at which he seems to teach that even believers indwelt by the Holy Spirit are totally unable to respond to the exhortations of Scripture. He reprimanded a fellow High Calvinist for his exhortations to Christians. Reviewing *The Moral Government of God* by James Wells he said: 'Nor are spiritual men one whit more able to perform spiritual actions than natural men, unless the Lord work in them to will and to do of his good pleasure.'[13]

What about the new creation? 'If any man be in Christ, he is a new creature: old things are passed away; behold all things

---

11. As quoted in B. A. Ramsbottom, *William Gadsby* (Harpenden, England: Gospel Standard Trust, 2004), p. 197.

12. James T. Dennison Jr., *Reformed Confessions of the Sixteenth and Seventeenth Centuries in English Translation, 1523–1693* (Grand Rapids: Reformation Heritage Books, 2008–2014), 4:252, 550.

13. *The Gospel Standard*, vol. 7 (1841), p. 82.

are become new' (2 Cor. 5:17). Philpot's teaching at this point left him open to the charge of antinomianism. Such an accusation was made by Frederick Tryon, another Strict Baptist pastor and former Anglican minister who complained that by 1847, there was 'a very great lack of reproof, rebukes and exhortations in the ministry most popular among us. The precepts of the Bible are much neglected through mock humility.'[14]

Philpot may have shunned direct exhortations, but with the passage of time there was an increased emphasis on practical godliness in his writings. In part this may have arisen as a result of criticism from fellow ministers, but before that he had to accept that while there must always be some awareness of personal sin and the need of a Savior, conviction does not always come in an overwhelming way.

Manifestations of Christ

In October 1839 Philpot received a letter from his elder sister, Frances Maria (Fanny). He writes: 'I was as much surprised at its contents as if she had written it in Greek'. It was a testimony to her unexpected conversion. She had been listening to a sermon by George Isbell, an Independent minister in Plymouth, when,

> she had a new view by faith of the Saviour and entered into the strait gate, after long groping for the wall. She hurried home, fell upon her knees, and could say without a doubt, 'My Lord and my Saviour'. She has been full of praise and blessing ever since. I never saw such an alteration in my life. Her letter is full of life and power, and I can scarcely believe she wrote it, so different is it from anything I ever heard her speak of.[15]

Philpot himself was clearly moved, he wrote: 'I trust it has stirred my spirit up, and led me to offer up many supplications by night and by day, that I may enjoy a blessing. She writes at present in the full assurance of faith, calls Jesus brother, and says whatever comes she is safe.' Fanny's language was not that normally employed in

---

14. Frederick Tryon, *Old Paths and New* (London, 1847), p. 16.
15. 'JCP to Joseph Parry, 17 October 1839', in *The Seceders*, 2:172–73.

Philpot's immediate circle. It caused him to write to his sister: 'May the promise spoken to your soul be fulfilled. My faith cannot rise so far. But continue in prayer and supplications, my dear sister for all whom you believe that promise to encircle, and for me also that I may have the love of God shed abroad in my heart, and the atoning blood of Jesus sprinkled on my conscience.'[16]

In the following January to a close friend who had visited Fanny he commented:

> If any cavil and say there was not this preliminary work, and that preliminary hell and damnation and terrors, all I can say, 'Who shall limit the Holy one of Israel?' As Hart says in his golden 'Preface'—in my opinion the most weighty piece of writing ever penned by man after the blessed Scriptures—'The dealings of God with his people though similar in the general, are nevertheless so various that there is no chalking out the paths of one child of God by those of another; no laying down of regular plans of Christian conversion, Christian experience, Christian usefulness or Christian conversation'. I heartily assent to what I have thus quoted, and though I believe that there is no revelation of Christ without previous condemnation by the law, who shall define the necessary degree of depth, or the indispensable period of length. Who shall take the compasses and scale, and mark out a circle for the Almighty to move in, or a line to walk by?[17]

Clearly Philpot himself was struggling with the subject of the full assurance of faith. He had not received what he described as a manifestation of Christ and since he was increasingly conscious of his own sinfulness but without a full experimental personal knowledge of the remedy his preaching lacked the balance to which Gadsby had called attention. It was in November 1844 during a time of illness and when he was being subjected to criticisms from friend and foe that he received what he had so long sought: a spiritual view of Christ as God and man that captivated and calmed his soul. He said:

---

16. *The Seceders*, 2:177.
17. 'JCP to J. Carby Tuckwell, 16 January 1840', in *The Seceders*, 2:190–91.

What I felt at the sight, I leave those to judge who have ever had a view by faith, of the Lord of life and glory, and they will know best what holy desires and tender love flowed forth, and how I begged of him to come and take possession of my heart. It did not last very long, but it left a blessed influence upon my soul; and if ever I felt that sweet spirituality of mind which is life and peace, it was the fruit of that view by faith of the glorious Person of Christ, and as the effect of that glorious manifestation.[18]

A Puritan Approach

The problem of false conversions was not new. Our Lord had warned in such parables as those of 'the Sower' and 'the Wise and Foolish Virgins' that the appearance of grace is not necessarily the reality. The Puritans had sought to deal with it in the aftermath of the Reformation when many people had made a profession of reformed Christianity without a change of heart. The early English Separatists had identified the problem as the state settlement of religion which accepted all citizens as Christians. Henry Barrow (c.1546–1593), the Separatist martyr wrote: 'all these people with all these manners, were in one day, with the blast of Queen Elizabeth's trumpet, of ignorant Papists and gross idolaters, made faithful Christians and true professors'.[19]

John Owen had expressed his concerns about a notional non-experimental knowledge of the truth. Writing in Restoration England in the late 1670s, he warned: 'Many live in a profession of the faith of the letter of the Gospel, yet—having no light, guide, nor conduct but that of reason—they do not, they cannot, really behold the glory of God in the face of Jesus Christ; nor hath the revelation of it any efficacy of it on their souls.'[20]

---

18. J. C. Philpot, *New Years' Addresses, Answers to Inquiries: A Treatise on the Eternal Sonship of Jesus Christ and Two Sermons* (London: Frederick Kirby, 1902), pp. 590–91.

19. As quoted in R. W. Dale, *History of English Congregationalism* (London, Hodder & Stoughton, 1907), p. 148.

20. John Owen, *The Person of Christ*, in *The Works of John Owen*, ed. William Goold (Edinburgh: T&T Clark, 1862), 1:77.

Owen was exegeting 2 Corinthians 4:6, arguing that a true sight of the glory of God in the face of Jesus Christ has a progressive transforming effect on the soul. Careful doctrinal preaching will help to draw a distinction between what is false and what is genuine. Such discrimination seeks to confirm the true believer, while the deluded should be pressed to repent. The preacher depends on the power of the Holy Spirit to bring this about:

> Men profess that they know the truth; but they know it not in its proper order, in its harmony and use. It leads them not to Christ, it brings not Christ unto them; and so it is lifeless and useless. Hence, oft-times none are more estranged from the life of God than such that have much notional knowledge of the doctrine of Scripture. For they are all of them useless, and subject to be abused, if they are not improved to form Christ in the soul and transform the whole person into his likeness and image.[21]

Like Philpot, Owen was aware of the difference between 'letter' preaching and that which is delivered in the power of the Holy Spirit.

Owen urged resolution and diligence in situations when the soul is 'dull in prayer, wandering in meditations, rare in thoughts of him [Christ].' This is a time to be all the more diligent in the means of grace:

> When it finds him not in any private endeavours, it makes vigorous application to the ordinances of public worship; in prayer, in preaching, in administration of the seals, doth it look after Christ. Indeed, the great enquiry the souls of believers is after Christ. So much as they find of him, so much sweetness and refreshment have they, and no more. Especially when under any desertion, they rise up to this inquiry; they listen to every word, to every prayer, to find if anything of Christ, any light from him, any light, any love, appears to them. 'Oh, that Christ would at length meet me in this or that sermon, and recover my poor heart to some sight of his love—to some taste of his kindness![22]

---

21. Owen, *The Person of Christ*, in *Works*, 1:84.
22. Owen, *Communion with God*, in *Works*, 2:130.

Christ is sovereign and does not limit His manifestations to public worship. Sometimes He may draw near to the soul in a totally unexpected situation, but public worship must not be neglected. The believer who is faithful in attending the congregations of God's people is most likely to be blessed in secret.

In 1858, Philpot reviewed this work of John Owen warmly, commenting: 'Dr Owen in the work before us, has penetrated into the depths of this divine subject as few but himself could have done'[23] Although Philpot may have had reservations about Owen's use of exhortations, clearly the two men agreed on the realities of manifestations of Christ and in the necessity of experimental godliness.

Conclusion

Philpot continued in his pastorates until 1864 when ill health precipitated his retirement to Croydon where he attended Providence Chapel, West Street, then under the pastorate of his friend, Francis Covell (1808–1879). He continued to write and to edit, combining literary work with occasional preaching. Some of his most enduring sermons date from these years. He was undoubtedly the most scholarly and erudite Strict Baptist minister of his generation, possibly the most able leader the Gospel Standard group of churches have ever had. At home in the biblical languages, he was generally a most careful exegete of Scripture and widely read and able to address many of the issues of his time. More than competent in the classical languages, Philpot was a master of English prose, and although nineteenth century literary style is not always the most attractive, Philpot's writings flow with a careful elegance carrying his readers along with ease. After his death C. H. Spurgeon paid tribute to him: 'We have read Mr Philpot's sermons with much profit, he was incomparable on his one theme, and now that he has gone to his eternal reward, we will not write a word of that friendly criticism that we might be called upon to utter.'[24]

---

23. Philpot, *Reviews*, 2:104.

24. As quoted in I. H. Murray, *Spurgeon v. Hyper-Calvinism* (Edinburgh: Banner of Truth,1995), pp. 105–6.

Like Spurgeon, Philpot was an avid reader of the Puritans. He wrote warm reviews of the works of John Owen and Thomas Goodwin. He welcomed the Nichols republication of sets of Puritan divines, although he regretted the inclusion of Thomas Adams. The various Puritans commended by Philpot and he refers approvingly to Charnock, Sibbes and Manton, were all paedo-baptists. With the exception of Bunyan he never seems to mention the works of the first and second generation of Particular Baptists, possibly because very few of these were reprinted in the nineteenth century. William Collins, Nehemiah Coxe, Hercules Collins, William Kiffin and Benjamin Keach appear to be unknown. I have never come across any reference to the Second London Confession of Faith (1689) or the Baptist Catechism (1693).

Spurgeon was surely right that Philpot was incomparable on his one theme, which was a biblical knowledge of Christ, and there he can be read with profit even though sadly one has to part company with him in matters of presentation of the gospel.

CHAPTER FOURTEEN

Eminent Spirituality and Eminent Usefulness: True Spirituality According to Andrew Fuller

Michael A. G. Haykin

T HE most common interpretative grid for understanding English Calvinistic Baptist life and theology in the eighteenth century is an ecclesial one. Due to the ecclesiological differences between the Calvinistic Baptists and other Dissenting communities, like those of the Presbyterians and Congregationalists, it is often assumed that the best way to understand these Baptists is by focusing on issues of church polity. Ecclesiological distinctives did set the Calvinistic Baptists apart from these other Christian communities during this era, but these distinctives were penultimate. As B. B. Warfield and others have stressed, the Puritans and their heirs—that is, the Calvinistic Baptists, Presbyterians and Congregationalists—were men and women whose ultimate ardency was about the Christian experience of the Holy Spirit. As such, pneumatological concerns and spirituality are at the core of eighteenth-century English Calvinistic Baptist experience.[1]

---

1. B. B. Warfield, 'Introductory Note' to Abraham Kuyper, *The Work of the Holy Spirit* (1900; repr. Grand Rapids: Eerdmans, 1956), pp. xxxv, xxviii. See also the discussions by Irvonwy Morgan, *Puritan Spirituality* (London: Epworth Press, 1973), pp. 53–65; Dewey D. Wallace, Jr., *The Spirituality of*

'The Divine Spirit' and 'Divine Ordinances'

Many Calvinistic Baptists in this era were thus adamant that keeping in step with the Spirit was *the* vital matter when it came to the nourishment of the believer's soul or the sustenance of a congregation's inner life. As John Sutcliff (1752–1814) of Olney, Buckinghamshire, observed:

> The outpouring of the divine Spirit … is the grand promise of the New Testament …. His influences are the soul, the great animating soul of all religion. These withheld, divine ordinances are empty cisterns, and spiritual graces are withering flowers. These suspended, the greatest human abilities labour in vain, and the noblest efforts fail of success.[2]

On another occasion Sutcliff made the same point thus:

> Be earnest with God for the gift of his Holy Spirit, in an abundant measure. Seek his divine influences, to furnish you with *spiritual* ability, in order that you may be found in the discharge of that which is your indispensible [*sic*] duty. Highly prize his sacred operations. These are the real excellency of all religious duties.[3]

Eighteenth-century Calvinistic Baptist life and thought was clearly marked by what Richard Lovelace has termed 'a theology of radical dependence on the Spirit'.[4]

---

the Later English Puritans. An Anthology (Macon, GA: Mercer University Press, 1987), pp. xi–xiv; Garth B. Wilson, 'Doctrine of the Holy Spirit in the Reformed Tradition: A Critical Overview' in George Vandervelde, ed., *The Holy Spirit: Renewing and Empowering Presence* (Winfield, BC: Wood Lake Books, 1989), pp. 57–62; J.I. Packer, *A Quest for Godliness: The Puritan Vision of the Christian Life* (Wheaton, IL: Crossway Books, 1990), pp. 37–38.

In an older work on the Holy Spirit, published in 1882, George Smeaton observed: 'Except where Puritan influences are still at work, we may safely affirm that the doctrine of the Spirit is almost entirely ignored.' *The Doctrine of the Holy Spirit* (repr.; London: Banner of Truth, 1958), p. 1.

2. John Sutcliff, *Jealousy for the Lord of Hosts illustrated* (London: W. Button, 1791), p. 12.

3. John Sutcliff, *The Authority and Sanctification of the Lord's-Day, Explained and Enforced* (Circular Letter of the Northamptonshire Association, 1786), p. 8.

4. Richard Lovelace, 'Pneumatological Issues in American Presbyterianism,' *Greek Orthodox Theological Review*, vol. 31 (1986): 345–346.

Yet, these Baptists were also certain that to seek the Spirit's strength apart from the various means through which the Spirit normally worked was both unbiblical and foolish. Benjamin Keach (1640–1704), the most significant Baptist theologian at the cusp of the eighteenth century, put it this way in 1681, when, in an allusion to the Quakers, who dispensed with the ordinances of baptism and the Lord's Supper, he declared:

> Many are confident they have the Spirit, Light, and Power, when 'tis all meer [sic] Delusion. ... Some Men boast of the Spirit, and conclude they have the Spirit, and none but they, and yet at the same time cry down and villify his blessed Ordinances and Institutions, which he hath left in his Word, carefully to be observed and kept, till he comes the second time without Sin unto Salvation.... The Spirit hath its proper Bounds, and always runs in its spiritual Chanel [sic], viz. The Word and Ordinances, God's publick [sic] and private Worship.[5]

Keach here mentioned three central vehicles that the Holy Spirit uses to shape God's people: the Word and the ordinances of baptism and the Lord's Supper. Benjamin Beddome (1717–1795), pastor of the Baptist church in Bourton-on-the-Water, Gloucestershire, and whose life spanned most of the eighteenth century, discerned in the phrase 'Draw nigh unto my soul' (Ps. 69:18) five ways in which God draws near to His people, three of which are identical to the means of spiritual formation listed by Keach. God draws near to us and we to Him, Beddome said, in prayer, in 'hearing the Word', in the ordinances of baptism and the Lord's Supper, and also, he added, in 'the time of affliction' and death.[6]

'The Fire of Devotion'

These twin foci of Calvinistic Baptist spirituality—the Holy Spirit and the means of grace or spiritual formation—are also

---

5. Benjamin Keach, *Tropologia: A Key to Open Scripture-Metaphors* (London: Enoch Prosser, 1681), 2:312, 314.

6. Benjamin Beddome, *Communion with God our Security and Bliss* in his *Sermons printed from the manuscripts of the late Rev. Benjamin Beddome, A.M.* (London: William Ball, 1835), pp. 399–401.

prominent in the works of the leading Baptist divine of the late eighteenth century, Andrew Fuller (1754–1815). The nineteenth-century Welsh author David Phillips once aptly described Fuller as the 'elephant of Kettering',[7] an allusion to his weighty theological influence in both his own day and throughout the century following his death. Charles Haddon Spurgeon (1834–1892) considered him to be 'the greatest theologian' of his century,[8] and the Southern Baptist historian A.H. Newman, who taught church history at McMaster University from 1881 to 1901, on one occasion commented that Fuller's 'influence on American Baptists' was 'incalculable' for good.[9]

Fuller wrote major theological works on a variety of issues, many of them in the area of apologetics. For instance, he wrote refutations of such eighteenth-century theological aberrations as Socinianism (or Unitarianism) and Sandemanianism, and in 1799 published the definitive eighteenth-century Baptist response to Deism.[10] But it was through his rebuttal of Hyper-Calvinism that he made his most distinctive contribution.

---

7. David Phillips, *Memoir of the Life, Labors, and Extensive Usefulness of the Rev. Christmas Evans* (New York, NY: M. W. Dodd, 1843), p. 74.

8. Cited in Gilbert Laws, *Andrew Fuller, Pastor, Theologian, Ropeholder* (London: Carey Press, 1942), p. 127.

9. 'Fuller, Andrew' in Samuel Macauley Jackson, *et al.* ed., *The New Schaff-Herzog Encyclopedia of Religious Knowledge* (New York, NY/London: Funk and Wagnalls Co., 1909), 4:409.

10. Fuller's main refutation of Socinianism may be found in *The Calvinistic and Socinian Systems Examined and Compared, as to their Moral Tendency*, in *The Complete Works*, ed. Joseph Belcher, 3rd London ed. (repr. Harrisonburg, VA: Sprinkle Publications, 1988), 2:108–242. For his reply to Sandemanianism, see *Strictures on Sandemanianism, in Twelve Letters to a Friend*, in *Complete Works*, 2:561–646. His chief response to Deism, especially that of the popularizer Thomas Paine (1737–1809), is *The Gospel Its Own Witness* (*Complete Works*, 2:1–107). For examinations of Fuller's reply to these theological aberrations, see Michael A. G. Haykin, '"The Oracles of God": Andrew Fuller and the Scriptures', *Churchman*, vol. 103 (1989), pp. 60–76; *idem*, 'A Socinian and Calvinist Compared: Joseph Priestley and Andrew Fuller on the Propriety of Prayer to Christ', *Dutch Review of Church History*, vol. 73 (1993), pp. 178–198; Thomas Jacob South,

Philip Roberts, one-time President of Midwestern Baptist Theological Seminary, has noted in a study of Fuller as a theologian:

> [Fuller] helped to link the earlier Baptists, whose chief concern was the establishment of ideal New Testament congregations, with those in the nineteenth century driven to make the gospel known worldwide. His contribution helped to guarantee that many of the leading Baptists of the 1800s would typify fervent evangelism and world missions.... Without his courage and doctrinal integrity in the face of what he considered to be theological aberrations, the Baptist mission movement might have been stillborn.[11]

Fuller's life thus reveals a great truth linked with times of revival and awakening, namely, the vital role played by key leaders. To be sure, no great work for God is accomplished by men working in isolation. And Fuller had the ability to nurture and sustain deep, long-lasting, and satisfying friendships that enabled him and his friends to serve God powerfully in their generation and to be the vehicles of a tremendous revival. One sees the depth of this relationship in three simple words that William Carey said when he heard of Fuller's death in 1815: 'I loved him.' But it was Fuller's theology, known as Fullerism, that was central to this entire movement of revitalization. And undergirding his theology was his personal walk with God and his commitment to the Scriptures.

Consider in this regard the sermon that Fuller delivered at the installation of Robert Fawkner as the pastor of Thorn Baptist Church, Bedfordshire, on October 31, 1787, which was later entitled *The Qualifications and Encouragement of a faithful Minister illustrated by the Character and Success of Barnabas.*[12] Fuller took

---

'The Response of Andrew Fuller to the Sandemanian View of Saving Faith' (Th.D. thesis, Mid-America Baptist Theological Seminary, 1993).

11. Phil Roberts, 'Andrew Fuller' in Timothy George and David S. Dockery, ed., *Theologians of the Baptist Tradition*, rev. ed. (Nashville, TN: Broadman and Holman, 2001), pp. 46, 47.

12. The sermon was first published in 1787: Andrew Fuller and John Ryland, *The*

Acts 11:24 for his text, where the early Christian leader Barnabas is said to have been 'a good man, and full of the Holy Spirit, and of faith' (NKJV) and that as a result of his ministry 'much people was added to the Lord' in Antioch. Although Fuller's remarks regarding spiritual formation were delivered in the context of a charge to a pastor, there is much here, as he would have readily agreed, that has more general application.

Fuller began by expressing his conviction that the example of other people's lives can have 'a great influence upon the human mind' for good, and especially the examples of those illustrious figures found in the Scriptures. The latter, 'drawn with the pencil of inspiration', have what Fuller called 'an assimilating tendency', that is, the record of their lives has a way of inspiring emulation and imitation.[13] Like most in his Baptist community, Fuller deeply valued Christian biography for its instructive value. As he noted in another context: 'It is good to read the lives of holy men; and the more holy they have been the better.'[14]

Qualifications and Encouragement of a faithful Minister, illustrated by the Character and Success of Barnabas. And, Paul's Charge to the Corinthians respecting their Treatment of Timothy, applied to the Conduct of Churches toward Their Pastors. Being the Substance of Two Discourses, Delivered at The Settlement of The Rev. Mr Robert Fawkner, in the Pastoral Office, Over the Baptist Church at Thorn, in Bedfordshire, October 31, 1787 (London: Published for Thorn Baptist Church, 1787). It can be conveniently found in *The Complete Works*, 1:135–144.

    For a discussion of this sermon, see Nigel David Wheeler, 'Eminent Spirituality and Eminent Usefulness: Andrew Fuller's (1754–1815) Pastoral Theology in his Ordination Sermons' (PhD thesis, University of Pretoria, 2009), pp. 189–203.

13. *Qualifications and Encouragement of a Faithful Minister* in *Complete Works*, 2:135. See also Andrew Fuller, *Preaching Christ*, in *Complete Works*, 1:505; *idem, On An Intimate and Practical Acquaintance with the Word of God*, in *Complete Works*, 1:483: 'Example has a strong tendency to excite us to emulation.' The Calvinistic Baptist minister James Fanch (1704–1767) once referred to deep friendships as having 'a marvelous transforming assimilating nature.' *Ten Sermons on Practical Subjects* (London: G. Keith, 1768), p. 30.

14. Andrew Fuller, 'Memoirs of Rev. James Garie', in *Complete Works*, 3:756.

Fuller proceeded to examine the three characteristics mentioned in the description of Barnabas' character. First of all, Barnabas was a good man. Fuller extolled the importance of being marked by the virtue of goodness and noted various spheres in which goodness must be expressed. First and foremost in Fuller's mind was the home:

> Value [goodness] ... at home in your family. If you walk not closely with God there, you will be ill able to work for him elsewhere. You have lately become the head of a family. Whatever charge it shall please God, in the course of your life, to place under your care, I trust it will be your concern to recommend Christ and the gospel to them, walk circumspectly before them, constantly worship God with them, offer up secret prayer for them, and exercise a proper authority over them.[15]

The desire to be a good man must also be seen both in one's public demeanor—'prove by your spirit and conduct that you are a lover of all mankind,' Fuller told Fawkner—and as a main priority in one's life.[16]

The Bible and Prayer

But how is such goodness to be obtained? Alluding to another passage from Acts, namely, Acts 6:4, Fuller emphasized two key means of spiritual formation and spiritual vitality: Fawkner was to give himself to personal study of 'the word of God, and to prayer'. With regard to the Scriptures, right from the very beginning of his ministry Fuller built his life and thought on the Word of God—as he said in the first draft (1778) of *The Gospel Worthy of All Acceptation*: 'O Lord, impress thy Truth upon my heart with thine own seal.' Fuller was an ardent reader of the Scriptures that he regarded as 'the book by way of eminence, the book of books.'[17]

---

15. Fuller, *Qualifications and Encouragement of a Faithful Minister*, in *Complete Works*, 1:136.

16. Fuller, *Qualifications and Encouragement of a Faithful Minister*, in *Complete Works*, 1:137–38.

17. Andrew Fuller, 'The Apostolic Office', in *Complete Works*, 3:498–99.

It occupied such a place of pre-eminence in his mind because, unlike all other books, it is 'unerring'[18] and is characterized by 'Divine inspiration and infallibility'.[19] As Fuller commented:

> Many religious people appear to be contented with seeing truth in the light in which some great and good man has placed it; but if ever we enter into the gospel to purpose, it must be by reading the word of God for ourselves, and by praying and meditating upon its sacred contents. It is 'in God's light that we must see light' [cf. Ps. 36:9] .... The writings of great and good men are not to be despised, any more than their preaching: only let them not be treated as oracular. The best of men, in this imperfect state, view things *partially*, and therefore are in danger of laying an improper stress upon some parts of Scripture, to the neglect of other parts of equal, and sometimes of superior importance.... If we adopt the principles of fallible men, without searching the Scriptures for ourselves, and inquiring whether or not these things be so, they will not, even allowing them to be on the side of truth, avail us, as if we had learned them from a higher authority. Our faith, in this case, will stand in the wisdom of man, and not in the power of God.... Truth learned only at second-hand will be to us what Saul's armour was to David; we shall be at a loss how to use it in the day of trial.[20]

Fuller here differentiated between the books of fallible men, albeit good thinkers, and the truth of God in Scripture. The writings of fallible men are, at best, unable to provide the nourishment necessary for genuine spiritual growth. And because they stem from fallible minds, they are inevitably partial perspectives on the truth and inadequate to support the believer in a time of trial. By contrast, Scripture is a sure guide for the believer, it brings godly balance and perspective to his life, and provides him with a wholly

---

18. Andrew Fuller, *On Spiritual Declension and the Means of Revival*, in *Complete Works*, 3:629.

19. Andrew Fuller, *The Nature and Importance of an Intimate Knowledge of Divine Truth*, in *Complete Works*, 1:160.

20. Fuller, *Intimate Knowledge of Divine Truth*, in *Complete Works*, 1:164.

adequate support in the face of life's challenges. The importance Fuller accorded to the Scriptures as a vehicle of spiritual vitality is also evident from the fact that he made essentially the same point in an ordination or installation sermon based on Ezra 7:10. 'Learn your religion from the Bible,' Fuller told the prospective minister:

> Let that [i.e. the Bible] be your decisive rule. Adopt not a body of sentiments, or even a single sentiment, solely on the authority of any man—however great, however respected. Dare to think for yourself. Human compositions are fallible. But the Scriptures were written by men who wrote as they were inspired by the Holy Spirit.[21]

Also significant in the sermon for Robert Fawkner are Fuller's remarks about prayer:

> Beware also, brother, of neglecting secret prayer. The fire of devotion will go out if it be not kept alive by an habitual dealing with Christ. Conversing with men and things may brighten our gifts and parts; but it is conversing with God that must brighten our graces. Whatever ardour we may feel in our public work, if this is wanting, things cannot be right, nor can they in such a train come to a good issue.[22]

Enabling true ministry, as Fuller conceived it, was to be 'the fire of devotion'. And such devotion needed the fuel of prayer to keep it bright and aflame. Fuller is usually remembered today for either his activism in the genesis of the modern missionary movement or his acumen as an apologist for the Christian faith.[23] But undergirding

---

21. Andrew Fuller, *On an Intimate and Practical Acquaintance with the Word of God*, in *Complete Works*, 1:483.

22. Fuller, *Qualifications and Encouragement of a Faithful Minister*, in *Complete Works*, 1:137.

23. Both of these marks of Fuller's character and ministry were noticed during his lifetime. In an obituary at the time of his death in 1815, the question was asked: 'for clearness of conception, for strength and vigour of mind, for decision of character, for laborious exertion, for punctuality and promptness in all his measure, where shall we find his equal?' 'Obituary,' *The New Evangelical Magazine and Theological Review*, vol. 1 (1815), 192.

both his activism and his apologetics was a recognition that prayer had to be a priority in his own life and ministry if he were ever going to be useful for God. As he stressed in a charge given to John West at the latter's ordination to the pastorate of the Baptist cause in Carlton, Bedfordshire, in the same year as his Thorn sermon: 'Let all your private meditations [on the Bible] be mingled with prayer. You will study your Bible to wonderful advantage, if you go to it spiritually-minded. It is this which causes us to see the beauty and to feel the force of many parts of Scripture.'[24]

Other passages from Fuller's corpus show that he was convinced that a prayerful life was requisite for all Christians if they were to know spiritual growth. For instance, in a series of articles he wrote on the Sermon on the Mount, he noted regarding Jesus' words on prayer in Matthew 6:5–8:

> It is taken for granted that Christ's disciples are praying men. What he says is not to persuade them to prayer, but to direct them in it. Infidels may imagine that God does not concern himself with the affairs of mortals, and may excuse themselves by pretending that it were presumption in them to solicit the Supreme Being to do this or that; formalists may say their prayers, and be glad when the task is over; but Christians cannot live without communion with God.[25]

And again, in a circular letter that he drew up in 1785 for the Northamptonshire Association of Baptist Churches and which was sent out to all of its members, he urged his readers:

> Finally, brethren, let us not forget to intermingle prayer with all we do. Our need of God's Holy Spirit to enable us to do any thing, and everything, truly good, should excite us to do this. Without his blessing all means are without efficacy, and every effort for revival will be in vain. Constantly and earnestly, therefore, let

---

24. Fuller, *Intimate and Practical Acquaintance*, in *Complete Works*, 1:484. On West, see Michael A.G. Haykin, ed., *The Armies of the Lamb: The Spirituality of Andrew Fuller* (Dundas, ON: Joshua Press, 2001), p. 114, n.2.

25. Andrew Fuller, 'Sermon on the Mount: Alms-giving, and Prayer', in *Complete Works*, 1:576.

us approach his throne. Take all occasions especially for closet prayer. Here, if anywhere, we shall get fresh strength, and maintain a life of communion with God.[26]

And in one of his final sermons, preached at the funeral of his close friend, John Sutcliff, in 1814, Fuller hammered home the same point: 'There is no intercourse with God without prayer. It is thus that we walk with God.'[27]

'Full of the Holy Spirit and of Faith'

Barnabas was also a man, according to Luke's description of him in Acts 11, who was 'full of the Holy Spirit', which Fuller understood to mean that Barnabas was full of the fruit of the Spirit mentioned in Galatians 5:22–23. In his words:

> To be full of the Holy Spirit is to be full of the dove, as I may say; or full of those fruits of the Spirit mentioned by the apostle to the Galatians; namely, 'love, joy, peace, long-suffering, gentleness, goodness.'... A person that is greatly under the influence of the love of this world is said to be drunken with its cares or pleasures. In allusion to something like this, the apostle exhorts that we 'be not drunken with wine, wherein is excess; but filled with the Spirit' [Eph. 5:18]. The word 'filled,' here, is very expressive; it denotes, I apprehend, being overcome, as it were, with the holy influences and fruits of the blessed Spirit. How necessary is all this, my brother, in your work! Oh how necessary is 'an unction from the Holy One' [1 John 2:20]![28]

Fuller's interpretation here of the term 'unction' from 1 John 2:20 was taken directly from John Gill (1697–1771), the voluminous eighteenth-century Baptist exegete. In his commentary on this passage, Gill had delineated that the 'unction' or 'anointing' that

---

26. Andrew Fuller, *Causes of Declension in Religion, and Means of Revival*, in *Complete Works*, 3:324.

27. Andrew Fuller, *Principles and Prospects of a Servant of Christ*, in *Complete Works*, 1:344.

28. Andrew Fuller, *Qualifications and Encouragement of a Faithful Minister*, in *Complete Works*, 1:138–39.

believers received from the Holy One, that is, the Lord Jesus, was the 'Spirit, and his graces'.[29]

Fuller was further convinced that the doctrinal divisions between Christians was owing to a lack of such fullness of the Spirit: 'It is no breach of charity to say,' he declared forthrightly, 'that if the professors of Christianity had more of the Holy Spirit of God in their hearts, there would be a greater harmony among them respecting the great truths which he has revealed.'[30] Above all things, therefore, Fawkner should make Psalm 51:11 his prayer: 'Take not thy Holy Spirit from me.'[31] For, Fuller stressed: 'If we are destitute of the Holy Spirit, we are blind to the loveliness of the Divine character, and destitute of any true love to God in our hearts.'[32] Again, we see the radical need of the Spirit's help in the Christian life: it is He who opens out eyes to the unsurpassable beauty of God and it is He who fills our hearts with love for God.

The final characteristic of Barnabas' life was that he was full of faith. Fuller took this to be expressive of three ideas: Barnabas had a mind 'stored with divine sentiment,' that is, he had deep personal convictions about the vital truths of the Bible; then he was 'rooted and grounded in the truth of the gospel,' and finally, he was 'daily living upon it.'[33]

'Eminent Usefulness'

Fuller's spirituality was that of an activist. After the formation of the Baptist Missionary Society in October of 1793, Fuller became the first secretary of the society until his death in 1815. The work of

---

29. John Gill, *An Exposition of the New Testament* (London: George Keith, 1776), pp. 355–56.

30. Fuller, *Qualifications and Encouragement of a Faithful Minister*, in *Complete Works*, 1:139.

31. Fuller, *Qualifications and Encouragement of a Faithful Minister*, in *Complete Works*, 1:139.

32. Fuller, *Qualifications and Encouragement of a Faithful Minister*, in *Complete Works*, 1:139.

33. Fuller, *Qualifications and Encouragement of a Faithful Minister*, in *Complete Works*, 1:141.

the mission consumed an enormous amount of Fuller's time as he regularly toured the country, representing the mission and raising funds. On average he was away from home three months of the year. Between 1798 and 1813, for instance, he made five lengthy and arduous trips to Scotland for the mission as well as undertaking journeys to Wales and Ireland.[34] For example, on one of these trips, that made to Scotland in 1805, Fuller travelled thirteen hundred miles and preached fifty sermons in around sixty days. As the mission secretary he also carried on an extensive correspondence both to the missionaries on the field and to supporters at home. And finally, he had supervise the selection of missionary appointees and sought to deal with troubles as they emerged on the field. In short, he acted as the pastor of the missionaries sent out.[35] The amount of energy and time this took deeply worried his friends. As one of his friends, Robert Hall, Jr. (1764–1831), put it in a letter to Fuller's first biographer, John Ryland, Jr. (1753–1825), 'If he [i.e. Fuller] is not more careful he will be in danger of wearing himself out before his time. His journeys, his studies, his correspondcies [sic] must be too much for the constitution of any man.'[36]

It is not surprising, therefore, that Fuller concluded his sermon for Fawkner with a reference to serving Christ and His kingdom. As he put it, 'eminent spirituality in a minister is usually attended with eminent usefulness.'[37] Fuller stressed that this affirmation was not meant to imply that piety automatically guaranteed success: 'I do not mean to say our usefulness depends upon our spirituality, as an effect depends upon its cause; nor yet that it is always in proportion

---

34. On Fuller's trips to Scotland, see Dudley Reeves, 'Andrew Fuller in Scotland', *The Banner of Truth*, no. 106–107 (July/August 1972), pp. 33–40.

35. Doyle L. Young, 'Andrew Fuller and the Modern Mission Movement', *Baptist History and Heritage*, vol. 17 (1982), pp. 17–27.

36. Letter to John Ryland, Jr., May 25, 1801, cited in Geoffrey F. Nuttall, 'Letters from Robert Hall to John Ryland 1791–1824', *The Baptist Quarterly* 34 (1991–1992): 127.

37. Fuller, *Qualifications and Encouragement of a Faithful Minister*, in *Complete Works*, 1:143. See also Andrew Fuller, *Affectionate Concern of a Minister for the Salvation of his Hearers*, in *Complete Works*, 1:508.

to it. God is a Sovereign; and frequently sees proper to convince us of it, in variously bestowing his blessing on the means of grace.'[38]

On the other hand, Fuller was certain that 'our want of usefulness is often to be ascribed to our want of spirituality, much oftener than to our want of talents.' Men, who seemed destined to be greatly used by God because of their gifts, have turned out otherwise and that because their inner lives were marred by 'such things as pride, unwatchfulness, carnality, and levity.'[39]

Why did Fuller hold that usefulness in God's service cannot be divorced from spirituality or what he called 'eminency in grace'? First, he argued that where there is true spirituality the soul burns 'with holy love to Christ and the souls of men'. It gives the possessor an unquenchable passion to see God and Christ glorified and men and women converted. Fuller pointed to a number of men who were great examples in this regard: Old Testament saints like Hezekiah, Ezra and Nehemiah and various figures in the history of the Church, men such as Peter and Paul, John Wycliffe, Martin Luther and John Calvin, as well as '[John] Elliot [*sic*], and [Jonathan] Edwards, and [David] Brainerd, and [George] Whitefield.'[40] It is noteworthy that in the group of Christian worthies from the seventeenth and eighteenth centuries, three of them—Eliot, Brainerd, and Whitefield—were admired in Fuller's day for their activism, their ceaseless missionary endeavors to reach the lost with the gospel. The fourth figure, Edwards—rightly described by Miklós Vetö as 'the greatest Christian theologian of the eighteenth century'[41]—was Fuller's main theological and spiritual guide after the Scriptures.[42]

---

38. Fuller, *Qualifications and Encouragement of a Faithful Minister*, in *Complete Works*, 1:143. See also Wheeler, 'Eminent Spirituality and Eminent Usefulness,' p. 202.

39. Fuller, *Qualifications and Encouragement of a Faithful Minister*, in *Complete Works*, 1:143.

40. Fuller, *Qualifications and Encouragement of a Faithful Minister*, in *Complete Works*, 1:143.

41. 'Book Reviews: *America's Theologian: A Recommendation of Jonathan Edwards*, by Robert W. Jenson,' *Church History*, vol. 58 (1989), p. 522.

42. Fuller, *Qualifications and Encouragement of a Faithful Minister*, in *Complete*

Fuller's second reason was that when a believer grows in spirituality he or she also becomes focused on two great goals: 'the glory of God and the welfare of men's souls', both of which God Himself is pursuing. Thus, one can hope for God's 'blessing to attend our labours.' Finally, Fuller believed that a person who is marked by 'eminency in grace' will also be a person of genuine humility and it is safe for him or her 'to be much owned of God.' Success will not go to his or her head.[43]

Further Reflections to Benjamin Francis

Fuller's sermon was so well received that the church at Thorn urged its publication, along with one given by Fuller's friend, John Ryland on the same day. The following summer, in July of 1788, Fuller wrote to Benjamin Francis (1734–1799), the pastor of a Calvinistic Baptist congregation in Horsley, Gloucestershire, and mentioned that his Thorn sermon had been published. Recalling what he had preached, though, caused Fuller to reflect on the way in which he personally fell short of living according to what he had said on that October day in Thorn:

> My greatest difficulties arise from within. I am not what a servant of Christ should be. I want an unction from the Holy One. I have lately preached an ordination sermon or two, (that at Thorn, which is printed, for one[44]) in which I have endeavoured to come as home to the heart and conscience of my brethren as I knew how. But, oh, what shame covers my face when I turn my attention inward! I am the man who am too, too guilty of many of those things which I have cautioned them to avoid.[45]

Works, 1:144. For the influence of Edwards on Fuller, see Chris Chun, *The Legacy of Jonathan Edwards in the Theology of Andrew Fuller*, Studies in the History of Christian Traditions 162 (Leiden/Boston: Brill, 2012).

43. Fuller, *Qualifications and Encouragement of a Faithful Minister*, in *Complete Works*, 1:144.

44. The other sermon, based on Ezra 7:10, was *Intimate and Practical Acquaintance*, now in *Complete Works*, 1:483–86.

45. Andrew Fuller, Letter to Benjamin Francis, July 13, 1788, in *The Baptist Magazine*, vol. 34 (1842), pp. 637–38. This letter is also reprinted in Haykin, ed., *Armies of the Lamb*, pp. 111–13.

The clause 'unction from the Holy One' is, of course, a reference to 1 John 2:20, which, as has been noted above, Fuller understood to be a reference to the Holy Spirit. By lamenting his perceived lack of such a fullness of the Spirit, Fuller was obviously indicating his ardency for and prizing of such a blessing. Without such an unction, or fullness of the Spirit, he knew that he could not be a useful servant of Christ, for, as he had put it in his Thorn sermon, 'eminent spirituality in a minister is usually attended with eminent usefulness.'

Chronological Bibliography

Works of Joel R. Beeke

1980–2017

Books Authored (English)

Jehovah Shepherding His Sheep. Grand Rapids: Eerdmans, 1982.

Bible Doctrine Student Workbook: Teacher's Guide. Grand Rapids: Eerdmans, 1982.

Backsliding: Disease and Cure. Grand Rapids: Eerdmans, 1982.

Student Workbook on the Reformed Faith: Based on Rev. Hellenbroek's 'A Specimen of Divine Truths.' Vol. 1. Grand Rapids: Eerdmans, 1985.

Assurance of Faith: Calvin, English Puritanism, and the Dutch Second Reformation. New York: Peter Lang, 1991.

Holiness: God's Call to Sanctification. Edinburgh: Banner of Truth Trust, 1994.

Justification by Faith: Selected Bibliography. Grand Rapids: Reformation Heritage Press, 1995.

Heritage Netherlands Reformed Theological Training. Grand Rapids: Reformation Heritage Books, 1995.

Assurance of Faith: Divine Promises, Inward Evidences, and Witness of the Spirit. Dundas: Free Reformed Student Society, 1995.

Truth that Frees: A Workbook on Reformed Doctrine. Grand Rapids: Reformation Heritage Books, 1998.

The Quest for Full Assurance: The Legacy of Calvin and His Successors. Edinburgh: Banner of Truth Trust, 1999.

A Reader's Guide to Reformed Literature: An Annotated Bibliography of Reformed Theology. Grand Rapids: Reformation Heritage Books, 1999.

Puritan Evangelism: A Biblical Approach. Grand Rapids: Reformation Heritage Books, 1999.

Gisbertus Voetius. Grand Rapids: Reformation Heritage Books, 1999.

Bringing the Gospel to Covenant Children in Dependency on the Spirit. Family Guidance, No. 1. Grand Rapids: Reformation Heritage Books, 2001.

A Loving Encouragement to Flee Worldliness. Family Guidance, No. 2. Grand Rapids: Reformation Heritage Books, 2001.

Family Worship. Grand Rapids: Reformation Heritage Books, 2002.

Truth that Frees: Teachers' Guide. Grand Rapids: Reformation Heritage Books, 2002.

Puritan Reformed Spirituality. Grand Rapids: Reformation Heritage Books, 2004.

Portraits of Faith. Bridgend, Wales: Bryntirion Press, 2004.

The Family at Church: Listening to Sermons and Attending Prayer Meetings. Grand Rapids: Reformation Heritage Books, 2004.

Overcoming the World: Grace to Win the Daily Battle. Phillipsburg, N.J.: P & R, 2005.

Striving Against Satan. Bryntirion, Wales: Bryntirion Press, 2006.

Puritan Reformed Spirituality. Darlington, England: Evangelical Press, 2006 [paperback edition].

The Epistles of John. Darlington: Evangelical Press, 2006.

Walking as He Walked. Grand Rapids: Reformation Heritage Books, and Bridgend, Wales: Bryntirion Press, 2007.

The Heritage Reformed Congregations: Who We Are and What We Believe. Grand Rapids: Reformation Heritage Books, 2007.

Puritan Evangelism. Second edition. Grand Rapids: Reformation Heritage Books, 2007.

Striving Against Satan in Russian. Bridgend, Wales: Bryntirion Press, 2008.

Heirs with Christ: The Puritans on Adoption. Grand Rapids: Reformation Heritage Books, 2008.

Living for God's Glory: An Introduction to Calvinism. Orlando, Fla.: Reformation Trust, 2008.

Contagious Christian Living. Grand Rapids: Reformation Heritage Books, and Bryntirion, 2009.

Parenting by God's Promises. Orlando, Fla.: Reformation Trust, 2011.

Getting Back into the Race: The Cure for Backsliding. Adelphi, Md.: Cruciform Press, 2011.

A Faithful Church Member. Darlington, UK: Evangelical Press, 2011.

Friends and Lovers: Cultivating Companionship and Intimacy in Marriage. Adelphi, Md.: Cruciform Press, 2012.

What Is Evangelicalism? Darlington, Eng.: Evangelical Press, 2012.

How to Evaluate Sermons. Darlington, U.K.: Evangelical Press, 2012.

'Heidelberg Catechism Sermons,' 2 Volumes. Grand Rapids: Reformation Heritage Books, 2013.

Tough Questions About the Bible. Fearn, Ross-shire, Scotland: Christian Focus, 2013.

Developing Healthy Spiritual Growth: Knowledge, Practice, and Experience. Darlington, England: Evangelical Press, 2013.

What Did the Reformers Believe About the Age of the Earth? Petersburg, Ky.: Answers in Genesis, 2014.

How Should Teens Read the Bible? Grand Rapids: Reformation Heritage Books, 2014.

What is Resurrection? Phillipsburg, NJ: P&R Publishing, 2014.

How Should Men Lead Their Families? Grand Rapids: Reformation Heritage Books, 2014.

Piety: The Heartbeat of Reformed Theology. Phillipsburg, N.J. and Philadelphia: P&R and Westminster Seminary Press, 2015.

Fighting Satan: Knowing His Weaknesses, Strategies, and Defeat. Grand Rapids: Reformation Heritage Books, 2015. [revised edition of Striving Against Satan]

Why Should We Sing Psalms? Grand Rapids: Reformation Heritage Books, 2015.

Portraits of Faith: What Five Biblical Characters Teach Us About Our Life with God. Grand Rapids: Reformation Heritage Books, 2015. [revised edition]

How Can I Cultivate Private Prayer? Grand Rapids: Reformation Heritage Books, 2016.

The Lord Shepherding His Sheep. Grand Rapids: Reformation Heritage Books, 2015. [revised edition]

How Can I Practice Christian Meditation? Grand Rapids: Reformation Heritage Books, 2016.

Revelation. The Lectio Continua Expository Commentary of the NT. Grand Rapids: Reformation Heritage Books, 2016.

How Do We Plant Godly Convictions in Our Children? Grand Rapids: Reformation Heritage Books, 2016.

Debated Issues in Sovereign Predestination: Early Lutheran

Predestination, Calvinian Reprobation, and Variations in Genevan Lapsarianism, Reformed Historical Theology Series 42. Gottingen: Vandenhoeck and Ruprecht, 2017.

Knowing and Growing in Assurance of Faith. Ross-shire, Scotland: Christian Focus Publications, 2017.

Reformed Preaching: Proclaiming God's Word from the Heart of the Preacher to the Heart of His People. Wheaton, IL: Crossway, forthcoming 2018.

Books Authored (Other Languages)

Verachtering in de Genade: Kwaal en Genezing. Utrecht: De Banier, 1989.

A Tocha dos Puritanos: Evangelização Bíblica. Palestras proferidas no IV Sympósio OS PURITANOS em 1995. Sao Paulo: Publicações Evangélicas Selecionadas, 1996.

Cultivating Holiness [in Chinese]. Portage, MI: China Reformation Publishers, 2000.

Cultivando a Santidade. Recife, Brazil: Proecto Os Puritanos, pp. 33–68. [*Cultivating Holiness* in Portuguese with a chapter of Ryle on holiness], 2000.

La Santidad: El Ilamamiento de Dios a la santificación [*Holiness* in Spanish]. Edinburgh: Banner of Truth Trust, 2000.

Jehovah Shepherding His Sheep [in Korean]. Seoul: Word of Life Press, 2001.

Puritan Evangelism: A Biblical Approach [in Korean]. Translated by Anne-Mette VanToor. Seoul: The Puritan Faith Publishing Ministries, 2002.

A Busca da Plena Seguranca: O Legado de Calvino e Seus Successores [*Quest for Full Assurance of Faith: Calvin and His Successors* in Portuguese]. Recife: Projecto Os Puritanos, 2003.

Trazendo o Evangelho aos Filhos da Alianca [*Bringing the Gospel to Covenant Children* in Portuguese]. Sao Paulo: Campinas, 2003.

Family Worship [in Korean]. Seoul: Korea Christian Book House, 2004.

Backsliding: Disease and Cure [in Korean]. Seoul: Revival & Reformation Press, 2004.

Il Culto Di Famiglia. [*Family Worship* in Italian]. Mantova, Italy: Passagio, 2005.

Gods roeping tot heiligmaking. Arnemuiden: Stichting Herleving, 2005.

Dagelijkse Gezinsgodsdienst. Arnemuiden: Stichting Herleving, 2005.

Calvin's Passion for the Lost and the Puritans on Adoption and Meditation [in Korean]. Seoul: Korean Institute for Reformed Preaching [KIRP], 2006.

Aangaande mij en mijn huis: Het geloof gestalte geven in het gezin. Kampen: De Groot Goudriaan, 2006.

Het vijfde gebod. Arnemuiden: Stichting Herleving, 2006.

Geloven in de praktijk: Schetsen van het geloofsleven. Kampen: De Groot Goudriaan, 2007.

De Wereld Overwinnen. Kampen: De Groot Goudriaan, 2007.

Jesus navolgen [*Walking as He Walked* in Dutch]. Translated by Ruth Pieterman. Kampen: De Groot Goudriaan, 2008.

La Lucha Contra Satanás: Conociendo el Enemigo Sua Debilidades, Estratgims, y Derroth [*Striving Against Satan* in Spanish]. Graham, N.C.: Publicaciones Faro e Gracia, 2008.

La Espiritualidad Puritana y Reformada [*Puritan Reformed Spirituality* in Spanish]. Graham, N.C.: Publicaciones Faro e Gracia, 2008.

Vencendo o Mundo: Graça para Vencer a Batalha Diária [*Overcoming the World* in Portuguese]. São José dos Campos,

Brazil: Editora Fiel, 2009.

Reformatorische spiritualiteit: Een praktische studie naar de gereformeerde spirituele erfenis [*Puritan Reformed Spirituality* in Dutch]. Translated by Ruth Pieterman. Kampen: De Groot Goudriaan, 2009.

Puritan Reformed Spirituality [in Korean]. Seoul: Revival and Reformation Press, 2009.

Menjadi Auli WarisBersama Kristus [*Heirs with Christ: The Puritan View of Adoption* in Indonesian]. Translated by Edi Purwanto. Jakarta, 2009.

Pastors Live for a Purpose: Reformed Spirituality and Preaching [in Korean]. Seoul: SMART, 2009.

Heirdeiros com Christo: Os Puritanos sobre a Adoção [*Heirs with Christ: The Puritans on Adoption* in Portuguese]. São Paulo: Publicações Evangélicas Selecionadas, 2010.

Living for God's Glory: An Introduction to Calvinism [in Korean]. Seoul: Jiryung, 2010.

Calvinisme: een godgerichte en praletische levensvisia [*Living for God's Glory: An Introduction to Calvinism* in Dutch]. Kampen: De Groot Goudriaan, 2010.

Soli Deo Gloria: Un 'introduzione al Calvinismo [*Living for God's Glory: An Introduction to Calvinism* in Italian]. Caltanissetta, Italy: Alfa & Omega, 2010.

Vivendo para a Glória de Deus [*Living for God's Glory: An Introduction to Calvinism* in Portuguese]. São José dos Campos, Brasil: Editora Fiel, 2010.

Familia na Igreja: Ouvindo os Sermos e Participando das Reunioes de Oracao (translation of *The Family at Church* into Portuguese). Sao Paulo: Os Puritanos, 2011.

Bringing the Gospel to Covenant Children [in Korean]. Seoul: Subook, 2011.

Parenting by God's Promises [in Korean]. Seoul: Jipyung Publishing Co., 2012.

Amigos e Amantes: Como Cultivar a Amizade e a Intimidade No Casamento [*Friends and Lovers* in Portuguese]. Translated by Flavia Lopes. Sao Paulo: Vida Nova, 2012.

Membru Fidil Tal-Knisja [*What is a Faithful Church Member?* in Maltese]. Darlington: Evangelical Press, 2012.

Inchinarea In Familie [*Family Worship* in Romanian]. Societatea Misionara Coresi, 2013.

De Volta para os Braços do Pai: A cura para quem se desvia dos caminhos de Deus [*Getting Back in the Race: The Cure for Backsliding* in Portuguese]. São Paulo: Vida Nova, 2013.

Amigo e Amantes: Como Cultivar a Amizade e a Intimidade No Casemento [*Friends and Lovers* in Portuguese]. São Paulo: Vida Nova, 2013.

A Família Na Igreja: Ouvindo os Sermoes e Participando das Reunioes de Oraçao. São Paulo: Os Puritanos, 2013.

Opvoeden bij Gods Woord: Gods beloften voor ouders [*Parenting by God's Promises* in Dutch]. Translated by Ruth Pieterman. Kampen: Brevier, 2013.

Alles in Christus!: Het heil in Christus bij de puriteinen. [Addresses given in the Netherlands—not available in English.] Lunteren, The Netherlands: De Tabernakel, 2013.

PuritanII Si Abordarea Biblia A Evanghelizari [*Puritan Evangelism* in Romanian]. Translated by Ninel Lazar. www. wdjd.ro Romania: Coresi Missionary Society, 2013.

Espiritualidade Reformada: Uma Teologica Pratica para a Devocao a Deus [*Puritan Reformed Spirituality* in Portuguese]. Sao Jose dos Campos, Brazil: Fiel Editora, 2014.

Inchinarea in Familie [*Family Worship* in Romanian]. Bucharest, Romania: Societatea Misonara Coresi, 2014.

How to Read the Bible [in Korean]. Seoul: Word of Life Press, 2014.

Family Worship [in Hebrew]. Israel: Hagefen Publishing, 2015.

Portraits of Faith [in Persian-Farsi]. Translated by Niloufar Javid. Cheltenham, England: Parsa Trust, 2016.

Teologia Puritana: Doutrina Para a Vida. With Mark Jones (translation of Puritan Theology by Marcio Loureiro Redondo into Portuguese). Sao Paulo: Vida Nova, 2016.

John Bunyan and His Preaching [in Korean]. Seoul: Korea Institute for Reformed Preaching/The Banner of Truth Korea, 2016.

Weersta de Boze! Zijn Zwakheid, Zijn Stratejie en Zijn Nederlaag [*Fighting Satan* in Dutch]. Heerenveen: Uitgeverij Groen, 2016.

Living for God's Glory [translation by Denis Boris into Russian]. Minsk, Belarus: EP, 2016.

Puritan Evangelism: A Biblical Approach [in Indonesian]. Translated by Paulus Sulaeman. 2017.

Puritan Evangelism: A Biblical Approach [in Romanian]. Dascalu-Ilfov, Romania: Magna Gratia, 2017.

Family Worship [in Romanian]. Dascalu-Ilfov, Romania: Magna Gratia, 2017.

Family Worship [in Chinese]. Grand Rapids: Reformation Heritage Books, 2017.

Books Co-authored (English)

Bible Doctrine Student Workbook. With James W. Beeke. Grand Rapids: Eerdmans, 1982.

Building on the Rock, Book 1. Christian Stories for Children. With James W. Beeke and Diana Kleyn. Grand Rapids: Eerdmans, 1989.

Building on the Rock, Book 2. Christian Stories for Children. With James W. Beeke and Diana Kleyn. Grand Rapids: Eerdmans, 1990.

Building on the Rock, Book 3. With Jenny Luteyn and James W. Beeke. Grand Rapids: Reformation Heritage Books, 1993.

Knowing and Living the Christian Life. With James Greendyk. Grand Rapids: Reformation Heritage Books, 1997.

Building on the Rock, Book 4. With Diana Kleyn. Grand Rapids: Reformation Heritage Books, 2000.

God's Alphabet for Life: Devotions for Young Children. With Heidi Boorsma. Grand Rapids: Reformation Heritage Books, 2000.

The Truths of God's Word. With Diana Kleyn. Ross-shire: Christian Focus, and Grand Rapids: Reformation Heritage Books, 2002.

An Analysis of Herman Witsius's 'Economy of the Covenants'. With D. Patrick Ramsey. Ross-shire: Christian Focus, 2002.

Bible Doctrine Student Workbook. With James Beeke. Grand Rapids: Reformation Heritage Books, 2003. [revised edition]

How God Used a Thunderstorm. With Diana Kleyn. *Building on the Rock, volume 1*. Ross-shire: Christian Focus, and Grand Rapids: Reformation Heritage Books, 2003.

How God Stopped the Pirates. With Diana Kleyn. *Building on the Rock, volume 2*. Ross-shire: Christian Focus, and Grand Rapids: Reformation Heritage Books, 2003.

How God Used a Snowdrift. With Diana Kleyn. *Building on the Rock, volume 3*. Ross-shire: Christian Focus, and Grand Rapids: Reformation Heritage Books, 2003.

How God Used a Draught and an Umbrella. With Diana Kleyn. *Building on the Rock, volume 4*. Ross-shire: Christian Focus, and Grand Rapids: Reformation Heritage Books, 2003.

How God Used a Dog to Save a Boy. With Diana Kleyn. *Building on the Rock, volume 5.* Ross-shire: Christian Focus, and Grand Rapids: Reformation Heritage Books, 2003.

Meet the Puritans, With a Guide to Modern Reprints. With Randall Pederson. Grand Rapids: Reformation Heritage Books, 2006.

Reformation Heroes: A Simple, Illustrated Overview of People Who Assisted in the Great Work of the Reformation. With Diana Kleyn. Grand Rapids: Reformation Heritage Books, 2007.

Living by God's Promises. With James A. La Belle. Grand Rapids: Reformation Heritage Books, 2012.

Developing a Healthy Prayer Life: 31 Meditations on Communing with God. With James W. Beeke. Grand Rapids: Reformation Heritage Books, 2010.

A Puritan Theology: Doctrine for Life. With Mark Jones. Grand Rapids: Reformation Heritage Books, 2012.

Living Zealously. With James A. La Belle. Grand Rapids: Reformation Heritage Books, 2012.

Encouragement for Today's Pastors: Help from the Puritans. With Terry Slachter. Grand Rapids: Reformation Heritage Books, 2013.

Prepared by Grace for Grace: The Puritans on God's Ordinary Way of Leading Sinners to Christ. With Paul M. Smalley. Grand Rapids: Reformation Heritage Books, 2013.

Why Christ Came: 31 Meditations on the Incarnation. With William Boekestein. Grand Rapids: Reformation Heritage Books, 2013.

Acts Journible. With Rob Wynalda. Grand Rapids: Reformation Heritage Books, 2013.

Proverbs Journible. With Rob Wynalda. Grand Rapids: Reformation Heritage Books, 2014.

Matthew Journible. With Rob Wynalda. Grand Rapids:

Reformation Heritage Books, 2014.

Revelation Journible. With Rob Wynalda. Grand Rapids: Reformation Heritage Books, 2015.

William Perkins. With Stephen Yuille. Welwyn Garden City, UK: EP Books, 2015.

Mark Journible. With Rob Wynalda. Grand Rapids: Reformation Heritage Books, 2015.

How Should We Develop Biblical Friendship? With Michael A.G. Haykin. Grand Rapids: Reformation Heritage Books, 2015.

One Man and One Woman: Marriage and Same-Sex Relations. With Paul M. Smalley. Grand Rapids: Reformation Heritage Books, 2016.

Living in a Godly Marriage. With James A. La Belle. Grand Rapids: Reformation Heritage Books, 2016.

Genesis Journible, 2 vols.. With Rob Wynalda. Grand Rapids: Reformation Heritage Books, 2016.

A Puritan Theology Study Guide. With Mark Jones. Grand Rapids: Reformation Heritage Books, 2016.

Church History 101: The Highlights of Twenty Centuries. With Sinclair B. Ferguson and Michael A.G. Haykin. Grand Rapids: Reformation Heritage Books, 2016.

John Bunyan and the Grace of Fearing God. With Paul M. Smalley. Grand Rapids: Reformation Heritage Books, 2016.

Why Should I Be Interested in Church History? With Michael A.G. Haykin. Grand Rapids: Reformation Heritage Books, 2017.

Exodus Journible, 2 Volumes. With Rob Wynalda. Grand Rapids: Reformation Heritage Books, 2017.

Theology Made Practical: New Studies on John Calvin and His Legacy. With David W. Hall and Michael A.G. Haykin. Grand Rapids: Reformation Heritage Books, 2017.

Reformed Systematic Theology. With Paul M. Smalley. 4 vols. Wheaton, IL: Crossway, forthcoming 2019–2023.

Books Co-authored (Other Languages)

The Great Shepherd Caring for His Sheep [*Building on the Rock, Books 1–3* in Chinese], 1999.

Het Onweer. With Diana Kleyn. Kampen: De Groot Goudriaan, 2007.

Een Redder in Nood. With Diana Kleyn. Kampen: De Groot Goudriaan, 2007.

ABC de Deus para a Vida [*God's Alphabet* in Portuguese]. With Heidi Boorsma. Levilâamdoa. Brazil: Knox Publicaçöes, 2008.

Meet the Puritans [in Korean]. Seoul: Revival & Reformation Press, 2010.

Paixão pela Pureza [*Meet the Puritans* in Portuguese]. São Paulo: Publicações Evangélicas Selecionadas, 2010.

Purytanie: Biografie I Dzieta [*Meet the Puritans* in Polish]. Translated by Jacek Satachi. Edited by Dariusz M. Brycko. Grand Rapids: Tolle Lege Institute, 2010.

Wie Gott durch ein Gewitter wirkte und andere Andachtsgeschichten. With Diana Kleyn. Oerlinghausen, Germany: 2013.

Wie Gott durch die Piraten besiegte und andere Andachtsgeschichten. With Diana Kleyn. Oerlinghausen, Germany: 2013.

Wie Gott durch eine Schneewehe rettete und andere Andachtsgeschichten. With Diana Kleyn. Oerlinghausen, Germany: 2013.

Wie Gott bei Dürre einen Schirm sandte und andere Andachtsgeschichten. With Diana Kleyn. Oerlinghausen, Germany: 2013.

Taking Hold of God [in Korean]. Seoul: YWAM Publishing Korea, 2014.

Puritan Theology [in Korean]. Seoul, Korea: Revival and Reformation Press, 2015.

Como Deus Usou Uma Tempestade e Outras Historias Devocionais [*How God Used a Thunderstorm, and Other Devotional Stories* in Portuguese]. Ananindeua, Panama: Knox Publicacoes, 2015.

Books Translated into English

Translated with J. C. Weststrate, *Reformed Dogmatics*, by G. H. Kersten. 2 vols. Grand Rapids: Eerdmans, 1980, 1983.

Translated, *A Specimen of Divine Truths*, by Abraham Hellenbroek. Grand Rapids: Reformation Heritage Books, n.d.

Ed. and translated, *Forerunner of the Great Awakening: Sermons by Theodorus Jacobus Frelinghuysen* (1691–1747). The Historical Series of the Reformed Church in America, No. 36. Grand Rapids: Eerdmans, 2000.

Books Edited and Co-Edited

Ed., *Religious Stories for Young and Old*, Vol. 3. Grand Rapids: Eerdmans, 1981.

Ed., *Religious Stories for Young and Old*, Vol. 4. Grand Rapids: Eerdmans, 1983.

Ed., *The Twenty-fifth Mission Day*. Grand Rapids: Eerdmans, 1984.

Ed., *Sovereign Grace in Life and Ministry*. Grand Rapids: Eerdmans, 1984.

Ed., *Experiential Grace in Dutch Biography*. Grand Rapids: Eerdmans, 1985.

Ed., *Collected Writings of Reverend William C. Lamain*, volume

1. Grand Rapids: Neth. Reformed Book and Publishing Committee, 1986. (Biographical sketch, pp. 1–6; memorial oration, pp. 87–97.)

Ed. and introductions, *Doctrinal Standards, Liturgy, & Church Order*. Grand Rapids: Eerdmans, 1992.

Ed. and introductions, *The Psalter*. Grand Rapids: Eerdmans, 1992.

Ed., *Heaven Taken by Storm*, by Thomas Watson. Ligonier: Soli Deo Gloria, 1992.

Ed., *The Christian's Reasonable Service*, 4 vols., by Wilhelmus à Brakel. Translated by Bartel Elshout. Morgan, PA: Soli Deo Gloria, 1995–99.

Ed., *Memoirs of Thomas Halyburton*, intro. Sinclair Ferguson. Grand Rapids: Reformation Heritage Books, 1996.

Ed. and introduction, *The Pearl of Christian Comfort*, by Petrus Dathenus. Grand Rapids: Reformation Heritage Books, 1997.

Ed. with Sinclair Ferguson, *Reformed Confessions Harmonized*. Grand Rapids: Baker Books, 1999.

Ed., *The Path of True Godliness* by William Teellinck. Translated by Annemie Godbehere. Classics of Reformed Spirituality Series. Grand Rapids: Baker, 2003.

Ed., Octavius Winslow, *Evening Thoughts* (with Kate DeVries). Grand Rapids: Reformation Heritage Books, 2005.

Ed. and biographical preface, Andrew Gray's *Loving Christ and Fleeing Temptation*. With Kelly VanWyck. Grand Rapids: Reformation Heritage Books, 2007.

Ed. with Sinclair Ferguson. *Harmonia das Confissões Reformadas*. São Paulo: Editora Cultura Cristo, 2007.

Selected and ed.. With Michael Haykin, *365 Days with Calvin*. Leominster, U.K. Day One, and Grand Rapids: Reformation Heritage Books, 2008.

Ed., William Ames, *A Sketch of the Christian's Catechism.* Translated by Todd M. Rester. Classic Reformed Theology, vol. 1. Grand Rapids: Reformation Heritage Books, 2008.

Ed., *365 Dagen met Calvijn* [*365 Days with Calvin* in Dutch]. Translated by Ruth Pieterman. Kampen: De Groot Goudriaan, 2009.

Ed., *'The Soul of Life': The Piety of John Calvin.* Profiles in Reformed Spirituality, no. 6. Grand Rapids: Reformation Heritage Books, 2009.

Ed. with Mark Jones, *'A Habitual Sight of Him': The Christ-Centered Piety of Thomas Goodwin.* Profiles in Reformed Spirituality, no. 8. Grand Rapids: Reformation Heritage Books, 2009.

Ed., *Calvin for Today.* Grand Rapids: Reformation Heritage Books, 2010.

Contributor and ed., *Milk & Honey: A Devotional.* Grand Rapids: Reformation Heritage Books, 2010.

Ed., *Calvin: Theologian and Reformer.* With Garry Williams. Grand Rapids: Reformation Heritage Books, 2010.

Ed., *The Three Forms of Unity.* Vestavia Hills, Al.: Solid Ground Christian Books, 2010.

Ed. with Anthony T. Selvággio, *Sing a New Song: Recovering Psalm Singing in the Twenty-First Century.* Grand Rapids: Reformation Heritage Books, 2010.

Ed. with Brian Najapfour, *Taking Hold of God: Reformed and Puritan Perspectives on Prayer.* Grand Rapids: Reformation Heritage Books, 2011.

Ed., *The Beauty and Glory of Christ.* Grand Rapids: Reformation Heritage Books, 2011.

Ed. with Ray B. Lanning, *Reformed Thought: Selected Writings of William Young.* Grand Rapids: Reformation Heritage Books, 2011.

Ed. with Rob Wynalda, *1 and 2 Corinthians Journible*. Grand Rapids: Reformation Heritage Books, 2011.

Comp. and ed. with Paul M. Smalley, *Feasting with Christ: Meditations on the Lord's Supper*. Darlington, Eng.: Evangelical Press, 2012.

Ed. with Joseph A. Pipa, Jr., *The Beauty and Glory of the Holy Spirit*. Grand Rapids: Reformation Heritage Books, 2012.

Ed., Godefridus Udemans, *The Practice of Faith, Hope, and Love,* Grand Rapids: Reformation Heritage Books, 2012.

Ed. with Rob Wynalda, *Deuteronomy Journible,* Grand Rapids: Reformation Heritage Books, 2012.

Ed. and modernized with Scott Brown, William Gouge, *Building a Godly Home, Volume 1: A Holy Vision for Family Life*. Grand Rapids: Reformation Heritage Books, 2013.

Ed., *The Beauty and Glory of the Father*. Grand Rapids: Reformation Heritage Books, 2013.

Ed. with Nelson Kloosterman, Petrus Van Mastricht, *The Best Method of Preaching: The Use of Theoretical-Practical Theology*. Grand Rapids: Reformation Heritage Books, 2013.

Ed. with Derek W. H. Thomas, *The Holy Spirit and Reformed Spirituality*. Grand Rapids: Reformation Heritage Books, 2013.

Ed. with Scott Brown, William Gouge, *Building a Godly Home, Volume 2: A Holy Vision for a Happy Marriage*. Grand Rapids: Reformation Heritage Books, 2013.

Ed., *The Beauty and Glory of Christian Living*. Grand Rapids: Reformation Heritage Books, 2014.

Ed., *The Reformation Heritage KJV Study Bible*. Grand Rapids: Reformation Heritage Books, 2014.

Ed. with Scott Brown. William Gouge, *Building a Godly Home, Volume 3: A Holy Vision for Raising Children*. Grand Rapids: Reformation Heritage Books, 2014.

Ed., *Faith Seeking Assurance,* by Anthony Burgess. Grand Rapids: Reformation Heritage Books, 2015.

Ed., *The Beauty and Glory of Christ's Bride.* Grand Rapids: Reformation Heritage Books, 2015.

Ed., *The Happiness of Enjoying and Making a True and Speedy Use of Christ,* by Alexander Grosse. Grand Rapids: Reformation Heritage Books, 2015.

Ed. with Michael Barrett, Gerald Bilkes, and Paul Smalley. *Family Worship Bible Guide.* Grand Rapids: Reformation Heritage Books, 2016

Series Editor

Series ed., Classics of Reformed Spirituality Series, Grand Rapids: Baker/Reformation Heritage Books, 2003–.

Series ed. with Jay Collier. Reformed Historical-Theological Studies. Grand Rapids: Reformation Heritage Books, 2004–.

Series ed., Profiles in Reformed Spirituality. Grand Rapids: Reformation Heritage Books, 2006–2012.

Series ed., Classic Reformed Theology. Grand Rapids: Reformation Heritage Books, 2008–

Series ed. with Jay Collier. Puritan Treasures for Today. Grand Rapids: Reformation Heritage Books, 2009–.

General ed. with Derek W. H. Thomas. *The Works of William Perkins.* Grand Rapids: Reformation Heritage Books, 2014–.

Series ed. with Ryan M. McGraw. Cultivating Biblical Godliness. Grand Rapids: Reformation Heritage Books, 2014–.

Select Articles Published in Books

'Justification by Faith Alone: The Relation of Faith to Justification.' In *Justification by Faith Alone.* Edited by Don Kistler. Morgan, PA: Soli Deo Gloria, 1994. pp. 53–105.

'William Cunningham.' In *Historians of the Christian Tradition: Their Methodology and Impact on Western Thought.* Edited by Michael Bauman and Martin I. Klauber. Nashville: Broadman & Holman, 1995. pp. 209–226.

'The Transforming Power of Scripture.' With Ray Lanning. In *Sola Scriptura! The Protestant Position on the Bible.* Edited by Don Kistler. Morgan, PA: Soli Deo Gloria, 1996. pp. 221–76.

'Acronius, Ruardus.' 'Bastingius, Jeremias.' 'Taffin, Jean.' 'Venator, Adolphus.' 'Vorstius, Conradus.' In *The Oxford Encyclopedia of the Reformation.* Edited by Hans Hillerbrand. Oxford: University Press, 1996. 1:2–3, 127–28; 4:143, 224–25, 248–49.

'Glad Obedience: The Third Use of the Law.' With Ray Lanning. In *Trust and Obey.* Edited by Don Kistler. Morgan, PA: Soli Deo Gloria, 1996. pp. 154–200.

'The Order of the Divine Decrees at the Genevan Academy: From Bezan Supralapsarianism to Turretinian Infralapsarianism.' In *The Identity of Geneva: The Christian Commonwealth, 1564–1864.* Edited by John B. Roney and Martin I. Klauber. Westport, Conn.: Greenwood Press, 1998. pp. 57–75.

'Anthony Burgess on Assurance.' In *The Answer of a Good Conscience.* London: Westminster Conference Papers, 1998. pp. 27–52.

'Ursinus, Oxford and the Westminster Divines.' With R. Scott Clark. In *The Westminster Confession into the 21st Century.* Edited by Ligon Duncan and Duncan Rankin. Jackson: Reformed Academic Press, 1999.

'Gisbertus Voetius: Toward a Reformed Marriage of Knowledge and Piety.' In *Protestant Scholasticism: Essays in Reassessment.* Edited by Carl R. Trueman and R. Scott Clark, Paternoster Press, 1999.

'Making Sense of Calvin's Paradoxes on Assurance of Faith.' In *Calvin and Spirituality.* Grand Rapids: CRC Product Services, 1999. pp. 13–30.

'"Glorious Things of Thee Are Spoken": The Doctrine of the Church.' In *Onward Christian Soldiers: Protestants Affirm the Church*. Edited by Don Kistler. Morgan, Pa.: Soli Deo Gloria, 1999. pp. 23–67.

'Netherlands Reformed Congregations of North America.' In *Dictionary of the Presbyterian and Reformed Tradition in America*. Edited by D.G. Hart. Downers Grove, Ill.: InterVarsity Press, 1999. pp. 168–69.

'The Utter Necessity of a Godly Life: The Foundation of Pastoral Ministry.' In *Reforming Pastoral Ministry: Challenges for Ministry in Postmodern Times*. Edited by John W. Armstrong. Wheaton: Crossway Books, 2001. pp. 59–82.

'Evangelism Rooted in Scripture: The Puritan Example.' In *Whatever Happened to the Reformation?* Edited by Gary L.W. Johnson and R. Fowler White. Philipsburg, N.J.: Presbyterian and Reformed, 2001. pp. 229–52, 320–25.

'The Lasting Power of Reformed Experiential Preaching.' In *Feed My Sheep: A Passionate Plea for Preaching*. Edited by Don Kistler. Morgan, Penn.: Soli Deo Gloria, 2002. pp. 94–128.

'William Perkins on Predestination, Preaching, and Conversion.' In *The Practical Calvinist: An Introduction to the Presbyterian & Reformed Heritage*. Edited by Peter Lillback. Ross-shire: Christian Focus Publications, 2002. pp. 183–214.

'Seeing God's Glory' and 'The Puritan Practice of Meditation.' In *Reformed Spirituality: Communing with Our Glorious God*. Taylors, S.C.: Southern Presbyterian Press, 2003. pp. 19–28, 73–100.

'Unto You, and To Your Children.' With Ray Lanning. In *The Case for Covenantal Infant Baptism*. Edited by Gregg Strawbridge. Philipsburg, N.J.: P&R, 2003. pp. 49–69.

'Learn from the Puritans.' *Dear Timothy: Letters on Pastoral*

Ministry. Edited by Thomas K. Ascol. Cape Coral, Fla.: Founders Press, 2004. pp. 219–69.

'The Atonement in Herman Bavinck's Theology.' In *The Atonement: Biblical, Historical, & Practical Perspectives.* Edited by Charles E. Hill and Frank A. James III. Downers Grove, Ill.: InterVarsity Press, 2004. pp. 324–45.

'Ursinus, Oxford, and the Westminster Divines.' With R. Scott Clark. *The Westminster Confession into the 21st Century, Volume 2.* Edited by J. Ligon Duncan. Ross-shire: Christian Focus Publications, 2004. pp. 1–32.

'Calvin on Piety.' In *The Cambridge Companion to John Calvin.* Cambridge: University Press, 2004. pp. 125–52.

'Coping with Criticism.' In *Character Assassins.* Edited by Peter Hammond. Cape Town: Christian Liberty Books, 2004. pp. 75–78.

'Thomas Bedford,' 'Alexander Comrie,' and 'Thomas Wills.' In *The Oxford Dictionary of National Biography.* Edited by H.C.G. Matthew and Brian Harrison. Oxford: Oxford University Press, 2004.

'William Perkins and "How a man may know whether he be a child of God, or no".' *The Faith that Saves: Papers Read at the 2004 Westminster Conference.* London: Westminster Conference, 2005. pp. 7–31.

'The Fullness of Grace.' In *Assured by God: Living in the Fullness of God's Grace. Edited by* Buck Parsons. Philipsburg, N.J.: Presbyterian and Reformed, 2006. pp. 107–24.

'Theodorus Jacobus Frelinghuysen (1691–1747).' In *Encyclopedia of Religious Revivals in America.* Edited by Michael McClymond. Westport, Conn.: Greenwood Press, 2007. 1:178–80.

'Transforming Power and Comfort: The Puritans on Adoption.' In *The Faith Once Delivered: Celebrating the Legacy of Reformed Systematic Theology and the Westminster Assembly.* Edited by Anthony Selvaggio. Phillipsburg, New Jersey: P &

R, 2007. pp. 63–105.

'Appropriating Salvation: The Spirit, Faith and Assurance, and Repentance—*Institutes*, 3.1.3.' In *A Theological Guide to Calvin's Institutes: Essays and Analysis*. Edited by David W. Hall and Peter A. Lillback. Phillipsburg, N.J.: P&R, 2008. pp. 273–300.

'Evangelicalism in the Dutch Further Reformation.' In *The Emergence of Evangelicalism: Exploring Historical Continuities*. Ed. Michael A. G. Haykin and Kenneth J. Stewart. Nottingham, U.K.: Apollos, 2008. pp. 146–68. (Published later in the year in America as *The Advent of Evangelicalism: Exploring Historical Continuities*. Nashville: Broadman and Holman, pp. 146–68.)

'Experiential Preaching.' In *Feed My Sheep: A Passionate Plea for Preaching*. Edited by Don Kistler. Second ed. Orlando: Reformation Trust, 2008. pp. 53–70.

'The Communion of Men with God.' In *John Calvin: A Heart for Devotion, Doctrine & Doxology*. Edited by Burk Parsons. Orlando: Reformation Trust, 2008. pp. 231–46.

'Necessary Blood' and 'The Blood of Christ in Puritan Piety.' In *Precious Blood: The Atoning Work of Christ*. Edited by Richard B. Phillips Wheaton, Ill.: Crossway, 2009. pp. 15–34, 163–78.

'Defending Definite Atonement.' *Banner of Sovereign Grace Truth* 17, 10 (Dec):274–76, 278.

'The Transforming Power of Scripture.' With Ray Lanning. In *Sola Scriptura: The Protestant Position on the Bible*. Edited by Don Kistler. Hardcover reprint. Orlando: Reformation Trust, 2009. pp. 111–41.

'Cherishing the Church.' In *Preaching Like Calvin: Sermons from the 500th Anniversary of Calvin*. Edited by David W. Hall. Phillipsburg, N.J.: P&R, 2010. pp. 191–213.

'Psalm Singing in Calvin and the Puritans.' In *Sing a New Song:*

Recovering Psalm Singing in the Twenty-First Century. Grand Rapids: Reformation Heritage Books, 2010. pp. 16–40.

'John Calvin on Prayer and Communion with God'; 'Anthony Burgess on Christ's Prayer for Us'; 'Matthew Henry on a Practical Method of Daily Prayer'; 'Thomas Boston on Praying to Our Father'; 'Puritan Prayers for World Missions;' 'Prayerful Praying Today.' In *Taking Hold of God: Reformed and Puritan Perspectives on Prayer.* Grand Rapids: Reformation Heritage Books, 2011. pp. 27–42, 83–108, 141–58, 159–86, 207–222, 223–40.

'Thomas Goodwin on Christ's Beautiful Heart.' In *The Beauty and Glory of Christ.* Grand Rapids: Reformation Heritage Books, 2011. pp. 135–54.

'The Assurance Debate: Six Key Questions.' In *Drawn into Controversie: Reformed Theological Diversity and Debates within Seventeenth-Century British Protestantism.* Edited by Michael A. G. Haykin and Mark Jones. Göttingen: Vanderhoeck & Ruprecht, 2011. pp. 263–83.

'"Only for His Believers": Paedocommunion and the Witness of the Reformed Liturgies.' In *Children and the Lord's Supper.* Edited by Guy Waters and Ligon Duncan. Ross-shire, UK: Christian Focus Publications, 2011. pp. 163–79.

'Hallowing God's Name.' In *Let Us Pray.* Edited by Don Kistler. Orlando: Northampton Press, 2011. pp. 37–56.

'Richard Sibbes on Entertaining the Holy Spirit.' In *The Beauty and Glory of the Holy Spirit.* Grand Rapids: Reformation Heritage Books, 2012. pp. 227–45.

'Zealous But Not Legalistic.' In *Law & Liberty: A Biblical Look at Legalism. Edited by* Don Kistler. Orlando: Northampton Press, 86–101

'Holding Firmly to the Heidelberg: The Validity and Relevance of Catechism Preaching'; 'Preaching the Catechism Today.' In *A*

Faith Worth Teaching: The Heidelberg Catechism's Enduring Heritage. Edited by Jon D. Payne and Sebastian Heck. Grand Rapids: Reformation Heritage Books, 2013. pp. 35–61, 62–78.

'Reformed Orthodoxy in North America.' In *A Companion to Reformed Orthodoxy.* Edited by Herman J. Selderhuis. Leiden: Brill, 2013. pp. 232–49.

'The Apostle John and the Puritans on the Father's Adopting, Transforming Love.' In *The Beauty and Glory of the Father.* Grand Rapids: Reformation Heritage Books, 2013. pp. 79–105.

'What Did the Reformers Believe about the Age of the Earth?' In *The New Answers Book 4: Over 30 Questions on Creation/ Evolution and the Bible.* Edited by Ken Ham. Green Forest, Ark.: Master Books, 2013, pp. 101–110.

'The Illumination of the Holy Spirit.' In *The Holy Spirit and Reformed Spirituality.* Grand Rapids: Reformation Heritage Books, 2013. pp. 52–69.

'Laurence Chaderton: An Early Puritan Vision for Church and School.' In *Church and School in Early Modern Protestantism: Studies in Honor of Richard A. Muller on the Maturation of a Theological Tradition.* Edited by Jordan J. Ballor, David S. Sytsma, Jason Zuidema. Leiden: Brill, 2013. pp. 321–37.

'Bunyan's perseverance.' In *The Pure Flame of Devotion: The History of Christian Spirituality: Essays in Honour of Michael A. G. Haykin.* Edited by G. Stephen Weaver, Jr. and Ian Hugh Clary. Kitchener, Ont.: Joshua Press, 2013. pp. 327–46.

'Thomas Ridgley on the Trinity.' In *Triniteit en kerk: Bundel ter gelegenheid van het afscheid van prof. dr. A. Baars als hoogelaar aan de Theologische Universiteit Apeldoorn. Edited by* G. C. den Hertog, H. R. Keurhorst, and H. G. L. Peels. Heerenveen, The Netherlands: Groen, 2014. pp. 128–45.

'Calvin's Teaching Office and the Dutch Reformed

Doctorenambt.' In *Biblical Interpretation and Doctrinal Formulation in the Reformed Tradition: Essays in Honor of James De Jong.* Ed. Arie C. Leder and Richard A. Muller. Grand Rapids: Reformation Heritage Books, 2014. pp. 5–32.

'Die Verwendung des Heidelberger Katechismus auberhalb Europas.' In *Handbuch Heidelberger Katechismus.* Edited by Arnold Huijgen, John V. Fesko, and Aleida Siller. Utrecht: Netherlands: Kok, 2014. pp. 119–29.

'Implementing Family Worship'; 'Answers to Abortion Arguments'; 'Proclamations of God's Word and Abortion.' In *A Theology of the Family.* Ed. Jeff Pollard and Scott T. Brown. Wake Forest, N.C.: NCFIC, 2014, 91–99, 523–27, 534–38.

Numerous articles and notes. In *The Reformation Heritage KJV Study Bible.* Grand Rapids: Reformation Heritage Books, 2014.

'John Calvin and John Brown of Wamphray on Justification.' In *Reformed Orthodoxy in Scotland: Essays on Scottish Theology 1560–1775.* Edited by Aaron Clay Denlinger. London: T&T Clark, 2015. pp. 191–209.

'The Case for Adam'; 'Christ, the Second Adam.' In *God, Adam, and You.* Edited by Richard D. Phillips. Phillipsburg, NJ: P&R Publishing, 2015. pp. 15–43, 141–68.

'Letters of Samuel Rutherford.' In *You Must Read: Books That Have Shaped Our Lives.* Edinburgh: Banner of Truth, 2015. pp. 185–91.

'The Incarnate Word'; 'The Cross of Christ.' In *The Triune God.* Edited by Ronald L. Kohl. Phillipsburg, N.J.: P & R, 2015. pp. 135–59; 181–209.

'What is Biblical Christianity and Why Is It Different?' With Paul M. Smalley. In *World Religions and Cults: Counterfeits of Christianity, Volume 1.* Edited by Bodie Hodge and Roger Patterson. Green Forest, AK: Master Books, 2015. pp. 35–70.

'Perseverance by the Spirit'; 'Perseverance by the Word.' In

Shepherds After My Own Heart: Essays in Honour of Robert W. Oliver. Edited by Robert Strivens and S. Blair Waddell. Welwyn Garden City, UK: EP Books, 2016. pp. 35–51, 53–67.

'The Life and Vision of Abraham Kuyper.' In *By Common Confession: Essays in Honor of James M. Renihan.* Edited by Ronald S. Baines, Richard C. Barcellos, and James P. Butler. Palmdale, CA: RBAP, 2015. pp. 175–94.

'Revival and the Dutch Reformed Church in Eighteenth-Century America.' In *Pentecostal Outpourings: Revival and the Reformed Tradition.* Edited by Robert Davis Smart, Michael A.G. Haykin, and Ian Hugh Clary. Grand Rapids: Reformation Heritage Books, 2016. pp. 230–53.

'A Historical Pedigree: Sixteenth-Century Reformed Preaching.' *Pulpit Aflame: Essays in Honor of Steven J. Lawson.* Grand Rapids: Reformation Heritage Books, 2016. pp. 43–58.

'The Family Man: Luther at Home.' *The Legacy of Luther.* Edited by R. C. Sproul and Stephen J. Nichols. Orlando: Reformation Trust, 2016. Pp. 75–93.

'The Worldview of the Puritans.' With Paul Smalley. In *The Beauty and Glory of the Christian Worldview.* Grand Rapids: Reformation Heritage Books, 2017. pp. 25–54.

(Dr Beeke has also published numerous articles in various theological journals such as *Calvin Theological Journal* and *Westminster Theological Journal,* written many prefaces and introductions to reprints of classic Reformed and Puritan books, and has been a regular contributor to periodicals such as *Banner of Truth, Reformation and Revival, Tabletalk,* and his denominational magazine the *Banner of Sovereign Grace Truth,* of which he is editor.)

Also available from Christian Focus ...

"a treat for anyone with healthy spiritual taste buds."
SINCLAIR B. FERGUSON

PURITAN
PORTRAITS

○ ✤ ○

J. I. PACKER
ON SELECTED CLASSIC PASTORS
AND PASTORAL CLASSICS

ISBN 978-1-8455-0700-8

Puritan Portraits

J. I. Packer on Selected Classic Pastors and Pastoral Classics

J. I. PACKER

Here one of the leading authorities on the Puritans, J. I. Packer introduces us to their rich theology and deep spirituality. Packer gives us profiles of John Flavel, Thomas Boston, John Bunyan, Matthew Henry, Henry Scougal, John Owen and Stephen Charnock and two closer portraits of William Perkins and Richard Baxter. The writings of the Puritans continue to profoundly reward readers and here J. I. Packer brings them alive in an inspiring way to encourage a new generation to experience their delights.

Like many, I first met the Puritans through the writings of Dr Packer and thus owe him a debt of gratitude. In this volume he has once again excelled: here are thoughtful introductions to some key Puritan thinkers and their works, along with a Puritan manifesto for today's pastors. This is vintage Packer. In an age of trendy fluff, here is solid food for the church and for the soul.

Carl R. Trueman
Professor, Department of Biblical and Religious Studies,
Grove City College, Pennsylvania

The best way to meet great men is through a personal introduction by someone who knows them well. That's precisely what J. I. Packer does in this book, introducing us to several Puritan-minded men of the sixteenth through eighteenth centuries. But this is more than biography. As Packer does so well, in this book the Puritans become mirrors in which we see heavenly truths about the gospel, evangelism, spiritual growth, and suffering. I thank God for the gathering of this previously scattered material into one volume, and anticipate that it will bless many.

Joel R. Beeke
President, Puritan Reformed Theological Seminary, Grand Rapids,
Michigan

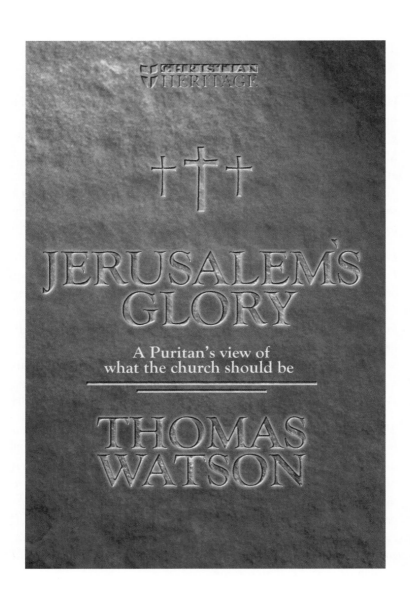

A Puritan's view of
what the church should be

ISBN 978-1-8579-2569-2

Jerusalem's Glory

A Puritan's View of What the Church Should Be

THOMAS WATSON

Written in 1661, this book contains all the hallmarks of what made the puritans great. It represents a clarion call to the church to recognize her failings and repent, turning to the Almighty God and casting herself on His mercy. Here we gain some insight to the virtue of a puritan preacher of the gospel, speaking plainly to the ills of society and in particular to the church, that according to the scripture is 'a city set on a hill'.

It revealed Thomas Watson's deep concern for the state of the Church and the prosperity of godliness and vital Christianity in a period of testing and decline. Watson did not merely write a religious polemic, but offered the fruits of many years of a successful preaching ministry, expounding issues such as when the Christian may rejoice, how to act in a godly manner when tested to the limit, and showing how glorious is Christ's Church when proven in the fires of affliction. It is a work that is aimed at helping the believer in a practical manner to live a life that glorifies God and places Christ at the centre of the Church both doctrinally and in practical everyday living. He challenges the reader at every turn to seek to prove these things according to the authority of the Scriptures, and to act upon it.

The text is simplified for the modern reader, with a biographical introduction added to the original work. It will, through time, come to be regarded as Watson at his most readable and best.

ISBN 978-1-8455-0978-1

Daily Readings – The Puritans

RANDALL J. PEDERSON

As you draw daily from the wisdom of the Puritans, you will find renewed joy for your daily service. This beautifully presented gift edition has 12 months of readings from Richard Baxter; John Bunyan; Stephen Charnock; Jonathan Edwards; John Flavel; William Gurnall; William Guthrie; Matthew Mead; John Owen; Samuel Rutherford; Thomas Watson; Thomas Vincent.

Christian Focus Publications

Our mission statement –

STAYING FAITHFUL

In dependence upon God we seek to impact the world through literature faithful to His infallible Word, the Bible. Our aim is to ensure that the Lord Jesus Christ is presented as the only hope to obtain forgiveness of sin, live a useful life and look forward to heaven with Him.

Our Books are published in four imprints:

CHRISTIAN
FOCUS

popular works including biographies, commentaries, basic doctrine and Christian living.

CHRISTIAN
HERITAGE

books representing some of the best material from the rich heritage of the church.

MENTOR

books written at a level suitable for Bible College and seminary students, pastors, and other serious readers. The imprint includes commentaries, doctrinal studies, examination of current issues and church history.

CF4•K

children's books for quality Bible teaching and for all age groups: Sunday school curriculum, puzzle and activity books; personal and family devotional titles, biographies and inspirational stories – Because you are never too young to know Jesus!

Christian Focus Publications Ltd,
Geanies House, Fearn, Ross-shire,
IV20 1TW, Scotland, United Kingdom.
www.christianfocus.com